*Helmut Graupner
Vern L. Bullough
Editors*

Adolescence, Sexuality, and the Criminal Law: Multidisciplinary Perspectives

Adolescence, Sexuality, and the Criminal Law: Multidisciplinary Perspectives has been co-published simultaneously as *Journal of Psychology & Human Sexuality*, Volume 16, Numbers 2/3 2004.

*Pre-publication
REVIEWS,
COMMENTARIES,
EVALUATIONS . . .*

"There is a great deal of interesting information that one can get from this publication."

Rudolf Müller, Judge
*Austrian Supreme Administrative Court Judge, Austrian Constitutional Court
Honorary Professor of Social Security Law and Labor Law
University of Salzburg*

*More pre-publication
REVIEWS, COMMENTARIES, EVALUATIONS...*

"CRITICAL AND COMPREHENSIVE.... INFORMATIVE AND THOUGHT-PROVOKING. This book is an excellent contribution to the literature in this important, but not much discussed, area. Sexologists, sex therapists, lawyers, social workers, and law enforcement officers will all find these pages most relevant to their work. In addition, the lay intelligentsia, including those concerned with human rights and responsibilities, will also find ideas and facts which are illuminating."

Padmal de Silva, MA, MPhil, FBPsS
*Consultant Clinical Psychologist
South London and Maudsley
National Health Service Trust
Senior Lecturer in Psychology
King's College
University of London
United Kingdom*

"REQUIRED READING FOR ALL HUMAN DEVELOPMENT STUDENTS and everyone interested in adolescence, sexuality, and societies. This important multidisciplinary volume dramatically illustrates how motives to protect children can harm them. It uses historical and current scientific information on adolescent sexual behavior to illustrate the potential dangers of making laws based not on scientific data but on moralistic principles."

Ronald Moglia, EdD
*Associate Professor
Department of Applied Psychology
Steinhardt School of Education
New York University*

The Haworth Press, Inc.

Adolescence, Sexuality, and the Criminal Law: Multidisciplinary Perspectives

Adolescence, Sexuality, and the Criminal Law: Multidisciplinary Perspectives has been co-published simultaneously as *Journal of Psychology & Human Sexuality*, Volume 16, Numbers 2/3 2004.

The *Journal of Psychology & Human Sexuality* Monographic "Separates"

Below is a list of "separates," which in serials librarianship means a special issue simultaneously published as a special journal issue or double-issue *and* as a "separate" hardbound monograph. (This is a format which we also call a "DocuSerial.")

"Separates" are published because specialized libraries or professionals may wish to purchase a specific thematic issue by itself in a format which can be separately cataloged and shelved, as opposed to purchasing the journal on an on-going basis. Faculty members may also more easily consider a "separate" for classroom adoption.

"Separates" are carefully classified separately with the major book jobbers so that the journal tie-in can be noted on new book order slips to avoid duplicate purchasing.

You may wish to visit Haworth's website at . . .

http://www.HaworthPress.com

. . . to search our online catalog for complete tables of contents of these separates and related publications.

You may also call 1-800-HAWORTH (outside US/Canada: 607-722-5857), or Fax 1-800-895-0582 (outside US/Canada: 607-771-0012), or e-mail at:

docdelivery@haworthpress.com

Adolescence, Sexuality, and the Criminal Law: Multidisciplinary Perspectives, edited by Helmut Graupner, JD, and Vern L. Bullough, PhD (Vol. 16, No. 2/3, 2004). *"There is a great deal of interesting information that one can get from this publication." (Rudolf Müller, Judge, Austrian Supreme Administrative Court; Judge, Austrian Constitutional Court; Honorary Professor of Social Security Law and Labor Law, University of Salzburg)*

Lesbian and Bisexual Women's Mental Health, edited by Robin M. Mathy, MSW, LGSW, MSc, MSt, MA, and Shelly K. Kerr, PhD (Vol. 15, No. 2/3/4, 2003). *Explores the interrelationship between lesbian and bisexual women's mental health and the diverse social contexts in which they live.*

Masturbation as a Means of Achieving Sexual Health, edited by Walter O. Bockting, PhD, and Eli Coleman, PhD (Vol. 14, No. 2/3, 2002). *"Finally, here is an excellent book filled with research illustrating how positive attitudes toward masturbation in history, across cultures, and throughout the life span can help in the achievement of sexual health. This book is an invaluable resource and I highly recommend it for all who are teaching health or sexuality education or are involved in sex counseling and therapy." (William R. Strayton, PhD, ThD, Professor and Coordinator, Human Sexuality Program, Widener University)*

Sex Offender Treatment: Accomplishments, Challenges, and Future Directions, edited by Michael H. Miner, PhD, and Eli Coleman, PhD (Vol. 13, No. 3/4, 2001). *An easy-to-read collection that reviews the major issues and findings on the past decade of research on and treatment of sex offenders. The busy professional will find this book a quick and helpful update for their practice. The reviews presented are succinct, but capture the main issues to be addressed by anyone working with sex offenders." (R. Langevin, PhD, CPsych, Director, Juniper Psychological Services and Associate Professor of Psychiatry, University of Toronto)*

Childhood Sexuality: Normal Sexual Behavior and Development, edited by Theo G. M. Sandfort, PhD, and Jany Rademakers, PhD (Vol. 12, No. 1/2, 2000). *"Important . . . Gives voice to children about their own 'normal' sexual curiosities and desires, and about their behavior and development." (Gunter Schmidt, PhD, Professor, Department of Sex Research, University of Hamburg, Germany)*

Sexual Offender Treatment: Biopsychosocial Perspectives, edited by Eli Coleman, PhD, and Michael Miner, PhD (Vol. 10, No. 3, 2000). *"This guide delivers a diverse look at the complex and intriguing topic of normal child sexuality and the progress that is being made in this area of research."*

New International Directions in HIV Prevention for Gay and Bisexual Men, edited by Michael T. Wright, LICSW, B. R. Simon Rosser, PhD, MPH, and Onno de Zwart, MA (Vol. 10, No. 3/4, 1998). *"Performs a great service to HIV prevention research and health promotion. . . . It takes* the words of gay and bisexual men seriously by locating men's sexual practice in their love relationships and casual sex encounters and examines their responses to HIV." (Susan Kippax, Associate Professor and Director, National Center in HIV Social Research, School of Behavioral Sciences, Macquarie University, New South Wales, Australia)

Sexuality Education in Postsecondary and Professional Training Settings, edited by James W. Maddock (Vol. 9, No. 3/4, 1997). *"A diverse group of contributers all experienced sexuality educators–offer summary information, critical commentary, thoughtful analysis, and projections of future trends in sexuality education in postsecondary settings. . . . The chapters present valuable resources, ranging from historical references to contemporary Websites."* (Adolescence)

Sexual Coercion in Dating Relationships, edited by E. Sandra Byers and Lucia F. O'Sullivan (Vol. 8, No. 1/2, 1996). *"Tackles a big issue with the best tools presently available to social and health scientists. . . . Perhaps the most remarkable thing about these excellent chapters is the thread of optimism that remains despite the depressing topic. Each author . . . chips away at oppression and acknowledges the strength of women who have experienced sexual coercion while struggling to eliminate sexist assumptions that deny women sexual autonomy and pleasure."* (Naomi B. McCormick, PhD, Professor, Department of Psychology, State University of New York at Plattsburgh)

HIV/AIDS and Sexuality, edited by Michael W. Ross (Vol. 7, No. 1/2, 1995). *"An entire volume on the topic of HIV and sexuality, bringing together a number of essays and studies, which cover a wide range of relevant issues. It really is a relief to finally read some research and thoughts about sexual functioning and satisfaction in HIV-positive persons."* (Association of Lesbian and Gay Psychologists)

Gender Dysphoria: Interdisciplinary Approaches in Clinical Management, edited by Walter O. Bockting and Eli Coleman (Vol. 5, No. 4, 1993). *"A useful modern summary of the state-of--the-art endocrine and psychiatric approach to this important problem."* (Stephen B. Levine, MD, Clinical Professor of Psychiatry, School of Medicine, Case Western Reserve University; Co-Director, Center for Marital and Sexual Health)

Sexual Transmission of HIV Infection: Risk Reduction, Trauma, and Adaptation, edited by Lena Nilsson Schönnesson, PhD (Vol. 5, No. 1/2, 1992). *"This is an essential title for understanding how AIDS and HIV are perceived and treated in modern America."* (The Bookwatch)

John Money: A Tribute, edited by Eli Coleman (Vol. 4, No. 2, 1991). *"Original, provocative, and breaks new ground."* (Science Books & Films)

∞ ALL HAWORTH BOOKS AND JOURNALS ARE PRINTED ON CERTIFIED ACID-FREE PAPER

Adolescence, Sexuality, and the Criminal Law: Multidisciplinary Perspectives

Helmut Graupner, JD
Vern L. Bullough, PhD, DSci, RN
Editors

Adolescence, Sexuality, and the Criminal Law: Multidisciplinary Perspectives has been co-published simultaneously as *Journal of Psychology & Human Sexuality*, Volume 16, Numbers 2/3 2004.

The Haworth Press, Inc.
New York • London • Victoria (AU)
www.HaworthPress.com

Adolescence, Sexuality, and the Criminal Law: Multidisciplinary Perspectives has been co-published simultaneously as *Journal of Psychology & Human Sexuality*™, Volume 16, Numbers 2/3 2004.

© 2004 by The Haworth Press, Inc. All rights reserved. No part of this work may be reproduced or utilized in any form or by any means, electronic or mechanical, including photocopying, microfilm and recording, or by any information storage and retrieval system, without permission in writing from the publisher. Printed in the United States of America.

The development, preparation, and publication of this work has been undertaken with great care. However, the publisher, employees, editors, and agents of The Haworth Press and all imprints of The Haworth Press, Inc., including The Haworth Medical Press® and Pharmaceutical Products Press®, are not responsible for any errors contained herein or for consequences that may ensue from use of materials or information contained in this work. Opinions expressed by the author(s) are not necessarily those of The Haworth Press, Inc. With regard to case studies, identities and circumstances of individuals discussed herein have been changed to protect confidentiality. Any resemblance to actual persons, living or dead, is entirely coincidental.

Cover design by Kerry E. Mack

The Haworth Press, Inc., 10 Alice Street, Binghamton, NY 13904-1580 USA

Library of Congress Cataloging-in-Publication Data

Adolescence, sexuality, and the criminal law : multidisciplinary perspectives / Helmut Graupner, Vern L. Bullough, editors.
    p. cm.
    "Co-published simultaneously as Journal of psychology & human sexuality, volume 16, numbers 2/3 2004."
    Chiefly papers presented at a symposium held in Vienna in 2002 as part of the biennial conference of the International Society for the Treatment of Sex Offenders.
    Includes bibliographical references and index.
    ISBN 0-7890-2780-1 (hard cover : alk. paper)–ISBN 0-7890-2781-X (soft cover : alk. paper)
    1. Teenagers–Sexual behavior–Congresses. 2. Teenagers–Legal status, laws, etc.–Congresses. 3. Teenagers and adults–Congresses. 4. Sexual consent–Congresses. 5. Child sexual abuse–Congresses. I. Graupner, Helmut, 1965- II. Bullough, Vern L. III. Journal of psychology & human sexuality.
HQ27.A3616 2004
305.235–dc22
                                                        2004026212

Indexing, Abstracting & Website/Internet Coverage

This section provides you with a list of major indexing & abstracting services and other tools for bibliographic access. That is to say, each service began covering this periodical during the year noted in the right column. Most Websites which are listed below have indicated that they will either post, disseminate, compile, archive, cite or alert their own Website users with research-based content from this work. (This list is as current as the copyright date of this publication.)

Abstracting, Website/Indexing Coverage . . . . Year When Coverage Began

- *Business Source Corporate: coverage of nearly 3,350 quality magazines and journals; designed to meet the diverse information needs of corporations; EBSCO Publishing <http://www.epnet.com/corporate/bsourcecorp.asp>* **2001**

- *Cambridge Scientific Abstracts is a leading publisher of scientific information in print journals, online databases, CD-ROM and via the Internet <http://www.csa.com>* **1992**

- *EBSCOhost Electronic Journals Service (EJS) <http://ejournals.ebsco.com>* **2002**

- *Educational Administration Abstracts (EAA)* **1995**

- *e-psyche, LLC <http://www.e-psyche.net>* **2001**

- *Family & Society Studies Worldwide <http://www.nisc.com>* **1996**

- *Family Index Database <http://www.familyscholar.com>* **2003**

- *Family Violence & Sexual Assault Bulletin* **1991**

- *GenderWatch <http://www.slinfo.com>* **1999**

- *Google <http://www.google.com>* **2004**

- *Google Scholar <http://www.scholar.google.com>* **2004**

(continued)

- *Health & Psychosocial Instruments (HaPI) Database (available through online and as a CD-ROM from Ovid Technologies)* . . . . *
- *Higher Education Abstracts, providing the latest in research and theory in more than 140 major topics* 1991
- *HOMODOK/"Relevant" Bibliographic database, Documentation Centre for Gay & Lesbian Studies, University of Amsterdam (selective printed abstracts in "Homologie" and bibliographic computer databases covering cultural, historical, social & political aspects) <http://www.ihlia.nl/>* 2002
- *IBZ International Bibliography of Periodical Literature <http://www.saur.de>* 1997
- *Index Guide to College Journals (core list compiled by integrating 48 indexes frequently used to support undergraduate programs in small to medium sized libraries)* 1999
- *Index to Periodical Articles Related to Law <http://www.law.utexas.edu>* 1991
- *Internationale Bibliographie der geistes- und sozialwissenschaftlichen Zeitschriftenliteratur . . . See IBZ <http://www.saur.de>* 1997
- *Lesbian Information Service <http://www.lesbianinformationservice.org>* 2003
- *National Clearinghouse on Child Abuse & Neglect Information Documents Database <http://nccanch.acf.hhs.gov>* 2001
- *OCLC ArticleFirst <http://www.oclc.org/services/databases/>* . . . . *
- *OCLC ContentsFirst <http://www.oclc.org/services/databases/>* . . . . *
- *Psychological Abstracts (PsycINFO) <http://www.apa.org>* 1988
- *Referativnyi Zhurnal (Abstracts Journal of the All-Russian Institute of Scientific and Technical Information–in Russian) <http://www.viniti.ru>* 1991
- *Sage Family Studies Abstracts (SFSA)* 1995
- *Sage Urban Studies Abstracts (SUSA)* 1995
- *Sexual Diversity Studies: Gay, Lesbian, Bisexual & Transgender Abstracts (Formerly Gay & Lesbian Abstracts) provides comprehensive & in-depth coverage of the world's GLBT literature compiled by NISC & published on the Internet & CD-ROM <http://www.nisc.com>* 2000
- *Social Work Abstracts <http://www.silverplatter.com/catalog/swab.htm>* 1991
- *Sociological Abstracts (SA) <http://www.csa.com>* 1991
- *Studies on Women and Gender Abstracts <http://www.tandf.co.uk/swa>* 1991

*Exact start date to come.

Special Bibliographic Notes related to special journal issues (separates) and indexing/abstracting:

- indexing/abstracting services in this list will also cover material in any "separate" that is co-published simultaneously with Haworth's special thematic journal issue or DocuSerial. Indexing/abstracting usually covers material at the article/chapter level.
- monographic co-editions are intended for either non-subscribers or libraries which intend to purchase a second copy for their circulating collections.
- monographic co-editions are reported to all jobbers/wholesalers/approval plans. The source journal is listed as the "series" to assist the prevention of duplicate purchasing in the same manner utilized for books-in-series.
- to facilitate user/access services all indexing/abstracting services are encouraged to utilize the co-indexing entry note indicated at the bottom of the first page of each article/chapter/contribution.
- this is intended to assist a library user of any reference tool (whether print, electronic, online, or CD-ROM) to locate the monographic version if the library has purchased this version but not a subscription to the source journal.
- individual articles/chapters in any Haworth publication are also available through the Haworth Document Delivery Service (HDDS).

Adolescence, Sexuality, and the Criminal Law: Multidisciplinary Persceptives

CONTENTS

Introduction   1
Helmut Graupner, JD
Vern L. Bullough, PhD, DSci, RN

The 17-Year-Old Child: An Absurdity of the Late
   20th Century   7
Helmut Graupner, JD

Age of Consent: A Historical Overview   25
Vern L. Bullough, PhD, DSci, RN

Adolescent American Sex   43
David Weiss, PhD
Vern L. Bullough, PhD, DSci, RN

An Empirical Examination of Sexual Relations
   Between Adolescents and Adults: They Differ from Those
   Between Children and Adults and Should Be Treated
   Separately   55
Bruce Rind, PhD

14 to 18 Year Olds as "Children" by Law? Reflections
   on Developments in National and European Law   63
Lilian Hofmeister, JD

Sexuality, Adolescence and the Criminal Law:
   The Perspective of Criminology   71
Michael C. Baurmann, PhD

Adolescence, Sexual Aggression and the Criminal Law *Lorenz Böllinger, JD, MA*	89
Prostitution of Young Persons: A Topic of Social Work and/or Penal Legislation *Thomas Moebius, MA*	105
Sexual Consent: The Criminal Law in Europe and Outside of Europe *Helmut Graupner, JD*	111
Index	173

ABOUT THE EDITORS

Helmut Graupner (www.graupner.at), Doctor in Law (University of Vienna), is *Rechtsanwalt* (attorney-at-law), admitted to the bar in Austria and in the Czech Republic. He is Vice President of the Austrian Society for Sex Research (ÖGS) and President of the Austrian lesbian and gay rights organisation Rechtskomitee LAMBDA (RKL); Vice President for Europe, International Lesbian and Gay Law Association (ILGLaw); Austrian member, European Group of Experts on Combating Sexual Orientation Discrimination working for the Commission of the European Union; member, Scientific Committee of the Center for Research and Comparative Legal Studies on Sexual Orientation and Gender Identity (CERSGOSIG), Turin; member, Editorial Board of the *Journal of Homosexuality*; member, World Association for Sexology (WAS); member, Expert Committee for the Revision of the Law on Sexual Offences, appointed by the Austrian Minister of Justice in 1996; 1996 and 2003, expert, Justice Committee of the Austrian Federal Parliament; 2002, lecturer, University of Innsbruck ("Sexuality & the Law"); 2001, winner of the Gay and Lesbian Award (G.A.L.A.) of the Austrian Lesbian and Gay Movement.

Vern L. Bullough is State of New York University Distinguished Professor of History and Sociology Emeritus, SUNY College, Buffalo. He was also a former Dean of Natural and Social Sciences there. He founded the Center for Sex Research at California State University, Northridge, and is also an Emeritus Professor from that institution. He has received the Distinguished Achievement Award as well as the Alfred Kinsey Award from the Society for the Scientific Study of Sex and was past president of the society. He has also received numerous other awards. He is the author or co-author or editor of more than fifty books, half of which deal with sex and gender issues, and more than a hundred refereed articles and many hundred more popular articles.

Introduction

Helmut Graupner, JD
Vern L. Bullough, PhD, DSci, RN

The essays in this special volume are, with two exceptions,[1] amended and updated versions of papers delivered to the biennial conference of the International Association for the Treatment of Sex Offenders (IATSO)[2] held in 2002 in Vienna. They were delivered at a symposion entitled: "Adolescence, Sexuality & the Criminal Law."[3]

The reason for holding this session was the draft for an European Union–"Framework Decision on combating the sexual exploitation of children and child pornography" presented by the European Commission in 2001, which, due to its indiscriminate labelling of all persons up to the age of 18 years as "children," was threatening to criminalize a good deal of consensual adolescent sexual behaviour throughout the European Union. Various speakers from various perspectives (history, law, criminology, psychology, child- and adolescent-psychiatry, social work, and pedagogy) pointed out the intrinsic differences between children on the one hand and adolescents on the other, which differences rule out to treat adolescents like children, and which differences call for respect for sexual autonomy of adolescents and of the partners they choose.

Sexual autonomy does encompass two sides. Correctly understood it enshrines both the right to engage in wanted sexuality and the right to be free and protected from unwanted sexuality, from sexual abuse, and sexual violence. Both sides of the "coin" have to be given due weight and neither one neglected. Only then can human sexual dignity be fully and comprehensively respected.

The very essence of human rights is respect for human dignity and freedom,[4] and the notion of personal autonomy is an important principle underlying the interpretation of the right to respect for private life (privacy).[5] Safe-guarding that respect has to be based upon present-day conditions and obligations arising from it have to be met at any time.[6] Attitudes of former times therefore may not serve as justification for lack of such respect today; moreover, states have to actively remove the negative effects which may materialize today as a result of such former attitudes.[7]

With regard to the right to freedom *from* unwanted sexual abuse and violence those rights should be construed as not only including the negative right to be left alone from state intervention but also the positive right to (active) protection of those rights, against the State as well as against other private individuals.[8] The right to respect for private life (privacy) should not be restricted to the classical right to do what you want, but be seen as a comprehensive personality right, including the right to physical and moral (psychological) integrity and security.[9] A right to adequate protection against sexual abuse and violence, and in grave cases even to the employment of the criminal law for the purpose of deterrence.[10] The right to fair trial for persons accused of sexual abuse has to be balanced against the right of victims of abuse to protection; defense rights may (and in some circumstances must) be reasonably limited in the interests of persons who are, or who are presumed to be, victims of sexual abuse.[11]

With regard to the other side of the coin, the freedom *to* engage in consensual sexual activity, the right to respect for private life (privacy) enshrines the right to personal development,[12] to free expression and the development of one's personality,[13] and to establish and develop relationships with other human beings especially in the emotional field for the development and fulfillment of ones own personality.[14] The purpose of the protection of private life (privacy) lies in safe-guarding an area for individuals in which they can develop and fulfill their personality,[15] and in securing the right to choose the way in which to lead a sexual life.[16] Sexuality and sexual life is at the core of private life (privacy) and its protection.[17] State regulation of sexual behavior interferes with this right, and such interference can only be justified, if demonstrably necessary for the prevention of harm to others. Whereby "necessity" in this context is linked to a democratic society, whose hallmarks are "tolerance, pluralism, broadmindedness",[18] those hallmarks requiring that there is a pressing social need for the measure and that the measure is proportionate to the aim sought to achieve.[19]

Attitudes of the majority can not serve as valid ground for justification.[20] It is the core task of human rights to protect the individual and minorities against unjustified interference by the majority, no matter–as John Stuart Mill put it[21]–how big the majority and how strong its moral rejection and repulsion of the acts, attitudes and values of the minority or the individual might be. Interferences solely based on the views of the majority Mill called a "betrayal of the most fundamental values of the political theory of democracy."[22]

Times passed since the IATSO-conference saw the *EU-Framework Decision*, mentioned above, entering into force by January 21st, 2004. On the other hand they also saw the *European Court of Human Rights* awarding considerable amount of compensation to an adolescent for, between the ages of 14 and 18, having been barred, by age-of-consent legislation, from entering into relations corresponding to his disposition for sexual contact with older, adult partners,[23] and they saw the *Supreme Court of the United States of America* setting aside, on the basis of his right to privacy, the conviction of an 18-year-old adult to 17 years of incarceration for consensual oral sex with a 14-year-old adolescent.[24]

Unfortunately, American law remains particularly ambiguous since age of consent is generally left to the states and is not a matter for federal legislation. In January, 2004, as this introduction is being written, Marcus Dixon, who is black, is serving a ten year term in a Georgia prison for engaging in sex with a girl nearly 16 when he was 18. The sex act took place in February, 2003, and according to Marcus was consensual, although two days later the girl accused him of rape. The jury who heard the case in May, 2003, composed of nine whites and three blacks took just 20 minutes to acquit Marcus of rape. They then had to consider a lesser charge of "aggravated child molestation," a charge that was applicable even if the sex was consensual. This statute had never been used before in Georgia to prosecute consensual sex with teenagers when both partners were close in age. Since Marcus had already admitted to having sex, it was easy to find him guilty. The judge then sentenced him to ten years, a sentence that shocked many of the jurors who later said they thought the charge was a minor one. The case is on appeal.[25]

Many, if not most states, usually are more tolerant, accepting consensual sex between teens with less then a three year sentence. The case even in Georgia probably would have been ignored if the rape charge had not been made which brought the matter into court in the first place. What the case emphasizes is the importance of serious consideration of what the age of consent should be. As it is emphasized throughout the book, adolescents are sexual beings and it is important for society to accept that. It was in Article 4 of the Declaration of Human and Citizen Rights that the French stipulated that "Liberty consists in being able to do all that does not harm others." Adolescents are people. Hopefully this book will provide a stimulus to serious thinking on the topic.

The book could not have been written without the dedicated help of our authors and contributors. We want to thank them for their efforts in writing and revising their papers and for giving us permission to publish them.

NOTES

1. The chapters by *HON Justice Lilian Hofmeister* and *Lorenz Böllinger*
2. http://www.medacad.org/iatso
3. *Max Friedrich*, Dean of child and adolescent psychiatry at Vienna University, unfortunately was not able submit his paper as a chapter. He presented a paper called "Adolescence, Sexuality & the Criminal Law–the Perspective of Child Psychiatry" and, from the perspective of child psychiatry, agreed with the position of the other contributors, favoured an age of consent of 14 and outlined that age-limits higher than 14 (also on so-called "seduction") are not in the best interests of adolescents and endanger their psychosexual development (see also Max Friedrich, Kein Reifezeugnis für die Koalition, *Der Standard* 11.07.2002). At the symposion he submitted the following abstract: *"Minors are not a coherent and uniform group. A 5-year old cannot be equated with a 12-year old and a 12-year old not with a 17-year old. To do so would ignore the findings of child psychiatry and cause considerable harm to a high number of young people. This paper will explore the impact of psychosexual development in children and adolescents on the need for differentiation between various age groups in sexual-offences-legislation."*
4. European Court of Human Right (ECHR): *Christine Goodwin vs. UK* (28957/95), judg. 11.07.2002 [GC] (par. 90); *I. vs. UK* (25680/94), judg. 11.07.2002 [GC] (par. 70)
5. ECHR: *Christine Goodwin vs. UK* (28957/95), judg. 11.07.2002 [GC] (par. 90); *I. vs. UK* (25680/94), judg. 11.07.2002 [GC] (par. 70)
6. See for instance ECHR: *L. & V. vs. Austria* (39392,98, 39829/98), judg. 09.01.2003 (par. 47); *S.L. vs. Austria* (45330/99), judg. 09.01.2003 (par. 39); *Wessels-Bergervoet vs. NL* (34462/97), judg. 04.06.2002 (par. 52f); for an analysis of the respective case-law of the *Court* see Helmut Graupner, *Sexualität, Jugendschutz und Menschenrechte: Über das Recht von Kindern und Jugendlichen auf sexuelle Selbstbestimmung* (Frankfurt/M., Peter Lang, 1997), Vol. 1, 75ff.
7. ECHR: *Wessels-Bergervoet vs. NL*(34462/97), judg. 04.06.2002 (par. 52f)
8. ECHR: *Z. & Others vs. UK* (29392/95), judg. 10.05.2001 [GC] (par. 73); *E. & Others vs. UK* (33218/96), judg. 26.11.2002 (par. 88)
9. ECHR: *Christine Goodwin vs. UK* (28957/95), judg. 11.07.2002 [GC] (par. 90: « physical and moral security »); *I. vs. UK* (25680/94), judg. 11.07.2002 [GC] (par. 70:

«physical and moral security"); *D.P. & J.C. vs. UK* (38719/97), judg. 10.10.2001 [GC] (par. 118: "physical and moral integrity"); *X. & Y. vs. NL* (8978/80), 26.03.1985 (par. 22: "physical and moral integrity"); *Ilaria Salvetti vs. Italy* (42197/98), dec. 09.07.2002 ("physical and psychological integrity")

10. If effective deterrence, in a case where fundamental values and essential aspects of private life are at stake, cannot be achieved otherwise: ECHR, *X. & Y. vs. NL* (8978/80), 26.03.1985 (par. 27);

11. ECHR: *S.N. vs. Sweden* (34209/96), judg. 02.07.2002 (par. 47); *Owen Oysten vs. UK* (42011/98), dec. 22.01.2002

12. ECHR: *Christine Goodwin vs. UK* (28957/95), judg. 11.07.2002 [GC] (par. 90); *I. vs. UK* (25680/94), judg. 11.07.2002 [GC] (par. 70); *Zehnalová & Zehnal vs. CZ* (38621/97), dec. 14.05.2002

13. ECHR: *Fretté vs. France*(36515/97), judg. 26.02.2002 (par. 32)

14. ECHR: *Zehnalová & Zehnal vs. CZ* (38621/97), dec. 14.05.2002; European Commission of Human Rights, *X. vs. Iceland* (6825/74), dec. 18.05.1976

15. European Commission of Human Rights, *Brüggemann & Scheuten vs. Germany* (6959/75), report 12.07.1977

16. ECHR: *Fretté vs. France*(36515/97), judg. 26.02.2002 (par. 32)

17. ECHR: *L. & V. v. Austria* (39392/98, 39829/98), judg. 09.01.2003, par. 36 («most intimate aspect of private life»); *S.L. v. Austria* (45330/99), judg. 09.01.2003, par. 29 («most intimate aspect of private life»); European Commission of Human Rights: *Sutherland vs. UK 1997* (25185/94), dec. 01.07.1997 (par. 57: "most intimate aspect of effected individuals 'private life'", also par. 36: "private life (which includes his sexual life)"; so also the ECHR in: *Dudgeon vs. UK* (7525/76), judg. 22.10.1981, par. 41, 52; *Norris vs. Ireland* (10581/83), judg. 26.10.1988 (par. 35ff); *Modinos vs. Cyprus* (15070/89), judg. 22.04.1993 (par. 17ff); *Laskey, Brown & Jaggard sv. UK* (21627/93; 21826/93; 21974/93) 19.02.1997, par. 36; *Lustig-Prean & Beckett vs. UK* (31417/96; 32377/96) (par. 82), 27.09. 1999; *Smith & Grady vs. UK* (33985/96; 33986/96), judg. 27.09.1999 (par. 90); *A.D.T. vs. UK* (35765/97), judg. 31.07.2000 (par. 21ff); *Fretté vs. France* (36515/97), judg. 26.02.2002 (par. 32); German Constitutional Court, BverfGE 47, 46 [73].

18. ECHR: *Dudgeon vs. UK* (7525/76), judg. 22.10.1981, par. 53; *Norris vs. Ireland* (10581/83), judg. 26.10.1988 (par. 44); *Modinos vs. Cyprus* (15070/89), judg. 22.04.1993 (par. 25); *Lustig-Prean & Beckett vs. UK* (31417/96; 32377/96) (par. 80), 27.09. 1999; *Smith & Grady vs. UK* (33985/96; 33986/96), judg. 27.09.1999 (par. 87)

19. ECHR: *Dudgeon vs. UK* (7525/76), judg. 22.10.1981, par. 51; *Norris vs. Ireland* (10581/83), judg. 26.10.1988 (par. 41f); *Modinos vs. Cyprus* (15070/89), judg. 22.04.1993 (par. 25); *A.D.T. vs. UK* (35765/97), judg. 31.07.2000 (par. 32f); For a detailed discussion of the requirements for interferences being justified according to Art. 8 par. 2 ECHR see Graupner (1997), *supra*, Vol. 1, 86ff.

20. ECHR: *Dudgeon vs. UK* (7525/76), judg. 22.10.1981; *Norris vs. Ireland* (10581/83), judg. 26.10.1988; *Modinos vs. Cyprus* (15070/89), judg. 22.04.1993; *Lustig-Prean & Beckett vs. UK* (31417/96; 32377/96), 27.09. 1999; *Smith & Grady vs. UK* (33985/96; 33986/96), judg. 27.09.1999; *L. & V. v. Austria* (39392/98, 39829/98), judg. 09.01.2003; *S.L. v. Austria* (45330/99), judg. 09.01.2003.

21. J. S. Mill, *On Liberty*

22. J. S. Mill, *On Liberty*, after de Tocqueville, *Democracy in America*.

23. *S.L. vs. Austria* (45330/99), judg. 09.01.2003 (par. 49, 52)

24. *Limon, Matthew R. v. Kansas*, U.S.-Supreme Court, 02.583, 27.06.2003

25. Marian Wright Edelman, "Old South Lingers in a Legal Lynching," *Los Angeles Times*, January 22, 2004, p. B17.

The 17-Year-Old Child:
An Absurdity of the Late 20th Century

Helmut Graupner, JD

Helmut Graupner (www.graupner.at), Doctor in Law (University of Vienna), is *Rechtsanwalt* (attorney-at-law), admitted to the bar in Austria and in the Czech Republic. He is Vice President of the Austrian Society for Sex Research (ÖGS); and President of the Austrian lesbian and gay rights organisation Rechtskomitee LAMBDA (RKL); Vice President for Europe, International Lesbian and Gay Law Association (ILGLaw); Austrian member, European Group of Experts on Combating Sexual Orientation Discrimination working for the Commission of the European Union; member, Scientific Committee of the Center for Research and Comparative Legal Studies on Sexual Orientation and Gender Identity (CERSGOSIG), Turin; member, Editorial Board of the *Journal of Homosexuality*; member, World Association for Sexology (WAS); member, Expert Committee for the Revision of the Law on Sexual Offences, appointed by the Austrian Minister of Justice in 1996; 1996 and 2003, expert, Justice Committee of the Austrian Federal Parliament; 2002, lecturer, University of Innsbruck ("Sexuality & the Law"); 2001, winner of the Gay and Lesbian Award (G.A.L.A.) of the Austrian Lesbian and Gay Movement.

This essay has been presented as a lecture at the 7th International Conference of the International Association for the Treatment of Sexual Offenders (IATSO), "Sexual Abuse and Sexual Violence–From Understanding to Protection and Prevention" (Vienna, September 11th-14th 2002), Symposion "Sexuality, Adolescence & the Criminal Law" (Friday, 13th September 2002), http://www.medacad.org/iatso; Last update: 22.01.2004.

Address correspondence to: Rechtskomitee LAMBDA, Linke Wienzeile 102, A-1160 Vienna, Austria (E-mail: hg@graupner.at).

[Haworth co-indexing entry note]: "The 17-Year-Old Child: An Absurdity of the Late 20th Century." Graupner, Helmut. Co-published simultaneously in *Journal of Psychology & Human Sexuality* (The Haworth Press, Inc.) Vol. 16, No. 2/3, 2004, pp. 7-24; and: *Adolescence, Sexuality, and the Criminal Law: Multidisciplinary Perspectives* (ed: Helmut Graupner, and Vern L. Bullough) The Haworth Press, Inc., 2004, pp. 7-24. Single or multiple copies of this article are available for a fee from The Haworth Document Delivery Service [1-800-HAWORTH, 9:00 a.m. - 5:00 p.m. (EST). E-mail address: docdelivery@haworthpress.com].

http://www.haworthpress.com/web/JPHS
© 2004 by The Haworth Press, Inc. All rights reserved.
Digital Object Identifier: 10.1300/J056v16n02_02

SUMMARY. Recently enacted EU-legislation will affect interferences with the sexual life of adolescents across Europe in an intensity so far not known in any of the European states. The "Framework-Directive on combating sexual exploitation of children and child-pornography" will oblige all member States of the European Union to create extensive offences of "child"-pornography and "child"-prostitution, defining as "child" every person up to 18 years of age, without differentiating between five-year-old children and 17-year-old juveniles. These offences go far beyond combating child pornography and child prostitution, thus making a wide variety of adolescent sexual behaviour, hitherto completely legal in the overwhelming majority of jurisdictions in Europe, serious crimes; for instance: sex between 16-year-olds for "remuneration", which includes invitations to cinema or to a dinner; "lascivious" drawings of a 17-year-old girl possessed by a 15-year-old boy; photographs of a 16 year-old girl in her bikini "lasciviously" exposing her pubic area, taken by her 17-year-old boyfriend on the beach; standard pornography involving younger looking 20-year-old adults or "webcam-sex" between 17-year-old-adolescents; even pictures of one's own adult spouse in "lascivious" poses, if this spouse looks younger than 18. No European jurisdiction so far has such a restrictive law. The massive criminalisation and the equation of adolescents with children caused heavy criticisms among experts but this criticism could not prevent the project from becoming law. This essay provides an analysis of the background, the legislative process and the content of the EU-Framework-Decision. *[Article copies available for a fee from The Haworth Document Delivery Service: 1-800-HAWORTH. E-mail address: <docdelivery@haworthpress.com> Website: <http://www.HaworthPress.com> © 2004 by The Haworth Press, Inc. All rights reserved.]*

KEYWORDS. Youth protection, youth rights, sexual offences, age of consent, sexual consent, sexual violence, sexual abuse, sexual exploitation, child sexual abuse, paedophilia, ephebophilia, child pornography, child prostitution, youth pornography, youth prostitution, juvenile prostitution, criminal law, human rights, sexual rights, European Union, European law

No language in the world ever used the term "child" for persons beyond their early teens (Friedenberg 1974, 21). No person beyond its early teens is a "child" (Baacke 1983, 70; Herbold 1977, 101; Kraemer et al., 1976, 40; Lautmann 1987, 66).[1] It was the *Convention on the Rights of the Child* of 1989[2] which first did away with the distinction between children and adolescents and labelled all minors under 18 "child" (Art. 1).

The European Commission took this concept over into the criminal law area when it proposed an *EU-Framework Decision on Combating the Sexual Exploitation of Children and Child Pornography* in December 2000.[3] This framework-decision obliges all the member states of the European Union to create certain sexual offences which would go far beyond what is known in that area in any European state today.[4]

The proposal of the Commission defined as "child" every person up to its 18th birthday (Art. 1 lit. a). It did not differentiate in any way between various age groups, i.e., it did not distinguish between children on the one hand and adolescents on the other. The proposal treated a 17 1/2 year old young man in the same way as a 5 year old child.

This implementation of the same criteria for sexual protection and abuse to a five-year-old child and a 17-year-old adolescent leads to absurd and dangerous consequences.[5]

DEFICIENT PROTECTION OF CHILDREN

The Commission in its proposal did not set a minimum age limit for consensual sexual activity, despite the fact that all the EU member states as well as all of the other European and non-European countries have determined such age limits, which limits are nowhere set under 12 years of age and, in most cases at 14 or 15.[6] According to the Commission proposal, member states will be obliged to outlaw sexual activity with children only in the context of pornography, prostitution, violence and inducement (Art. 2 & 3). The proposal (and the final text) did not cover sexual activity with a child outside the area of pornography and prostitution and committed without violence and without inducing the child. This deficiency in protection appears inconceivable, in that it would leave it open to the EU member states to even decriminalize pedosexual contacts, to the extent that no inducement or violence and no involvement into pornography or prostitution of the child takes place.

The Commission proposal also merely required the member states ". . . to *consider* prohibiting natural persons from exercising . . . activities involving supervision of children when they have been convicted for one of the criminal offences provided for . . ." (Art. 5 par. 5).[7] That this is not an *absolute requirement* is perplexing, indeed. As is the fact that only *private*–and not *public*–bodies can be held responsible for their offences (Art. 1 lit. d, Art. 6 & 7).

These insufficient and half-hearted measures for the protection of children stand in striking opposition to the near draconian limitations prescribed for the sex lives of adolescents. Both being the result of the same mistake: the equation of children with adolescents.

DRACONIAN LIMITATIONS ON THE SEX LIFE OF ADOLESCENTS

The Commission defines as "child"-pornography all visual depictions of explicit sexual conduct which (directly or indirectly) involves a person under 18 (Art. 1 lit. b). Explicit sexual conduct thereby includes even "lascivious exhibition"[8] not only of the genitals but also of the mere pubic area.[9] This phrase, as the whole definition of "child"-pornography, has been literally taken over from § 2256 of the U.S.-Federal Criminal Code. How extensive these phrases are can be inferred from the development in the U.S. In 1994 the Congress, in reaction to a Supreme Court case (United States vs. Knox 1992), expressly declared that in enacting this provision[10] it was and is the intent of Congress that "the scope of 'exhibition of the genitals or pubic area' is not limited to nude exhibitions or exhibitions in which outlines of those areas were discernible through clothing, and that for videotapes falling under this law it is not afforded that the genitals or the pubic area are visible in the tapes and that the minors pose or act lasciviously."[11] So the phrase now taken over into European law covers all kinds of allegedly erotic depictions of persons under 18, even if the young man or woman on the picture is fully clothed.

According to the Commission's proposal also fictitious depictions are covered, as for instance comic strips, drawings and paintings, even if totally unrealistic (Art. 3).[12] In addition it shall not be necessary to establish the true age of the actors; it shall suffice that for the viewer they appear to be under 18.[13] Given the very diverse views in estimating age and considered that according to this wide variety nearly every person of 18, 19, or in its early twenties can be judged to be possibly under 18, a good deal of standard pornography and standard erotic material faces the risk of prosecution under this provision.

The Commission's proposal aimed not only at a massive extension of sexual offences in the area of pornography. It wanted to oblige the member states also to criminalize sexual contacts with persons under 18 not just against money or other items of economic value but also in exchange for "other (non-economic) forms of remuneration" (Art. 2 lit. b ii), whatever that might be. In addition even "inducement" of young men and women under 18 to sexual acts should become a criminal offence (Art. 2 lit. b ii). The Commission did not define "inducement"[14] and gave no reason whatsoever for this proposed criminalization of sexual contacts of adolescents which are not initiated by themselves but by their partners.[15]

The proposal (as the final text) also contains no exception for juveniles, so the member states have to criminalize even adolescents themselves as perpetrators of these offences. And the penalties suggested by the Commission are draconian: the maximum penalty must be at least four years incarceration, with no differentiation between juvenile and adult offenders (Art. 5). So as victims, adolescents are treated as children, and as offenders, they are treated as adults.

According to the proposal of the Commission in all the member states of the European Union a 15-year-old will be liable to up to four years incarceration (at the minimum) for making a picture of his girlfriend of same age in tight bikinis exposing (not the genitals but) the "pubic area" and posing erotically (or in the words of the law: "lasciviously"). The same is true for a 14-year-old who, in private, draws a young beauty naked and in "lascivious" poses. As well it is for 17-year-olds, who exchange intimate pictures of themselves, or watch each other via live cams on the internet "lasciviously" exposing their "pubic area" (or even their genitals), not to mention watching each other during sexual activity (so called "webcam-sex"). Also adolescents asking other adolescents for sex would face prosecution, as they "induce" a "child" into sex. That would be the more so if they offer any reward for being accepted.

The *European Parliament* welcomed the proposal by a vast majority of 446 against 16 votes. It even called for extensions, as for instance the criminalization of "negligent" production of "child"-pornography and the criminalization of audiovisual, textual, or written material advocating sexual contacts with persons under 18.[16] It also wanted to criminalize images of adults who look younger than 18, even if it is proven that the person depicted was adult at the time of depiction.[17,18]

WIDESPREAD EXPERT CRITICISM

Among experts the proposal caused widespread criticism. In particular the *World Association for Sexology (WAS)*,[19] the *Austrian Society for Sex Research (ÖGS)*,[20] and all three German sexological associations[21] as well as the *European Region of the International Lesbian and Gay Association (ILGA-Europe)*[22] and the *German Lesbian and Gay Association (LSVD)*[23] expressed their opposition to such a wide-ranging criminalization of juvenile sexuality. The *German Society for Sex Research* even spoke of "moral colonialism" as the definition of "child"-pornography has been literally taken over from § 2256 of the U.S.-Federal Criminal Code.[24] In a public hearing of experts in the *Austrian parliament* experts (in law, child psychiatry, psychotherapy, and child sexual exploitation) unanimously criticized the framework-decision and Austrian implementation legislation for its extensive and overbroad criminalization.[25]

The associations and experts called for respect of adolescents' sexual autonomy by lowering the age limit of 18 and, above all, to differentiate between children and adolescents. They asked for a complete deletion of the offence of "inducement" of a person under 18 into sex and the deletion of the offence of sexual contact against "non-economic" remuneration. In addition they asked to bear in mind that giving a reward is not necessarily prostitution; it could also cover the invitation to cinema or a dinner.[26] The associations suggested to consider also that criminal investigations whether a reward has been causative for an intimate contact or not would do more harm than good to the juveniles involved. Finally even in the case of real youth-prostitution criminalization would remarkably impair social-work with young prostitutes, which turned out as the only effective mean of support and relief for them.[27]

These concerns, also raised by more than half of the member-states, to some extent have been taken into account during the deliberations in the EU-Council of Ministers, which is the competent body to finally pass the frame-work-decision. The offence of "inducement" of under 18-year-olds into sexual contacts and the reference to non-economic forms of remuneration have been deleted at the first discussion of the proposal.[28] And the offence of sexual contact against remuneration has been amended[29] so that the remuneration or consideration has to be given as payment in order to induce a 'child' (a person under 18) to engage in sexual activity.[30] This wording excludes from the offence situations where the juvenile initiates the contact or readily agrees to a respective offer. Later on in the deliberations of the Council, however, the English (and Italian) version of the text, for reasons not known, returned back to the wording "remuneration or consideration given as payment in exchange for the 'child' engaging in sexual activities," which wording again seems to cover all cases of sex against consideration.[31] The German,[32] the French,[33] the Spanish,[34] the Portuguese,[35] and the Dutch[36] versions, however, still involve inducement.[37]

As regards pornography the Council established certain exceptions, which the member-states can, but need not, apply.

INSUFFICIENT EXCEPTIONS

While under the Commission's proposal it was always possible to avoid punishment by proving that the person depicted in fact was over 18 at the time the picture was taken (Art. 3 par. 2), the Council changed that to a mere option for the member-states (Art. 3 par. 2 lit. a). They can also establish that the mere impression that a depicted person looks like a person under 18 suffices for conviction, and that a younger look and impression alone constitutes the offence. Several member-states wanted to go even further, exclude the exception totally and oblige all the member-states to render also depictions of adults, who look like a minor, a criminal offence.[38] That despite the fact that the U.S.-Supreme Court in a recent judgment held that the criminalization of fictitious or virtual (child-) pornography violates fundamental rights (Ashcroft vs. Free Speech Coalition 2002). As the definition of "child"-pornography has been taken over from the U.S.-Federal Criminal Code one might have expected that such a judgment of fundamental importance by the Supreme Court would matter. It did not.

Another exception the Council introduced is that the member-states can (but again need not) exclude from criminal liability the production and possession of images of persons of the age of sexual consent or older with their consent and solely for their own private use (Art. 3 par. 2 lit. b). This exception turns out as far too narrow. It does exempt from criminal liability just production and possession[39] which is solely for the use of the adolescent depicted. So it seems highly questionable whether other persons than mere photographers and depositaries without any interest in the images on their own could benefit from this exception. So, for instance, the 15-year-old who possesses a "lascivious" picture of his girlfriend for joint (!) use with her or for his bedside table; or a (even also himself adolescent) "Webcamsex-Partner" of a juvenile on whose computer the image of his juvenile partner is displayed primarily for his use, and only secondarily for the use of the juvenile partner who sends the picture mainly in exchange to see the other one himself over the cam. In all these cases the image is possessed or produced not solely (!) for the use of the depicted person.[40] Definitely outside of the scope of the exception is an adolescent who hands over or even just shows a "lascivious" picture of him- or herself to another person, a 15- or 16-year-old doing so is liable to harsh sentences for producing, making accessible, and distributing "child"-pornography. Also outside of the scope of the exception is a couple of two 17-year-olds exchanging intimate pictures of themselves,[41] let alone if they show it to third persons.

Italy persistently resisted even this extremely narrow exception.[42] So, as a compromise,[43] a paragraph has been included saying, that "[E]ven where the existence of consent has been established, it shall not be considered valid, if for example superior age, maturity, position, status, experience, or the victim's dependency on the perpetrator has been abused in achieving the consent" (Art. 3 par. lit. ii). It is not hard to imagine that in each and every relation between two people at least one of those elements exists: either one is older, or more mature, or in a higher position, or more experienced than the other. This way, and given also the ambiguity of the term "abused," the application of this, anyhow extremely narrow, exception is left up to the unfettered discretion of police authorities, prosecutors and judges, without any legal certainty for adolescents and their partners.

The third exception regards fictitious or virtual images. The Council (different than the Commission) restricted the scope of the frame-work-decision to fictitious images, which are "realistic,"[44] and stipulated that the member-states could (but again need not) exclude from liability production and possession for the own private use of the producer (Art. 3 par. 2 lit. c). Also, here the judgment of the U.S.-Supreme Court had no, or just a minor, impact. The 14-year-old mentioned before, may now (if his member-state allows for that exception) draw the naked young beauty in "lascivious poses," but he becomes liable to prosecution and harsh sentences for making accessible "child"-pornography if he shows this drawing to a friend. Italy again also persistently resisted this exception.[45] And also here, as a compromise, the exception has been narrowed further.[46] The exception has been made[47] contingent upon the condition that in the production of the virtual material no depiction of a real person is used and that the act (production and possession) involves no risk for the dissemination of the material (Art. 3 par. 2 lit. c). So a 17-year-old (if her member-state allows for that exception)[48] may generate and store a lascivious virtual animation of an adolescent on her computer but she becomes criminally liable under "child"-pornography legislation if she uses a picture of her 16-year-old boyfriend in the production of the animation or if she does not lock the file with a password.

All this seems absurd. As it seems absurd to treat 17-year-olds as "children" and to criminalize a person for acquiring or possessing an erotic ("lascivious") picture of a 17 1/2 year old fully developed young man or of a 17 1/2 year old fully developed young woman.

Even more so as the Council inserted a provision into the framework-decision prohibiting member-states to make investigations or prosecution dependent on the report or accusation by the juvenile or his/her legal guardian (Art. 9 par. 1).[49]

To make it utmost clear. The fight against sexual exploitation of children is extremely important. In this respect the upcoming frame-work-decision is to be welcomed. As shown at the beginning, it even does not go far enough in this area. The decision, however, goes very far beyond combating child-pornography and child-prostitution and infringes deeply into people's sex lives. Insofar it has to be criticized and rejected.

Initially six member-states raised concerns regarding the indiscriminate age-limit of 18 years.[50] It is difficult to understand why they gave in.[51] On 22nd December 2003, the Council of Ministers of the European Union formally adopted the framework-decision, which entered into force on 21st January 2004.[52]

CITED CASES

Ashcroft vs. Free Speech Coalition, United States Supreme Court, opinion 16.04.2002, 535 U.S., No. 00-795, *http://www.supremecourtus.gov*
United States vs. Knox, No. 92-183, 1992

REFERENCES

American Psychiatric Association (APA), *Diagnostic and Statistical Manual of Mental Disorders (Fourth Edition), DSM-IV*, USA 1994, *http://www.psych.org/public_info/dsm.pdf*
Baacke, Dieter, *Die 13-bis 18jährigen, Einführung in die Probleme des Jugendalters*, Weinheim/Basel 1983
Bleibtreu-Ehrenberg, Gisela, Der pädophile Impuls–Wie lernt ein junger Mensch Sexualität?, *Der Monat neue Folge*, 294, 175ff, 1984

Bundesrat, Niederschrift über die 9. Sitzung des Ausschusses für Frauen nd Jugend am 4. März 1992 in Bonn, Öffentliche Anhörung, Protokoll Nr. 93, Bonn 1993

Deutscher Bundestag, *28, 29. und 30. Sitzung des Sonderausschusses für die Strafrechtsreform,* 6. Wahlperiode, Stenographischer Dienst, Bonn 23., 24. und 25. November 1970, Bonn 1970

Dür, W. et al., *Aids-Aufklärung bei Jugendlichen,* Vienna 1990

Eich, Holger, *Der Kuβ der Macht, Zur kindlichen und erwachsenen Wahrnehmung von Sexualität,* in: Perner, Zuliebe, Zuleibe, S. 50ff, Bad Sauerbrunn 1991

Friedenberg, Edgar Z., *The Vanishing Adolescent,* NY/USA 1974

Graupner, Helmut, *Sexualität, Jugendschutz & Menschenrechte–Über das Recht von Kindern und Jugendlichen auf sexuelle Selbstbestimmung,* 2 Volumes, Peter Lang, Frankfurt, M/Berlin/Bern/New York/Paris/Vienna, 1997

Graupner, Helmut, Sex in the Böhmdorfer-City, *Der Standard,* 39, 11.12.2003

Herbold, H., Einige delikttypische Veränderungen bei sexuellem Mißbrauch von Kindern (§ 176 StGB) in den letzten Jahren, *Monatsschrift für Kriminologie und Strafrechtsreform (MschrKrim),* 60, 90f, 1977

Kraemer, W., *The Forbidden Love: the Normal and Abnormal Love of Children,* London 1976

Lautmann, Rüdiger, *Die heterosexuelle Verführung–sexuelle Interaktion und Kriminalisierung bei § 182 StGB,* in: Jäger, H. & Schorsch, E., Sexualwissenschaft und Strafrecht, S. 54ff, Stuttgart 1987

Maier, Erne, Sexualerziehung und Jugendschutz, *Unsere Jugend* 5, 9, 385ff, 1953

Müller-Luckmann, Elisabeth, *Über die Glaubwürdigkeit kindlicher und jugendlicher Zeuginnen bei Sexualdelikten,* Stuttgart 1959

Peters, J., Children Who are Victims of Sexual Assault and the Psychology of Offenders, *American Journal of Psychotherapy,* 398ff, 1976

Reinhardt, Heinz, *Die Bestrafung der Unzucht mit Kindern unter besonderer Berücksichtigung des Verhaltens und der Persönlichkeit des Opfers,* Berner kriminologische Untersuchungen 4, Bern 1967

Schultz, L. G., *Sexual Emancipation–An Introduction,* in: Schultz, L. G., The Sexual Victimology of Youth, p. 355f, Springfield/Illinois/USA 1980

Working Group of Experts on Sexual Offences (1997-1999), *Protocols of Deliberations,* Ministry of Justice, Vienna (unpublished)

World Health Organisation (WHO), *International Statistical Classification of Diseases and Related Health Problems,* 10th Revision, 1992, http://www.who.int/whosis/icd10/

Wyatt, G. E. & Powell, G. J., *Lasting Effects of child sexual abuse,* Newburry Park et al. 1988

NOTES

1. "Sexually mature human beings are no children anymore but potential parents" (Eich 1991, 55, translation by the author [tba]); "Quite a number of problems arise from the fact that the adolescent is less a developing person than an already developed one [...] He cannot be treated as a child and he must not accept if that happens" (Maier 1953, 398, tba). "By 12 years of age, as Eugen Verhellen of the University of Gent, Bel-

gium, reports about psychological studies, children do not differ in social competence sigificantly from adults" (profil 39/1993, 87, www.profil.at; tba). "Both the court and legislature ultimately must come to grips with the fact that the basic intellectual capacities are present very young and that complex moral and political reasoning can take place least by age twelve or fourteen" (Schultz 1980, 366, citing *Governor's Special Commission on the Age of Majority*, Summary, 1971, at 2, State of Michigan/USA; E. Boulding, *Childrens Rights*, Society, 15 (1):40, 1977). "Contacts between–culturally defined–'adults' and 'children' are not subsumed under the term pedophilia, *if both partners have reached puberty*, since then those contacts are just contacts between adults of different ages" (Bleibtreu-Ehrenberg 1984, 175, tba). Also the *American Psychiatric Association (APA)* and the *World Health Organisation (WHO)* do not qualify sexual relations with adolescents beyond early puberty as "pedophilic"(WHO 1992: ICD 10: F65.4; APA 1994: "diagnostic criteria for 302.20 pedophilia"). Cf. *Swiss legal history*: "After publication of the draft 1908 again numerous opinions have been filed with the Ministry of Justice. Most of them, coming mainly from feminist or religious associations, called for a rise in the age of consent to 18. Girls of 16 would not be mature enough to discern the meaning of sexual intercourse, and the age should also be raised to prevent prostitution. On the other side Wilhelm in his commentary on sexual offences law is of the opinion that indiscriminate child protection up to the age of 16 is inexpedient, since adolescents between 14 and 16 could not be seen as 'children' anymore and could not be put on the same footing with 8-year-olds [...] Zürcher, Gautier, Thormann und Calame oppose raising the age of consent to 18 because children over 16 should already have a certain maturity in character and a girl between 16 and 18 could not be seen as a child anymore" (Reinhardt 1967, 31ff, tba)

2. General Assembly resolution 44/25 (20 November 1989), entered into force 2nd September 1990, www.unhchr.ch

3. COM [2000] 854, OJ C 62 E/327-330, 27.02.2001, http://europa.eu.int/prelex/rech_simple.cfm?CL=en

4. See the other chapter of Graupner in this book for details. In Europe in nearly 1/2 of the jurisdictions consensual sexual relations with 14 year old adolescents are legal; in almost 2/3 with 15 year olds; in a majority also when the older partner has started the initiative and also when the initiative contains an offer of remuneration. In nearly all European jurisdictions such relations are legal from the age of 16 onwards. Nearly all European jurisdictions set the same age limit in the criminal law for depicting sexual activity as for the sexual activity itself. Only *Estonia*, *France* (Art. 227-23 CC), *Italy* (Art. 600ter CC; exploitation afforded), *Latvia* (Art. 165 CC), *Spain* (Art. 189 CC) *and Sweden* (Ch. 6 § 7 (2) CC; restricted to seduction to making depictions) have an age limit in the criminal law for depicting sexual activity that is higher than the general age-limit for sex. And none of the provisions of these countries are nearly as extensive as the offences prescribed by the EU-Framework-Decision. Also the *Cybercrime-Convention* of the Council of Europe (ETS 185, 23.11.2001; http://conventions.coe.int) and the 2000 *Optional Protocol* to the UN-Convention on the Rights of the Child "*on the sale of children, child prostitution and child pornography*" (General Assembly resolution A/RES/54/263 of 25 May 2000, entered in to force 18th January 2002, www.unhchr.ch) do not proscribe such extensive offences. Both do not require possession for private purposes and depictions of (younger looking) adults neither virtual productions to be made crimes. And the *Cybercrime-Convention* does not oblige member-states to criminalize depictions of persons of 16 years of age and above.

5. Both adolescents and adults experience the age group of 13- to 18-year-olds essentially as a "sensuous unity" (Baacke 1983, 22). In addition to that due to the "approximation between generations", which took place during the past years, adolescents "today largely view adults not anymore different than themselves [...] One treats them exactly the same as peers" (Müller-Luckmann 1959, 85, tba). "There are real friendships between adolescents and adults in contemporary society, especially in America; it is taken for granted that there should be" (Friedenberg 1974, 24). "Shortly before physical onset of puberty, a different quality of feeling suffuses one's perception of certain other individuals. They are loved. Children and juveniles do not love in this sense, because they are rarely interested in the complete personalities of other persons" (Friedenberg 1974, 47). "Intimacy means a close relationship over a longer period and the ability to exchange personal information based upon a sense of mutual understanding. This structure of experience first emerges at the age of 12 to 13" (Keller in Bundesrat 1992, 122, tba). See also Peters (1976, 413: "thirteen as a cut-off-point"); Wyatt & Powell (1988, 12, "Children age 12 and under often do not have the cognitive processes to understand the severity of the incidents"). "In principle it can be said that the discussion among adults whether adolescents may have sexual intercourse or not has already been decided by the adolescents themselves a long time ago and unambiguous. [...] If one asks 16- and 17-year-old students, at which age a boy or a girl may have sexual intercourse, the majority says either: 'as soon as one has the desire to do so' or 'as soon as one is mature' or 'by 15 at the latest'" (Sigusch in Deutscher Bundestag 1970, 864, tba). "Already for the first sexual intercourse one finds the same kind of relationships which are typical for sexual behaviour of adults." "Adolescents determine their sexual life–as adults–essentially on personal and individual criteria" (Dür 1990, 8, tba). "They want participation not protection. The sexually emancipated minor is here now" (Schultz 1980, 368). Many more references in Graupner 1997 (i.e. Vol. 1, 260ff).

6. See the other chapter of Graupner in this book for details.

7. Also the final text of the framework decision proscribes the exclusion of perpetrators from professional supervision of children only "if appropriate" (Art. 5 par. 3).

8. During deliberations in the Council France and Belgium, unsuccessfully, wanted to change that term into "sexually explicit position" (Council of the European Union, Working Party on Substantive Criminal Law, 8112/01, DROIPEN 35, MIGR 36, 27.04.2001, http://register.consilium.eu.int)

9. COMMUNICATION FROM THE COMMISSION TO THE COUNCIL AND THE EUROPEAN PARLIAMENT: Combating trafficking in human beings and combating the sexual exploitation of children and child pornography, page 23, 22.01.2001, http://europa.eu.int/eur-lex/en/com/pdf/2000/en_500PC0854_01.pdf

10. The legislation was introduced in 1978 with an age limit of 16 (Pub.L. 95-225, § 2(a), Feb. 6, 1978, 92 Stat. 7, 8). 1984 the age was raised to 18 (Pub.L.98-292, §§ 4, 5, 7(2), May 21, 1984, 98 Stat. 204, 205, 206).

11. §§ 2251-2256 Federal Criminal Code; Confirmation of Intent of Congress in Enacting Section 2252 and 2256 (Section 160003 of Pub.L. 103-322).

12. COMMUNICATION FROM THE COMMISSION TO THE COUNCIL AND THE EUROPEAN PARLIAMENT: Combating trafficking in human beings and combating the sexual exploitation of children and child pornography, page 23, 22.01.2001, http://europa.eu.int/eur-lex/en/com/pdf/2000/en_500PC0854_01.pdf

13. COMMUNICATION FROM THE COMMISSION TO THE COUNCIL AND THE EUROPEAN PARLIAMENT: Combating trafficking in human beings and com-

bating the sexual exploitation of children and child pornography, page 23, 22.01.2001, http://europa.eu.int/eur-lex/en/com/pdf/2000/en_500PC0854_01.pdf

14. In some language versions "inducement" was even translated as "persuasion," while it was omitted in the French and Spanish texts.

15. COMMUNICATION FROM THE COMMISSION TO THE COUNCIL AND THE EUROPEAN PARLIAMENT: Combating trafficking in human beings and combating the sexual exploitation of children and child pornography, pages 22f, 22.01.2001, http://europa.eu.int/eur-lex/en/com/pdf/2000/en_500PC0854_01.pdf

16. European Parliament legislative resolution on the proposal for a Council Framework Decision on combating the sexual exploitation of children and child pornography (COM[2000] 854-C5-0043/2001-2001/0025[CNS]), A5-0206/2001, 12.06.2001, http://www.europarl.eu.int/plenary/default_en.htm (Amendment 42: "encourage, incite, or instigate"

17. Amendment 10.

18. In the Council "no delegation thought that the draft should be modified in the light of that opinion" (Council of the European Union, Working Party on substantive criminal law, 7536/02 DROIPEN 18 MIGR 20, 27.03.2002; Council of the European Union, COREPER, 8135/02 DROIPEN 26 MIGR 35, 19.04.2002; http://register.consilium.eu.int.

19. Letter to the European Commission (17.09.2001), http://www.rklambda.at/eu_plan_en.htm

20. Letter to the European Commission (29.05.2001), http://www.rklambda.at/eu_plan_en.htm

21. German Society for Social Scientific Research (DGSS), Letter to the European Commission (27.06.2001); German Society for Sex Research (DGfS), Letter to the European Commission (July 2001); German Society for Sexology (GSW), Letter to the European Commission (06.11.2001); all three at http://www.rklambda.at/eu_plan_en.htm

22. "Combating sexual exploitation of children", Ilga-Europe-Newsletter, vol. 1, issue 3, 15f, November 2001, www.ilga-europe.org

23. Letter to the European Commission (03.08.2001), http://www.rklambda.at/eu_plan_en.htm

24. German Society for Sex Research (DGfS), Letter to the European Commission (July 2001); http://www.rklambda.at/eu_plan_en.htm

25. Austrian National Council, Committee of Justice, Public Hearing of Experts, 11.12.2003 (minutes to be published at http://www.rklambda.at/eu_plan.htm).

26. For what reason Denmark felt bound to formally declare that it will apply the provision for contacts with prostitutes only ("person below the age of 18, who fully or in partially makes a living through prostitution": Annexes to Council of the European Union, COREPER 29.11.2001, 148647/01 DROIPEN 104 MIGR 93, ADD 1, 05.12.2001; and to Working Party on substantive criminal law, 7536/02 DROIPEN 18 MIGR 20, 27.03.2002, http://register.consilium.eu.int).

27. For more detailed arguments and references regarding these issues see the chapter of Moebius in this book, Graupner (1997, vol. 1, 260-308, 357-414) and the expert testimony of specialized social workers in Working Group of Experts on Sexual Offences (1997-1999);

28. Council of the European Union, Working Party on Substantive Criminal Law, 8112/01, DROIPEN 35, MIGR 36, 27.04.2001, http://register.consilium.eu.int

29. Primarily due to reservations of France. See Council of the European Union, Working Party on Substantive Criminal Law, 8112/01, DROIPEN 35, MIGR 36, 27.04.2001, http://register.consilium.eu.int

30. Council of the European Union, Working Party on Substantive Criminal Law, 10458/01, DROIPEN 59, MIGR 58, 02.07.2001, http://register.consilium.eu.int ("payment in order to obtain the sexual activity from the child"); Council of the European Union, Presidency, 10854/01, DROIPEN 68, MIGR 61, 13.07.2001, http://register.consilium.eu.int ("payment in order to induce a child to engage in sexual activities"); Council of the European Union, Presidency, 11311/01, DROIPEN 72, MIGR 66, 30.07.2001, http://register.consilium.eu.int ("payment in order to induce a child to engage in sexual activities").

31. Council of the European Union, COREPER, 14864/01, DROIPEN 104, MIGR 93, 04.12.2001; Council of the European Union, Council (06./07.12.2001), 5298/02, DROIPEN 2, MIGR 4, 17.01.2002; Council of the European Union, Working Party on Substantive Criminal Law, 7536/02, DROIPEN 18, MIGR 20, 27.03.2002, http://register.consilium.eu.int; Council Framework Decision 2004/68/JHA, OJ 13 L/44-48, 20.01.2004, http://europa.eu.int/eur-lex/en/archive/2004/l_01320040120en.html (Art. 2 lit. c ii); Council Framework Decision 2004/68/JHA, OJ 13 L/44-48, 20.01.2004, http://europa.eu.int/eur-lex/it/archive/2004/l_01320040120it.html ("dia in pagamento denaro, o ricorra ad altre forme di remunerazione o compenso in cambio del coinvolgimento del bambino in attività sessuali").

32. Council of the European Union, Working Party on Substantive Criminal Law, 7536/02, DROIPEN 18, MIGR 20, 27.03.2002, http://register.consilium.eu.int ("Geld oder sonstige Vergütungen oder Gegenleistungen dafür geboten werden, dass sich das Kind zu den sexuellen Handlungen bereit findet"); Council Framework Decision 2004/68/JHA, OJ 13 L/44-48, 20.01.2004, http://europa.eu.int/eur-lex/de/archive/2004/l_01320040120de.html ("Geld oder sonstige Vergütungen oder Gegenleistungen dafür geboten werden, dass sich das Kind an den sexuellen Handlungen beteiligt").

33. Council Framework Decision 2004/68/JHA, OJ 13 L/44-48, 20.01.2004, http://europa.eu.int/eur-lex/fr/archive/2004/l_01320040120fr.html ("en offrant de l'argent ou d'autres formes de rémunération ou de paiement pour les activités sexuelles auxquelles se livre l'enfant").

34. Council Framework Decision 2004/68/JHA, OJ 13 L/44-48, 20.01.2004, http://europa.eu.int/eur-lex/es/archive/2004/l_01320040120es.html ("ofrecer al niño dinero u otras formas de remuneración o de atenciones a cambio de que se preste a practicar actividades sexuales").

35. Council Framework Decision 2004/68/JHA, OJ 13 L/44-48, 20.01.2004, http://europa.eu.int/eur-lex/pt/archive/2004/l_01320040120pt.html ("se ofereça dinheiro ou outras formas de remuneração ou pagamento, em troca da prática de actividades sexuais pela criança").

36. Council Framework Decision 2004/68/JHA, OJ 13 L/44-48, 20.01.2004, http://europa.eu.int/eur-lex/nl/archive/2004/l_01320040120nl.html ("geld of andere vormen van beloning of vergoeding, aangeboden in ruil voor seksuele gedragingen van het kind").

37. The author did not check the Danish, Swedish, Finnish and Greek version.

38. The Netherlands, Belgium, Portugal and Germany. See Council of the European Union, Working Party on Substantive Criminal Law, 8112/01, DROIPEN 35, MIGR 36, 27.04.2001; Council of the European Union, Working Party on Substantive Criminal Law, 10458/01, DROIPEN 59, MIGR 58, 02.07.2001; Council of the European

Union, Presidency, 10854/01, DROIPEN 68, MIGR 61, 13.07.2001, *http://register. consilium.eu.int*.

39. Greece, Austria and Finland wanted to include also "acquisition" into the exception, but have not been successful. See Council of the European Union, Presidency, 10854/01, DROIPEN 68, MIGR 61, 13.07.2001; Council of the European Union, Presidency, 11311/01, DROIPEN 72, MIGR 66, 30.07.2001, *http://register.consilium. eu.int*

40. Inititally the exception was not restricted to the sole use by the depicted minor. Only as late as October 2002 the exception, as a result of the persistent opposition of Italy against the exception, has been so narrowed (Council of the European Union, Working Party on Substantive Criminal Law, 10458/01, DROIPEN 59, MIGR 58, 02.07.2001 ["all those involved are over the age of sexual consent, and they have consented to the production, and where the images are only intended for and being used for the involved persons own use"]; Council of the European Union, Presidency, 10854/01, DROIPEN 68, MIGR 61, 13.07.2001 [images of persons over the age of sexual consent are produced and possessed with their agreement and solely for their own private use]; Council of the European Union, Presidency, 11311/01, DROIPEN 72, MIGR 66, 30.07.2001 [images of persons over the age of sexual consent are produced and possessed with their agreement and solely for their own private use]; Council of the European Union, Working Party on substantive criminal law, 7536/02 DROIPEN 18 MIGR 20, 27.03.2002, [images of persons of the age of sexual consent or older are produced and possessed with their agreement and solely for their own private use]; Council of the European Union, COREPER, 8135/02 DROIPEN 26 MIGR 35, 19.04.2002 [images of persons of the age of sexual consent or older are produced and possessed with their agreement and solely for their own private use]; Council of the European Union, Council, 9140/1/02 DROIPEN 32 MIGR 43, 27.05.2002 [images of persons of the age of sexual consent or older are produced and possessed with their agreement and solely for their own private use]; Council of the European Union, Presidency, 12413/02, DROIPEN 67, MIGR 86, 02.10.2002, [images of children having reached the age of sexual consent are produced and possessed with their consent and solely for their own private use], *http://register.consilium.eu.int*).

The Dutch version of the final text however still does not restrict the exception to the use by the depicted minor (Council Framework Decision 2004/68/JHA, OJ 13 L/44-48, 20.01.2004, *http://europa.eu.int/eur-lex/nl/archive/2004/l_01320040120nl. html* ("indien die afbeeldingen met instemming van de betrokkenen en uitsluitend voor persoonlijk gebruik worden vervaardigd en in bezit worden gehouden").

41. Funny enough the two minors fall under the exception if both of them are depicted on the pictures they exchange. Then the pictures are produced and possessed solely for the use of a depicted minor. So a 17-year old is criminally liable if he has a "lascivious" picture of his 17-year-old girlfriend on his bedside table but he would not have any problem with the law if he keeps a "lascivious" picture of both of them there. Also in the latter case he would not be allowed to show it to anyone else than the girlfriend. If he takes no care that the picture on his bedside table cannot be seen by anyone coming to his room, he would be liable for making accessible "child"-pornography.

42. Council of the European Union, Council (06./07.12.2001), 5298/02, DROIPEN 2, MIGR 4, 17.01.2002; Council of the European Union, Working Party on substantive criminal law, 7536/02 DROIPEN 18 MIGR 20, 27.03.2002; Council of the European Union, COREPER, 8135/02 DROIPEN 26 MIGR 35, 19.04.2002; Council of the European Union, Council, 9140/1/02 DROIPEN 32 MIGR 43, 27.05.2002; *http://register. consilium.eu.int*.

43. Council of the European Union, Presidency, 12413/02, DROIPEN 67, MIGR 86, 02.10.2002, *http://register.consilium.eu.int.*

44. The restriction to "realistic" images applies to images of non-existent persons only (Art. 1 lit. b iii). The framework decision obliges the member-states to criminalize depictions of existing adolescents, even if the picture is unrealistic (as paintings, drawings, comics, etc.) (Art. 1 lit.b ii).

45. See Council of the European Union, Working Party on substantive criminal law, 7536/02 DROIPEN 18 MIGR 20, 27.03.2002; Council of the European Union, COREPER, 8135/02 DROIPEN 26 MIGR 35, 19.04.2002; Council of the European Union, Council, 9140/1/02 DROIPEN 32 MIGR 43, 27.05.2002; *http://register. consilium.eu.int.*

46. Funny enough, Italy initially, as Denmark and Finland, opposed the criminalization of virtual pornography and called for an exception (Council of the European Union, Working Party on Substantive Criminal Law, 8112/01, DROIPEN 35, MIGR 36, 27.04.2001; Council of the European Union, Working Party on Substantive Criminal Law, 10458/01, DROIPEN 59, MIGR 58, 02.07.2001; Council of the European Union, Presidency, 10854/01, DROIPEN 68, MIGR 61, 13.07.2001, *http://register. consilium.eu.int*).

47. In May 2002. See Council of the European Union, Council, 9140/1/02 DROIPEN 32 MIGR 43, 27.05.2002; *http://register.consilium.eu.int.*

48. Five member-states (United Kingdom, Belgium, Germany, Ireland, Greece), upon adoption of the framework-decision, officially stated that they "see no distinction between real and virtual images of children, and consider it essential to take strong action against both", they will therefore not apply the exception of Art. 3 par. 2 lit. c. Portugal however declared, that "it cannot accept the importance of child protection being devalued by assimilation to virtual images", it "will therefore provide for harsher sentences for all acts involving children or other human beings than apply in cases of virtual pornography" (Council of the European Union, Meeting 22.12.2003, Addendum to the minutes, Council of the European Union, Secretariat, 15992/03, DROIPEN 87 MIGR 110, 12.12.2003, *http://register.consilium.eu.int*).

49. Five member-states (France, the Netherlands, Finland, Spain, Belgium) opposed that prohibition. So finally it has been restricted to offences committed within the territory of the member-state. See Council of the European Union, Working Party on Substantive Criminal Law, 8112/01, DROIPEN 35, MIGR 36, 27.04.2001, *http://register.consilium.eu.int*

50. During the first discussion in the Council on the proposal of the Commission, in April 2001, 8 member-states objected to the extensive width of the offences proposed by the Commission. 6 member-states expressed concerns regarding the unconditional age-limit of 18 (United Kingdom, Austria, Denmark, Germany, Finland and Portugal) and 5 member-states (Finland, Germany and Austria from the group which opposed the age-limit of 18, plus France and Greece) wanted to criminalize production (and possession) of pornographic material only "for the purpose of distribution." Denmark opposed the criminalization of "acquisition" and "possession" in principle and Greece wanted to restrict the application of "acquisition" and "possession" to computer systems only. See Council of the European Union, Working Party on Substantive Criminal Law, 8112/01, DROIPEN 35, MIGR 36, 27.04.2001, *http://register.consilium. eu.int.*

France and Germany initially questioned the legal basis and the fulfilment of the requirement of subsidiarity as regards offences of abuse of authority or influence over a child (Art. 2 lit. b iii) (Council of the European Union, Working Party on Substantive Criminal Law,

8112/01, DROIPEN 35, MIGR 36, 27.04.2001, *http://register.consilium.eu.int*). The European Union however, as the German Society for Sexual Research (DGfS) in its opinion stressed so clearly, exceeded its competencies on a much broader basis. Art. 29 and 31 of the Treaty on European Union [EU], on which articles the Commission and the Council relied in enacting the frame-work decision, do allow for approximation of material criminal law regulations only in the field of organised crime. As far as the framework decision proscribes offences in the area of non-organised crime it has no legal basis in the treaty.

"Without prejudice to the powers of the European Community, the Union's objective shall be to provide citizens with a high level of safety within an area of freedom, security and justice by developing common action among the Member States in the fields of police and judicial cooperation in criminal matters and by preventing and combating racism and xenophobia.

That objective shall be achieved by preventing and combating crime, organised or otherwise, in particular terrorism, trafficking in persons and offences against children, illicit drug trafficking and illicit arms trafficking, corruption and fraud, through:

closer cooperation between police forces, customs authorities and other competent authorities in the Member States, both directly and through the European Police Office (Europol), in accordance with the provisions of Articles 30 and 32,

closer cooperation between judicial and other competent authorities of the Member States including cooperation through the European Judicial Cooperation Unit ("Eurojust"), in accordance with the provisions of Articles 31 and 32,

approximation, where necessary, of rules on criminal matters in the Member States, in accordance with the provisions of Article 31(e)."

(Art. 29 of the Treaty on European Union [EU])

"1. Common action on judicial cooperation in criminal matters shall include:

 a. facilitating and accelerating cooperation between competent ministries and judicial or equivalent authorities of the Member States, including, where appropriate, cooperation through Eurojust, in relation to proceedings and the enforcement of decisions;

 b. facilitating extradition between Member States;

 c. ensuring compatibility in rules applicable in the Member States, as may be necessary to improve such cooperation;

 d. preventing conflicts of jurisdiction between Member States; *progressively adopting measures establishing minimum rules relating to the constituent elements of criminal acts and to penalties in the fields of organised crime, terrorism and illicit drug trafficking.*

2. The Council shall encourage cooperation through Eurojust by:

 a. enabling Eurojust to facilitate proper coordination between Member States' national prosecuting authorities;

 b. promoting support by Eurojust for criminal investigations in cases of serious cross-border crime, particularly in the case of organised crime, taking account, in particular, of analyses carried out by Europol;

 c. facilitating close cooperation between Eurojust and the European Judicial Network, particularly, in order to facilitate the execution of letters rogatory and the implementation of extradition requests."

(Art. 31 of the Treaty on European Union [EU])

"The Community shall act within the limits of the powers conferred upon it by this Treaty and of the objectives assigned to it therein.

In areas which do not fall within its exclusive competence, the Community shall take action, in accordance with the principle of subsidiarity, only if and in so far as the objectives of the proposed action cannot be sufficiently achieved by the Member States and can therefore, by reason of the scale or effects of the proposed action, be better achieved by the Community.
Any action by the Community shall not go beyond what is necessary to achieve the objectives of this Treaty."
(Art. 5 of the Treaty establishing the European Community [EC])
Denmark and Finland opposed the criminalization of virtual child pornography, where no real child has been abused (paintings, drawings and similar material).

51. Germany, until the final stage of the law-making process, kept on to oppose the unconditional age-limit of 18 and wanted to add age-limits to the definition of "child" (Art. 1 lit. a), but after the first discussion no other delegation supported Germany anymore in this respect. France, Spain, Portugal Belgium and the Commission even explicitly stressed their opposition to calling into question the age limit of 18. See Council of the European Union, Presidency, 11622/01 ADD1, DROIPEN 75, MIGR 71, 11.09.2001, *http://register.consilium.eu.int*. Also Denmark kept on to voice its opposition against the criminalization of "acquisition" and "possession," but received no support. Finland, Denmark and Germany continued in their support for France in its intention to criminalize production (and possession) of pornographic material only "for the purpose of distribution," but Ireland, the Netherlands, Portugal, Belgium, Spain and the Commission, successfully in the end, resisted that proposal. See Council of the European Union, Working Party on Substantive Criminal Law, 10458/01, DROIPEN 59, MIGR 58, 02.07.2001; Council of the European Union, Presidency, 10854/01, DROIPEN 68, MIGR 61, 13.07.2001, *http://register.consilium.eu.int*.

52. Council Framework Decision 2004/68/JHA of 22 December 2003 on combating the sexual exploitation of children and child pornography, OJ 13 L/44-48, 20.01.2004, *http://europa.eu.int/eur-lex/en/archive/2004/l_01320040120en.html*.

Age of Consent:
A Historical Overview

Vern L. Bullough, PhD, DSci, RN

SUMMARY. Age of Consent throughout history has usually coincided with the age of puberty although at sometimes it has been as early as seven. Early on age of consent was a familial or tribal matter and only became a legal one in the Greco-Roman period. The Roman tradition served as the base for Christian Europe as well as the Christian Church itself which generally, essentially based upon biological development, set it at 12 or 14 but continued to set the absolute minimum at seven. In the past century there has been a tendency to raise the age of consent but the reasons for the change have not always been clear and the issue has been further complicated by the reluctance of many contemporary historians to recognize what the actual age of consent in the past has been. This failure has distorted the importance of biology on age of consent in the past. *[Article copies available for a fee from The Haworth Document Delivery Service: 1-800-HAWORTH. E-mail address: <docdelivery@haworthpress.com>*

Vern L. Bullough is State of New York University Distinguished Professor, History and Sociology Emeritus, SUNY College, Buffalo. He was also a former Dean of Natural and Social Sciences there. He founded the Center for Sex Research at California State University, Northridge, and is also an Emeritus Professor from that institution. He has received the Distinguished Achievement Award as well as the Alfred Kinsey Award from the Society for the Scientific Study of Sex and was past president of the society. He has also received numerous other awards. He is the author or co-author or editor of more than fifty books, half of which deal with sex and gender issues, and more than a hundred refereed articles and many hundred more popular articles.

[Haworth co-indexing entry note]: "Age of Consent: A Historical Overview." Bullough, Vern L. Co-published simultaneously in *Journal of Psychology & Human Sexuality* (The Haworth Press, Inc.) Vol. 16, No. 2/3, 2004, pp. 25-42; and: *Adolescence, Sexuality, and the Criminal Law: Multidisciplinary Perspectives* (ed: Helmut Graupner, and Vern L. Bullough) The Haworth Press, Inc., 2004, pp. 25-42. Single or multiple copies of this article are available for a fee from The Haworth Document Delivery Service [1-800-HAWORTH, 9:00 a.m. - 5:00 p.m. (EST). E-mail address: docdelivery@haworthpress.com].

http://www.haworthpress.com/web/JPHS
© 2004 by The Haworth Press, Inc. All rights reserved.
Digital Object Identifier: 10.1300/J056v16n02_03

Website: <http://www.HaworthPress.com> © 2004 by The Haworth Press, Inc. All rights reserved.]

KEYWORDS. Age of consent, sexual consent, age of marriage, statutory rape, sexual violence, sexual abuse, child sexual abuse, paedophilia, ephebophilia, adolescent-adult sexual relations, sex history, legal history, biology

Trying to use historical data to explain present day problems is a doubtful enterprise. Time and conditions change and yesterday's answers and solutions are not necessarily valid for today. The situation is somewhat different, however, when looking at human physical development from a historical perspective. If evolutionary psychology has any validity, then the traditional ages at which puberty appeared and sexual activity was acceptable could be regarded as an indicator of biological programming, programming which should be taken into account in dealing with some sexual issues of today. It has pertinence not only in helping to explain adolescent sexual activity, but perhaps also might suggest a different approach to those adults involved in ephebephilia, adult interaction with pubescent young people.

Traditionally the age at which individuals of opposite sex could come together in a sexual union was something either for the family to decide or a matter of tribal custom. Probably, in most cases, this coincided with the beginning of puberty. Perhaps the first effort to establish any kind of regulation came from religious groups but when this happened is unclear. In ancient Egypt, for example, no mention has so far been discovered in the sources of any legal or religious ceremony to formalize a marriage. The sole significant act seems to have been the cohabitation, and in particular, the entry of one party, usually the female, into the household of another (Robbins, 1993). Even if it is not always clear at what age such a change concerned, it early involved the consent of the female involved. Consent usually had at least two meanings for females, i.e., a willingness first to leave their father's house, and second to engage in sexual union. For example, in the Jewish scripture when Abraham's representative asked for the hand of Rebecca for his son Isaac, even though her father and brother gave their consent, she also had to give her consent (Genesis, 24:50-51). Interestingly there is not much concern in the early records about the male age of consent. Usually, however, the male appears to have been older than the female.

While there were differences among peoples and cultures (Westermarck, 1922) consent almost universally coincided with the onset of puberty, the physical signs of which are clearly visible. In most cultures this took place between 12 and 14 for girls, and at a slightly older age for boys. In girls, the physical signs included enlargement of breasts and areola, growth of pubic hair, and the onset of the menses; in boys by appearance of pubic hair, the wrinkling of the scrotum, and increase in the size of the penis and scrotum, as well as the appearance of inconvenient erections (Tanner, 1962).

In the case of females, early pregnancy was desirable, with first babies coming at least in the middle teens, 15 or 16, if not before. Biologically it was particularly important to encourage females to become pregnant as early as possible since in the past as females aged in many, if not all societies, they were less likely to bring babies to full term. This is because of their greater likelihood of becoming anemic, a condition brought on by an iron deficiency, and which was more likely to occur as people moved from hunting and gathering to settled agricultural environments. My data comes from medieval Europe but I think it can apply to earlier periods as well. In the later Middle Ages, the average absorption of iron by both sexes was, at the most optimistic calculation, from 0.25-0.75 mg per day. This intake is marginal for men and less than adequate for women. The loss of iron in the menstrual flow adds to the potential for deficiency in women. To avoid anemia they would need between 1 and 2 mg of iron per day, and only a few could achieve this since it would take a diet high in protein. Meat, the major source of protein, was not widely available to most of the population on a regular basis. Since a milliliter of blood contains approximately 0.5 mg of iron, even a mild increase in the menstrual flow increases iron loss significantly. Therefore, a woman after menarche and until menopause, even without getting pregnant, probably would need about twice as much iron as a man. During pregnancy, a woman's need for replacement iron is even greater than when she is not pregnant due to the fetal needs for iron and the loss of blood and lochia at delivery. During the last two trimesters of pregnancy, iron requirements are said to be from 3.5 to 7.5 mgs per day. This is an amount greater than the amounts available in the ordinary diet in the medieval world and I think also in most of the classical world. The total loss of iron during an average pregnancy was probably 680 mg. of iron, or 2.4 mg per day. Lactation itself causes an additional loss of approximately 0.50 mg per day. This means that a woman's iron requirement during her lifetime would be nearly three times that of the iron required by men. The lack of iron results in anemia, the likelihood of which increased with age and pregnancy, and this results in greater probability of spontaneous abortion and more difficult pregnancies as the female entered her twenties. Anemia also diminishes the oxygen carrying capacity of the blood and makes females more susceptible to diseases such as pneumonia, bronchitis, and emphysema, all of which further diminished the supply of oxygen in the blood (Bullough, 1980; Bullough, 1987).

While the cause of such occurrences was unknown to our ancestors, the results were observable since women in their early twenties would be less likely to survive pregnancies than those much younger because of their lower iron count. A female, in terms of child bearing potential, was at her height within a year or two of reaching puberty. Though some physicians today argue that adolescents of fourteen are not physically mature enough to bear a child since skeletal growth continues beyond early adolescence (Stekle, 1975), the dangers of anemia were so much greater that his had little noticeable effect at the time, and age of women at first births on the average was in their middle teens since age of menarche was between 12 and 14. (Amundsen and Diers, 1969; Bullough, 1981). Moreover, other physicians, including those involved in the Austrian national commission on the revision of the criminal law argue that most girls at 14 are physically mature enough to bear a child (Graupner 1997, 1, 251 note 2). Did this emphasis on early adolescence as the age of consent carry over to boys as well? To some extent it did and the best evidence for this is among the Greeks, especially archaic Greece, where boys entered into a relationship with an older man when they began to enter puberty. The early age at which males entered into such relationships has generally been ignored or denied by historians of Greece, and only recently have detailed investigations into the topic been undertaken. The most recent studies demonstrated that Greek boys entered into such relationships when pubertal changes were observable and the average age of consent was probably about twelve years of age (Percy, 1996), the same age as girls. It is not that the data about such relationships has not been available before since this male initiation into sex and adulthood was described in some detail by the classical writer Strabo (*Geographica*) in his account of the mock abduction and subsequent honeymoon of a youth coming of age. The fact is that such data was simply ignored, perhaps because of the hesitation of most classicists to deal with same sex relationships, or to believe that such contacts took place a the onset of puberty. In the Greek world same-sex relationships perhaps had political and economic value since the practice made it easier for marriage to be delayed for males until much later (usually at

30) when they often married pubescent young girls.. This consensual male sex relationship, at least according to William Percy, was institutionalized throughout Greek culture by the sixth century B.C.E., and survived well into the Roman period among some elements of society (Percy, 1996). In his *On the Education of Children*, Plutarch (c. 46/47-c.120) stated that though fathers might view the society of those who admired youth as an "intolerable outrage to their sons," he himself felt inclined to emulate such past followers as Socrates, Plato, Xenophon, and others in the practice. The Greek example emphasizes that marriage age and age for sexual relations could be different things. This is still true.

Finding data to document age of consent in Western culture, the sources of most of my data, is not always easy. When we do find a specified example or examples of age of consent, it seems unclear how safe it is to generalize from one or two examples. In Athens, for example, we have at least one betrothal agreement for a girl age five, but we also know that betrothal agreements, though they involved payments, did not always lead to marriage or sexual relationships. Though Plato in his *Republic* recommended somewhere between eighteen and nineteen as suitable age for marriage of a female, most authorities feel that this did not reflect Greek practice since the Greeks had such fanatical emphasis on female chastity at marriage, the average appears to be much younger and either twelve or fourteen appears in the sources for different areas of Greece (Lacey, 1968)

In republican Rome, where family law material is more available, a girl was held ready for marriage at twelve and a boy at fourteen. Age of marriage, however, was not always the same as age of consent for sexual activity. Though the poorer families might have delayed marriage because of the difficulty of getting a dowry, the evidence of both literature and inscriptions established that fourteen was the *average* age of girls at first marriage (Balsdon, 1962). The term average should be emphasized since there were both younger and older cases. Marriage and age of consent remained private matters between the families involved until the time of Augustus in the first century when the state began to intervene. Marriage then legally became a two step process, a betrothal which involved an enforceable agreement between the heads of two households, followed by marriage itself. Women who were not yet of age could be married with the consent of their fathers. While the women's consent was not necessary for betrothal, it was for marriage. Usually if a girl was betrothed before she had her first menses, the couple were to wait for this before consummating the marriage which can be regarded as the age of consent. But such a delay was not necessarily enforceable and was not always observed (Friedlander, 1913). It was only late in the Empire that it became law that children must be able to understand what they were consenting to if they married, and this came to be accepted as occurring by age seven (Balsdon, 1962). Often there was considerable age disparity between husbands and wives or would-be wives and in most areas while chastity requirements were very severe for females, they were less strict for males. In some cases, sexual intercourse was deferred until puberty in the female, but this was not always the case. It was, however, the case with one of the more famous persons, namely St. Augustine (354-439 M.E.), one of the founders of the Western Christian Church.

Augustine, though born of a Christian mother, converted as a young man to Manichaeism, a religion which emphasized abstinence from sex for its adepts, the highest level of believers. Augustine, a believer, strove mightily to obtain the status of an adept but found sexual abstinence difficult. Though he reported that he prayed daily for his god to help him achieve abstinence, he himself states that he always ended his prayer saying "Give me chastity, but not yet." Finally giving up on his attempts to achieve abstinence, he decided to marry and have a legitimate family. Once he made this decision, he kicked out his mistress and his son by her and became betrothed to a pre-pubertal girl, i.e., under 12. Unable to remain abstinent, and unwilling to have sex with his betrothed since she had not yet had her first period, he visited a prostitute to satisfy his sexual needs. This turn of events led him to have a crisis which led him to convert to Christianity and swear off sex for the rest of his life (Augustine, 1955). There is nothing to indicate that betrothal or even marriage to a pre-pubertal girl was unusual although sexual relations in most cases depended on the appearance of the menses. There was usually an age disparity between the female and the male who was usually much older, although this was not always the case.

Roman law, as the case of Augustine illustrates, was not always clear. Where laws did exist they were not hard and fast. The Roman tradition and its ambivalence entered into most of the Western world through the major law code of the later Roman Empire, the *Corpus Juris Civilis*, the collection compiled under the direction of the Emperor Justinian in the sixth century. This stipulated that to be married, the parties must at least be *puberes*, i.e., girls twelve and boys fourteen. If both or either parties were *impuberes* at the time of their marriage, however, it could still be legal if each partner had stated his or her intention to live together and, if they did, it became a legal marriage (Institutes,1910, I, tit. X). In short, the law stated one thing but there were legal ways around it. It was the Roman law tradition which was adopted into both European civil law and canon law and became the standard when it could be enforced. Under canon law the marriage age was individual biological maturity (first menstruation, ejaculation). Only as late as 1563, during the Council of Trient, a fixed age limit was introduced, which had been set at 12 for girls and 14 for boys. At the same Council of Trient "marriage by consensus" (entering into marriage by just living together in the will to marry) was outlawed, and it was established that marriage could only be engaged into by a formal ceremony before a priest (Graupner 1997, 1, 126, 127). Probably in most cases, however, it was tradition which most people followed rather than law, even when the power of the canon law was at its height from the twelfth to the fifteenth centuries, an exception could always be made. That was what canon lawyers were for.

Whether it was the Roman tradition or traditional Arabic customary law which influenced the prophet Muhammed (570-632 M.E.) to follow the same path as Augustine is unclear, but he too became betrothed to a prepubescent girl. In Muhammed's case it came after the death of his first wife, Khadijah, which seemed to have left him inconsolable. His friends, worried about his condition, advised him to marry again, believing that this might help him to more easily overcome his grief. Although reluctant to agree, the prophet eventually was persuaded to marry Ayssha, a young girl who was then believed to be seven years of age (some say nine). It was reported that just watching her play with her dolls proved uplifting to him. Most Islamic authorities hold that the marriage was not consummated until Ayesha began to menstruate, the traditionally acceptable time for actual intercourse, around twelve years old (Bullough, 1976), but there is no definite evidence either way.

It is worthy of comment that Augustine, the most influential of the Christian fathers, and Muhammed, the founder of Islam, saw nothing wrong in being betrothed to a pre-pubertal girl. Neither for that matter did others, although they might abstain from sex until the girl had her first menses. In fact, officially the Medieval Catholic Church honored any vow made between a male and female, so long as they were not related (or already married) regardless of where they were made, or in whose presence. Though Gratian, the influential founder of Canon law in the twelfth century, accepted the traditional age of puberty (12 for girls and 14 for boys) for marriage, he also said consent was meaningful if the children were older than seven. This point was disputed, not because it was so low, but because it was too high and some authorities allowed marriages at still younger ages. Such a child marriage would be permanent as long as neither party sought annulment before reaching puberty or consummated it earlier. What made the marriage legal was each had consented (Brundage, 1987) and even if the husband had technically raped his wife before she reached puberty, the marriage was regarded as consummated. It was this policy which was carried over into English law, and although consent was necessary, force and influence seemed to have been permissible elements of persuasion (Brundage, 1987; Howard, 1986; Sheehan, 1878; Helmholz, 1974). In the English tradition, age of consent was particularly elastic when property was involved or family alliances at stake. This was true even in the early modern period. For example, in 1564, a three year old named John was married to a two year old named Jane in the Bishop's Court in Chester, England (Furnivall, 1897). This was certainly not the norm but it was possible, although marriage had to ultimately be consummated, usually at 12, the age of consent for sexual activities. Though Shakespeare set his *Romeo and Juliet* in Verona, the fact that Juliet was thirteen probably reflects the reality in England. Her mother, who was twenty-six, calls her almost an old maid. We do not know how old Romeo was, but the Church sanctified Juliet's marriage to Romeo, even without parental consent on the grounds she was old enough to do consent on her own.

In examining English cases, it seems clear that the law could at best be called a guide that could be ignored when it was in the best interests of the family to do so. Let me examine some other cases which occurred in England and in those English colonies in what became the United States to illustrate this. One of the more interesting cases was recently publicized by Holly Brewer (Brewer and Bullough, 2001), namely the case of Mary Hathaway, the only daughter and heir of the deceased Thomas Hathaway. In Virginia in 1689, when she was nine, she was married to William Williams. We know her case only because two years later she sued for divorce which she was allowed to do since the marriage had not been consummated, and was released from the covenant she had made because the marriage had not been consummated. If, however, her husband, two years older than she, had raped her, she probably could not have been given a divorce (Stafford County, 1691). Consent, however, was desirable.

Just how common were such relationships? I strongly believe that they were not uncommon. Information about such cases, however, only becomes public when for some reason, such as a divorce, the courts became involved. The only reliable data on age at marriage in England comes from *Inquisitions Post Mortem*, records which involved only those who left property (Walker, 1982; Post, 1974; Russell, 1948). This means that we lack data on the overwhelming majority of the English population. Still, perhaps indicative of the extent of very young marriages and early age of consent among those who inherited property in medieval and early modern England is the fact that the more complete the records are, the more common it is to uncover young marriages. Judges even honored marriages based on mutual consent at ages younger than seven, the age that Gratian offered as the minimum age for meaningful consent. Even the marriage vows of two-year old Jane Brerton and three-year old John Somerford, where others had to speak for them, were accepted. When the two a few years later wanted a divorce, they had to go to court to annul the marriage (Furnivall, 1897). At least one seventeenth century lawyer, Henry Swinburne, distinguished between the marriages of those under seven and those between seven and puberty. He wrote that those under seven who had said their vows had to ratify it afterwards by giving kisses, embraces, lying together, exchanging gifts or tokens, or calling each other husband or wife. If they did not do some of these things, the marriage could not be accepted. The same standards also applied to those who were over seven when they married, but after taking such actions, if they wanted an annulment, they had to go to court since they had been of the ripe age to marry (Swinburne, 1686). While many of those who married early and for whom we have records were of the greater or lesser nobility some were of royal blood. For example, one of Charles II's illegitimate sons, whom he created the Duke of Southampton in 1671, married Mary Wood when he was nine and she was seven. Mary, an only child, was an heiress much desired for her wealth and the king obviously wanted it for his son. The pre-marriage contract drawn up by Mary's father and the king stipulated that her father would pay the duke 20,000 pounds if she refused to follow through on the marriage implying that she still had to consent. Among the elite, semi-arranged marriages at fairly young ages were common, and though the children might have been given some choice, the marriages were actually brokered and negotiated by parents and usually involved complicated settlements (Habakkuk, 1940; Staves, 1990; Salmon, 1986). Not all records of marriage are of the upper class, and for example, there is a record of a George Hulse, listed as an apprentice, being married at 7 (Furnivall, 1897). As Holly Brewer has argued, young marriages had everything to do with lineage, with maintaining inherited status, with the ideologies underlying social stability, order, and monarchy. Controlling marriage was a way of stabilizing the patriarchal system (Brewer and Bullough, 2002) and when family interests were at stake, age of consent was unimportant. Philip Stubbes in the seventeenth century wrote that in East Anglia there

> is over great liberty permitted therein; for little infants, in swaddling clowts, are often married by their ambitious Parents and friends, when they know neither good nor evil, and this is the origin of much wickedness, & directly against the word of God, and examples of the primitive age. (Stubbes, 1583) [The spelling is Stubbes, not mine]

Stubbes was most concerned not with the marriage of the elites, but the fact that their example encouraged the poor to do likewise. This was of particular concern in the American colonies where many people arrived as indentured servants. Their masters wanted them to work off their indenture and in fact in many of the colonies, the age of indenture was extended to 24, in order to curtail younger marriages. Servants who married earlier were denounced with harsh penalties and if they had children they were regarded as illegitimate, although this aspect of the law was short lived.

The most influential legal text of the seventeenth century in England and its colonies was that of Sir Edward Coke who made it clear that marriage of girls under 12 was normal, and the age at which a girl who was a wife was eligible for a dower from her husband's estate was nine even though her husband be only four years old (Coke, 1719). But it is not only two children being married, it is not infrequently older men marrying young girls. The most popular sex manual of the eighteenth century (and for much of the nineteenth as well), *Aristotle's Masterpiece* (1745?), talks of the joys of older men having young virgins as marriage partners. Though the author says the ripe age for virgins is 14 or so, he states that in his imaginary country Campania, men in their 80s either marry or seek out ever younger young virgins with whom to have sex and perhaps children. The search of the older man for a young girl or women is a common theme in English fiction from Chaucer to Sheridan to Aphra Behn and even into the more squeamish twentieth century when Nabokov's *Lolita* still continues to intrigue. Though technically sex with girls under ten was considered "rape" in most areas of Europe, (18 El, 1576) there is little evidence the law was enforced with any regularity. Giovanni Jacopo Casanova de Seingalt, for example, counted a nine year old among his hundreds of sexual partners although he indicated she was not a very good lay (Bullough, 1976).

Could a six-year-old child give consent? A local jury found John Bennet guilty of having sex with six-year-old Nancy Geer and sentenced him to one year in jail. This was shortly after Virginia had revised its law code, stipulating that raping a girl under ten carried a sentence of not less than one nor more than ten years. Interestingly, the same revision imposed a more severe penalty for raping a woman above ten–the sentence was not less than ten years, nor more than 21 years (Henning, 1825). When Bennet appealed his case, the court decided that a child under ten was not capable of consenting and even though she had refused his advances, the rape of a girl under ten was not a crime of the same degree as forcing an older girl or woman who could give consent. In short, a girl–child under ten–was incapable of giving consent and therefore could not be forced and this meant that the penalty should be less (Brockenbrough, 1826).

This paper could go on and list other cases to illustrate that in many jurisdictions in both English Church law and in English Common law (and ultimately American), the age of consent was not a very meaningful distinction. This raises the question of whether laws about age of consent should be accepted at face value when in fact there are so many loop holes in them. The age of consent quite simply was more variable than a summary of the law seems to imply. Why has this not been emphasized in most studies? One of the answers is because we have a tendency to rely on statistics for data about the age of consent. Peter Laslett (1984), for example, on the basis of records he examined, argued marriage and child bearing in the late teens was not common in England and marriage at twelve was virtually unknown. I believe his statement is erroneous although much of his data might be accurate. This is because his statistics are based on skewed samples. In England only a small portion of marriages were registered, less than one third, and on those registrations it is extremely difficult to tell if they recorded first or second or later marriages. A second marriage by a man in his late > fifties or a woman in her early > thirties, skews the data. Not all the records even bother to record the age. Unrecorded are marriage without parental consent, private weddings, and many others, and the quality of the data varies from region to region in England. For example, in the parish register of Middlesex County, Virginia, there is a record of 14-year-old Sarah Halfhide marrying 21-year-old Richard Perrot. Only in the last sentence of the register does it indicate that she was a widow. Did the compiler of data read that far? We simply do not know what her age at first marriage was, or even if the marriage had been consummated, or whether she had been pregnant (Parish Register, 1897) (Parish Register, 1897). Of the 98 girls on the register, perhaps as many as three married at age eight, one was married at 12, one at 13, and two at 14. Since the list of marriages ceases for a ten year period, it is not possible to know what happened to the girl children who more or less disappear. Often also individuals are only identified by a given name and their last name and since mothers and unmarried daughters often had the same first name as did other relatives, it is hard to distinguish identities. In St. Paul's register for Stafford County, a Stephen Chandler was born to John and Behethland Chandler in July 1768. Aside from this family, no other Chandlers appear on the record. On December 24, 1774, a Stephen Chandler married Elizabeth Bunbury. How should this be counted on a statistical sampling. If this is the same person he would only be six, but probably it seemed so unreasonable that the case was either ignored or reinterpreted by those gathering statistics. This is not a unique case and it is often impossible to determine whether someone with the same name or different person who appears on the birth and is recorded as marrying someone eight, ten, or fourteen years later. In short, quantifying data requires certain assumptions about marriage ages or age of consent. It is also assumed that people whose names do not appear on the records are similar to those who do. Unfortunately, also, the persons involved in making these decisions about age in the past might well be influenced by their own assumptions. Quite simply, historians of today, perhaps ever fearful of child sexual abuse, are also loath to recognize the existence of child marriages since it goes against what they think should have been the case... Though there is not the aversion to heterosexual relationships of youths in western culture as there has been to same sex ones, the twentieth century saw a growing tradition of hostility to childhood sexuality, and a corresponding reluctance of society to deal with it. Since historians are inculcated with the current mores of society, and even though the changing opinions has allowed us to begin to deal with homosexuality in a more open way than in the past, there is still great difficulty in dealing with sex and the age of consent, of accepting the idea that many societies had different standards than ours or even that earlier generations had different views than we do.

A good example is the case of Thomas Jefferson. An increasing number of historians have more or less reluctantly concluded that the American president, Thomas Jefferson, had intimate relations with Sally Hemmings, a black slave, and that miscegenation reached even into the White House. They have been even more reluctant to accept or publicize the fact that if such a relationship existed, that Sally Hemmings was 15 years old when it began while Jefferson, of course, was much older, old enough to be her father. One historian, Annette Gordon-Reed, distressed at such conduct, wrote that we just can't talk about our founding fathers that way (Gordon-Reed, 1997).

Natalie Davis, a former president of the American Historical Association, and the author of a popular book which also became a movie, *The Return of Martin Guerre*, is another example of proper thinking, that is a refusal to deal with what seems reality of early age of consent and marriage (Davis, 1983). Her book is based on a real historical incidence and concerns the plight of a woman, Bertrande, whose husband, Martin, had been gone for many years. Not accepted as widow and without children to support her, her position in the village was tenuous. She eventually accepted a stranger posing as Martin as her long lost husband to be her real husband and by whom she had a son. This is not the place to describe the plot in any detail but only to indicate that the source material described Bertrande as a young girl, nine to ten years old, when she married, and Martin near the same age. Davis, simply refuses to accept such ages, even when it corresponds with other data in the trial record. Instead she implies she was married much later and that the trial record is simply erroneous.

Concerned with outmoded laws and inconsistencies, the French in 1804 enacted the *Code Civil*, establishing two criteria, age and consent, as the markers for determining marriage age. They, however, did not change the age. Many countries followed the example of France in revising their law codes to meet the new problems of the nineteenth century. The new Italian government adopted *Codice civile* in 1865 while the older Spanish one adopted *Códgo civile* in 1865. The united Germany, after tumultuous debate in the Reichstag, approved the *Bürgerliches Gesetzubch* in 1895. Countries such as Turkey (in 1926) and Japan (1898), and most Latin American countries also adopted new code. Importantly, however, there was little change in the age of consent (Zeriger and Kotz, 1992; Wieacker, 1995; Graupner, 1997; see tables in the appendix). When Magnus Hirschfeld surveyed the age of consent of some 50 countries at the beginning of the twentieth century, he found it to be 12 in fifteen countries (including Scotland), 13 in seven, 14 in five, 15 in four, and 16 in five. In the remaining countries it remained unclear (Hirschfeld, 2000). The Vatican was one of those with age 12, an age it still maintains, which means that technically most of the priests in the U.S. being accused of having sex with pubescent youth, were not doing anything illegal by Vatican standards except for violating their vows of clerical celibacy.

Neither England nor the United States had a major code revision at this time, although modifications were made. Since the sixteenth century England had a law defining sex with any girl under ten as rape, which more or less remained the law (although not much enforced) until the end of the nineteenth century The precipitating incident for bringing about a change was the issue of child prostitution where girls as young as 12 were allegedly being sold into prostitution. There were several attempts to raise the age of consent to 16 for girls but bills proposed in 1883 and 1885 failed to do so. The legislative impasse was broken largely through the efforts of W.T. Stead, editor of the *Pall Mall Gazette* who staged a mock seduction of a young girl whom he had purchased from her mother for one pound. The publicity (and his subsequent trial and imprisonment) led to the raising of the age of consent in England to 16 for vaginal penile intercourse. For oral and manual sex the age remained at 13 and was not raised to 16 until the 1920s. The same bill also made homosexual activities illegal (Stead, 1885; Bullough, 1964; Terrot, 1960). In the United States, where age of consent remained a state issue, ages continued to range from 12 to 16 throughout much of the twentieth century (Posner and Silbaugh, 1998). Only in the last two decade was there a movement to raise it.

In the twentieth century, however, we began extending the age of adolescence to meet the demands of modern society for greater education and job training. Age of leaving school was raised as was the age for driving, for drinking, for smoking, and numerous other aspects of life. Age of marriage has also risen, not necessarily because of laws, but because of changing roles of women and men in society. College education is the norm in an increasing percentage of our society. This is the reality. What we have not done, however, is rid ourselves of our biological programming that is still part of being human. As times change, we find ever more reasons to advance the age of consent, and the process we have classified many past activities as unacceptable David Finkelhor (1984), for example, who has written extensively on childhood sexuality as well as integenerational sex, has held that it is impossible for a child to give "true consent" to sexual activities because he or she is not aware of the (1) social rules concerning sexuality, (2) rules concerning the acceptability of a sexual partner, (3) the natural history of a sexual relationship, and (4) the reaction of others to one's sexual contacts. This definition ignores biology and implies age of consent is dependent upon social and developmental issues. There is, however, great variance in these in both the adolescent population and the population as a whole and this variability works against any setting any common standard.

Quite clearly, age of consent is an issue today, not only for sexual relations among peers but more importantly in determining prosecution of those who engage in an intergenerational sex. Several national commissions in Europe and elsewhere have attempted to come up with answers to both questions. Most of these commissions recommended a minimum age limit of 14 as the age of consent although the parliaments of the various countries did not always agree with the commissions. The Dutch "Melai" Commission, for example, recommended 12. A number of private groups have recommended 14 as the age at which a child could give consent including the German Sexological Association, the Howard League of the United Kingdom, the Sexual Law Reform Society of the United Kingdom, the National Council of Civil Liberties in the United Kingdom, the Catholic Youth Council in the Netherlands, the Dutch Bar association, the British Criminological Society (Graupner, 1997; Graupner 1999; Graupner, 2000). One believed there should be a differentiation between consent with peers or near peers and those for intergenerational sex where the age should be higher.

IMPLICATIONS

The purpose of this paper is not to try to recommend an age of consent, but to emphasize that biologically adolescents are programmed to enter into sexual relations as they reach puberty. This has to be taken into account in any kind of realistic sex education as well as any legislation. Post pubertal youth need to distinguished from prepubertal children. In the past, puberty for the most part coincided with the age of consent. It no longer does and this has led to societal debate about what the age of consent should be. Society has changed the rules about all sorts of things which were once acceptable from the holding of slaves, to smoking in public places to sexual harassment. Many parts of the world have also raised the age of consent but in the process of doing so have not recognized the full force of adolescent sexuality which is an important part of how they define themselves. To try to ignore human biological programming or repress such problems as the Catholic Church in the United States did with its own sexual crisis over priestly sexual activity is only to invite greater problems. History can be a guide, but it cannot give any final answer. It can only emphasize that age of consent was traditionally 12 to 14. Hopefully our laws can meet the reality of our period in history even though we might end up with a slightly different age of consent than most people of the past. The first step, however, is to recognize the biological programming which exists in all of us and to devise means to fully respect the sexual autonomy of adolescents and their partners while establishing societal norms.

REFERENCES

Amundsen, D.W. and Diers, C. J. (1969). "The Age of Menarche in Classical Greece and Rome," *Human Biology* 41: 125-32.

Aristotle's Compleat Masterpiece in Three Parts (1745). npl. Many editions.

Augustine (1955). *Confessions*. Trans. A. C. Outler. London: SCM Press.

Balsdon, J.P.V.D. (1962). *Roman Women: Their History and Habits*. London: The Bodley Head.

Brewer, H. and V.L. Bullough, (2001). "She Feared a Sin? Girls and Sex in Virginia and England, 1500-1820." Unpublished Paper given at a conference on Sexuality in Early America sponsored by the McNeill Center for Early American Studies and the Omohundro Institute of Early America History and Culture. Philadelphia, PA.

Brockenbrough, W. (1826). *Virginia Cases, or Decisions of the General Court of Virginia, Chiefly on the Criminal Law of the Commonwealth, Commencing June Term, 1815, and Ending June term, 1826*. Richmond, VA: 2 VA. Cases, Commonwealth v. John Bennet 235-40.

Brundage, J. (1987). *Law, Sex, and Society in Christian Europe*. Chicago: University of Chicago Press.

Bullough, V. L. (1964). *A History of Prostitution*. New York: University Books.

Bullough, V. L. (1976). *Sexual Variance in Society and History*. Chicago: University of Chicago Press.

Bullough, V. L. (1980). "Female Longevity and Diet in the Middle Ages," *Speculum*, 55: 317-25

Bullough, V. L. (1981). "Age at Menarche: A Misunderstanding," *Science*, 213 (17 July) 365-66.

Bullough, V. L. (1987). "Nutrition, Women, and Sex," *Perspectives in Biology and Medicine* 30 (Spring), 450-80.

Coke, E. (1719). *The First Part of the Institutes of the Laws of England*. 11th ed. London. npl.

Davis, N. (1983). *The Return of Martin Guerre*. Cambridge: Harvard University Press.

Friedlander, L. (1913). *Roman Life and manners Under the Early Empire*. London: Gough.

Furnivall, F. J. (1897). *Child Marriages, Divorces, and Ratifications. &c in the Diocese of Chester, A.D. 1561-66*. London: npl. .

Gordon-Reed, A. (1997). *Thomas Jefferson and Sally Hemings: An American Controversy*. Charlottesville: University of Virginia Press.

Graupner, H. (1997). *Sexualität Jugendschutz und der Menschenrechte–Über das Recht von Kindern und der Jugenlichen aux sexualle Selbstbestimmung*. 2 vols., Berlin: Peter Lang.

Graupner, H. (1999). "Love versus Abuse: Cross Generational Sexual Relations of Minors; A Gay Rights Issue?" *Journal of Homosexuality*, 23 (4, 1999), 21-36.
Graupner, H. (2000). "Sexual consent: The Criminal Law in Europe and Overseas," *Archives of Sexual Behavior*, 29 (5), 415-61.
Helmholz, R.H. (1974). *Marriage Litigation in Medieval England* Cambridge: Cambridge University Press.
Habakkuk, J. (1994). *Marriage, Debt, and the Estate Systems: English Landownership 1650-1950*. Oxford: Oxford University Press.
Henning, W. W. (1825). *The Virginia Justice, Comprising the Office and Authority of a Justice Of the Peace, in the Commonwealth of Virginia, Together with a Variety of Useful Precedents Adapted to the Laws Now in Force*. Richmond.
Hirschfeld, Magnus (2000). *The Homosexuality of Men and Women.*. Translated by Michael Lombardi Nash. Buffalo: Prometheus Books.
Institutes of Justinian (1910). Edited and translated by Thomas C. Sandars. London: Longmans, Green, and Co.
Lacy, W. K. (1968). *The Family in Classical Greece*. Ithaca, NY: Cornell University Press.
Laslett, P. (1984). *The World We Have Lost: Further Explored*. New York:
McFarland, A. (1986). *Marriage and Love in England, 1300-1840*. Oxford: Oxford University Press.
Parish Register of Christ church, Middlesex County, Virginia, from 1653 to 1812. (1897). Richmond, VA.
Percy, W.A. (1996) *Pederasty and Pedagogy in Archaic Greece*. Urbana: University of Illinois Press.
Posner, R.A. and Silbaugh, K. B. (1998) *A Guide to America's Sex Laws*. Chicago: University of Chicago Press.
Post, J. B. (1974) "Another Demographic Use of Inquisitions Post Mortem," *Journal of the Society of Archivists*, 5110-14.
Robbins, G. (1993). *Women in Ancient Egypt*. Cambridge: Harvard University Press.
Russell, J.C.D. (1948). *British Medieval Population*. Albuquerque: University of New Mexico Press.
Salmon, M. (1986). *Women and Law*. Chapel Hill: University of North Carolina Press.
Sheehan, M. (1978). "Choice of Marriage Partner in the Middle Ages," *Studies in Medieval and Renaissance History*. 1:3-33
Staves, S. (1990). *Married Women's Separate Property in England 1660-1833*. Cambridge: Harvard U. Press.
Stead, W.T. (1885). "The Maiden Tribute of Modern Babylon," *Pall Mall Gazette*. July 6.
Stekle, G. (1975). "Pregnancy in Adolescents: Scope of the Problem," *Contemporary OG/GYN*, 5, (6):85-91.
Stafford County [Virginia] Order Book.. Dec.. 16, 1691.
Stubbes, P. (1583). *Anatomie of Abuses in Ailgna [Anglia]* London: npl.
Swinburne, H. (1686). *Treatise of Spousal or Matrimonial Contracts*. London: npl.
Tanner, J. M. (1962). *Growth at Adolescence*. 2d ed. Oxford: Blackwell Scientific Publications.
Terrot, C. (1960). *Traffic In Innocents*. New York: E.P. Dutton.

Walker, S.S. (1982). Free Consent and Marriage of Feudal Wards in Medieval England, *Journal of Medieval History*, 8:123-24.

Westermarck, E. (1922). *The History of Human Marriage*. 3 vols., 5th ed: New York: Allerton Book Company.

Wieacker, F. (1995). *A History of Private Law in Europe*. Ed. and trans. Tony Weir. Oxford: Clarendon Press.

Zweigert and H Kötz, (1992). *An Introduction to Comparative Law* 2d ed., ed and trans. Tony Weir. Oxford: Clarendon Press.

Adolescent American Sex

David Weiss, PhD
Vern L. Bullough, PhD, DSci, RN

SUMMARY. Though there has been a decline in the percentage of sexually active high school students in the past decade in the United States, the rate of adolescents engaging in sexual behavior leading to orgasm has actually increased. Such orgasms are achieved without penetration and penetration is how most American adolescents define sex. Most adolescent sex also occurs within intimate relationships with partners at or near their own age but definitions of what constitutes intimacy is different than in the past. Sexuality is very important in the life of adolescents in the United States, and sexual activity broadly defined begins fairly early among teenagers although actual sexual intercourse usually takes place much later. *[Article copies available for a fee from The Haworth Document Delivery Service: 1-800-HAWORTH. E-mail address: <docdelivery@haworthpress.com> Website: <http://www.HaworthPress.com> © 2004 by The Haworth Press, Inc. All rights reserved.]*

David Weiss, who died in September of 2002 after completing a rough draft of his article, was a professor of human relations and family studies at Bowling Green State University in Ohio. He was the author of numerous articles in professional journals on adolescent sexuality, marital exclusivity, and peer counseling among other topics. He received the Hugo Beigel Award from the *Journal for Sex Research* for his study of the emotional reactions to first intercourse.

The Weiss manuscript was edited and added to by Vern L. Bullough.

[Haworth co-indexing entry note]: "Adolescent American Sex." Weiss, David, and Vern L. Bullough. Co-published simultaneously in *Journal of Psychology & Human Sexuality* (The Haworth Press, Inc.) Vol. 16, No. 2/3, 2004, pp. 43-53; and: *Adolescence, Sexuality, and the Criminal Law: Multidisciplinary Perspectives* (ed: Helmut Graupner, and Vern L. Bullough) The Haworth Press, Inc., 2004, pp. 43-53. Single or multiple copies of this article are available for a fee from The Haworth Document Delivery Service [1-800-HAWORTH, 9:00 a.m. - 5:00 p.m. (EST). E-mail address: docdelivery@haworthpress.com].

http://www.haworthpress.com/web/JPHS
© 2004 by The Haworth Press, Inc. All rights reserved.
Digital Object Identifier: 10.1300/J056v16n02_04

KEYWORDS. Age of consent, sexual consent, sexual violence, sexual abuse, child sexual abuse, paedophilia, ephebophilia, adolescent-adult sexual relations

One of the most popular and controversial areas of sex research in the U.S.A. continues to be adolescent sexual behavior. As a general guide, we can suggest there is increasing recognition that social context, interpersonal relationships, and physical development all have an influence on whether sexual intercourse occurs, at what age, and with outcomes or consequences. Susan Newcomer (2002) has provided a useful summary of recent research. She notes that (1) boys tend to begin having intercourse earlier than girls, (2) youths who reach puberty earlier tend to have intercourse earlier, (3) African American youth tend to have intercourse earlier than either Hispanic or other Americans, (4) youth from poor households tend to have intercourse earlier, (5) youths who have intercourse for the first time before the median age are less likely to use protection against disease or pregnancy, (6) girls tend to have male partners for intercourse who are slightly older than the girl (this is true of marriage, as well), and (7) condom use by adolescents has increased in the last decade. She also notes that, while it is popular to blame the media for the sexual adventuring of youth, there are no scientifically sound studies which demonstrated that consumption of sexually explicit media has any effect on sexual behavior. It should be noted, however, that Newcomer's comments apply specifically only to sexual intercourse (i.e., penetration).

Much has been made, in some quarters, of a decline in the percentage of sexually active high school students in recent years than two decades ago (Centers for Disease Control, 2002). By 2001, the percentage of high school students who have had sexual intercourse dropped by about six percent over the past decade or so to slightly below 50%. The drop was more pronounced for black teens. But there is contradictory evidence. For example, 55% of 11th graders in a recent study in Toledo, Ohio, reported having had intercourse. One-third said they had intercourse with a friend. The rate, moreover, would have been higher if questions about oral sex had been included which is regarded by them as different (Stepp, 2003). A recent poll by the *New York Times* found that 20% of American teens had sexual intercourse by age 15. Interestingly, most of these sexually active 12-14 year olds were using contraceptives. The sex was not all in secret since about one-third of their parents knew they were having intercourse. Data in the report came from the National Survey of Family Growth, the National Longitudinal Survey of Adolescent Health and the National Longitudinal Survey of Youth (Lewin, 2003). The implication of this is that reports of a possible decrease in sexual intercourse among teenagers should be interpreted with caution.

This assumption needs to be considered in the light of two additional findings. One is the evidence that American teens may only be postponing the onset of intercourse (which has mistakenly come to be described as sexual debut), catching up to the levels of the late 1980s by age 21 (CDC, 2002). There have been no published studies (as of this writing) documenting any such decline among college students. Perhaps more importantly, the concentration on sexual intercourse as the only sexual behavior of interest severely distorts adolescent sexual development, a point which I (Weiss) made two decades ago (Weiss, 1985). Teens engage in a wide variety of non-coital sexual behaviors before they have intercourse. In fact, the constant focus on intercourse, to the exclusion of other sexual behaviors, tends to hide one of the major trends in adolescent sexuality of the last decade. This is the tremendous growth of oral sex as a practice in its own right (Paul & Hayes, 2002). In fact, the rate of American adolescents engaging in sexual behaviors leading to the orgasm of one or both partners has actually increased in the last 15 years. About one-third of the 15-17 year olds, and two thirds of the 18-24 year olds in a recent Kaiser Foundation study reported they had oral sex (Hoff & Greene, 2000). The reality is that there is a major development in adolescent sexual practices that does not involve penetration and penetration is the definition which most of them use for actually defining sex. One study found that over 80% of youths had participated in non coital, partnered sexual activities (typically mutual masturbation and oral-genital contact) before age 16 (Bauserman & Davis, 1996). Over 60% of such activities were pursued with a partner of roughly the same age, and 92% were heterosexual in nature. The question is whether such behaviors serve as a "lead up" to intercourse. Most researchers think it does have some correlation and empirical data directly addressing this question are contained in a survey for first incidences of various behaviors. These suggest the following sequential behavior: holding hands, kissing, necking (kissing for a long time), feeling breasts over clothes, feeling breasts under clothes or with no clothes on, feeling penis over clothes, feeling penis under clothes or with no clothes on, feeling a girl's genitalia over clothes, feeling them under clothes or with no clothes on, and then finally engaging in penile/vaginal intercourse (Halpern, Joyner et al., 2000). Whether this "progression" characterizes a particular encounter or represents a series of unfolding activities across many encounters is undocumented. Overall, however, the temporal gap among sexual behaviors at the "end" of the sequence is small. For example, mutual masturbation, oral sex, and coitus were all pursued at around age 17 for men and 16 for women (Weinberg, Lottes, and Shave, 1995). It is important to bear in mind, however, that the reporting of the most sensitive behaviors are the most susceptible to inconsistent or non-responses on surveys (Rodgers, Billy, and Udry, 1982).

The most reliable data, with some cross cultural validity, suggests a historic trend B more pronounced among girls than boys B toward progressively earlier initiation of coitus (Centers for Disease Control, 2002; Davis & Lay-Yee, 1999; DeLamater & Fredrich, 2002; Laumann, Gagnon, Michael and Michaels et al., 1994). By the time youth are between 18 and 24 years old, only 12% of the men and 6% of women had not had intercourse (Laumann, Gagnon, Michael and Michaels et al., 1994).

The focus of the percentage of teens having (or not having) intercourse tends to obscure two additional trends of the last decade. Contraceptive behavior has increased and pregnancy rates decreased among high school students in the 1990s (Meschke, Bartholomae, & Zentall, 2000). The United States now has the lowest teenage pregnancy rate in more than a half century.

Since the issue of teenage sex is highly political, there is also at times contradictory data which seems to be politically influenced in its interpretation. For example, the very conservative Heritage Foundation Reports, using Health Data sets (age 14-17), but not citing any prior refereed studies nor reporting any actual statistical analyses, claimed that teenagers who have sexual intercourse are more likely to report suffering from depression and to attempt suicide than abstinent teens (Rector, Johnson & Noyes, 2003). Other studies, however, based on limited empirical evidence, suggest that an early onset in partnered sex which is not experienced as abusive or coercive, has a positive impact on adolescent and adult sexual arousal, pleasure, satisfaction, and acceptance or various sexual behaviors for self and others (Bauserman & Davis, 1996; Rind, 2001; Sandfort, 1992; Savin William, 1998).

One change in U.S. teenagers from the past is the growing knowledge base about sex among them. A 2000 report of national surveys of teenagers, parents, teachers, and school principal by the Kaiser Foundation provides impressive evidence of the strides that have been made in providing American youth a comprehensive sex education in schools. In contrast to fifty years ago, virtually all American public schools now offer some form of sex education. By far, the most common approach is to provide a comprehensive perspective that includes information about contraceptives, sexually transmitted diseases, and basic anatomy and physiology, in addition to recommendations to remain abstinent. Less than one-half of the programs, however, provided any information about homosexuality or how to discuss sex with a partner. About one-third of the principals described their programs as abstinent-only (Hoff & Green, 2000). In spite of this, comprehensive sex education seems to be growing and has made important gains since 1970 when I (Weiss) entered the field. Kirby (2002) has also noted that involvement in education is associated with lower pregnancy rates and lower sexual risk-taking, that sex education programs are not associated with increases in sexual behavior, but are associated with increased contraceptive and condom use. One way of reading recent studies, however, is to say that teens who believe sexual activity is appropriate and acceptable are, in fact, more likely to engage in sexual behavior, particularly if they have opportunities (Gilmore, Archibald, Morrison, Wilsdon, Wells, Hoppe, Naliom & Murowchick, 2002; Whitbeck, Yoder, Hoyt & Conger, 1999). However one reads the data, it is clear that 80% of American youth have engaged in sexual intercourse by age 19 (Singh and Daroch, 1999).

One noticeable change in research on teenage sex in the United States is an expansion of research on teenagers beyond the standard WASP (White, Anglo-Saxon, Protestant), a rather misused term for mainstream Americans (Moore & Chase-Lansdale, 2001; O'Sullivan and Meyer-Bahlburg, 2003; Raffaelli & Green, 2003). There even has been some expansion of the creativity of hypotheses tested and explanations investigated. Using National Longitudinal Study of Adolescent Health data, for example, it has been found that there are two predictable peaks of coital debut during each year. One is a summer peak, not associated with involvement in a romantic relationship. The other is a holiday peak, occurring in December and associated with involvement in a romantic relationship, especially for girls (Savin-Willliams and Diamond, 2002).

Another change is an emphasis on relationships surrounding adolescent sexuality, an important factor since most adolescent sexual experiences occurred within intimate relationships. At one time, there was an assumption that adolescent males and females went through a fairly predictable sexual and courtship sequence. Bailey (1989) summarized this well: couples met, were attracted, began dating, went steady, eventually became engaged, and were ultimately married. Through the course of the twentieth century, the stage where sexual intercourse began moved to earlier points in the sequence. As late as the 1970s, sexual experimentation tended to take place during the college years. This courtship system can be traced as far back as the 1920s and flourished through the 1950s and 1960s, extending into the 1980s (Bailey, 1989). In fact, the pattern of going steady or going together (exclusive intimate relationships) seems to have remained popular until well into the 1980s. Essentially, however, such a description applied mainly to the college students, and was not necessarily descriptive of working class or other groups (Horowitz, Weis, and Laflin, 2001; Harris, 2004).

Nearly two decades ago, Carol Cassell (1984) used the term, swept away, to describe what she maintained was a chief sexual fantasy (script) for women in America at that time. She argued that young women were socialized to pair sexual excitement with passion, to wrap sexual desire in a cloak of romance. This is the stuff of song, movies, books, and magazines. It was the very core in her mind of the entire romance industry. Such a script, she said, allowed women to deny responsibility for their own sexual decisions and activity and allowed them to gain sexual experience in a society that was still uncomfortable with female sexuality. It is questionable whether such a script is relevant today, and if so, for whom?

In fact, several recent studies call this understanding of the twentieth century concept of courtship into question for today's relationships (Glenn & Marquardt, 2001; Hall, 2003; Harris, 2003; Stepp, 2003). Each of these authors indicate that young people today tend to "hang-out" in small groups, because "there is nothing to do" (Hall, 2003). Quite often, this happens in house parties accompanied by drinking where people "hook up" with whomever. Hooking up is intentionally vague and may be used to refer to kissing, petting, oral sex, or intercourse. One can, as mentioned above, however, not be certain about its precise meaning (Glenn & Marquardt, 2001; Hall, 2003). Few young people consider oral sex to be sex at all (the Bill Clinton standard) and intimate relationships are widely seen as a great responsibility. Apparently, hooking up, is seen as the way to do it (Hall, 2003).

Despite the prominence of this hanging out script, most college women today still appear to hold marriage as a major life goal. This was an easier goal to achieve earlier when men greatly outnumbered women on college campuses but this is no longer true. In 1997, for example, there were 79 male college students for every 100 female. Male-female relationships are now either characterized by a high degree of commitment (exclusive) or very little (non-exclusive) friendship. Hooking up is widely seen as a "sex without commitment" interaction. College men rarely ask women for dates as they earlier did. Only about 50% of college women report they had been asked for as many as six dates during their four years of college. Coed dorms are the most common place to meet partners and to hang out. The culture of courtship has largely become the culture of hook ups (Glenn and Marquardt, 2001). Within this culture, it appears that many young people today may make a distinction between casual sex and relationship sex, and may have both. Casual sex may occur with friends, what Stepp (2003) called "buddy sex." Young women, in particular, now appear to believe that they have every right to enjoy sex in whatever form they choose–as in the popular television show *Sex in the City* (Glenn & Marquardt, 2001; Stepp, 2003). Inevitably also, at pre-college age, much teen sex may no longer be connected to the traditional courtship system, especially since dating implies exclusivity and serious involvement for most young people and is no longer a major factor in relationships until they are well advanced.

In one of the few actual studies of these patterns, Glenn and Marquardt (2001) reported that college women whose parents were divorced were more willing and more likely to hook up, although they were also more eager to marry earlier. Given that the current generation of adolescents and young adults have grown up against the background of a high divorce rate and given that the median age of first marriage is now in the late twenties, it makes sense that new forms of male-female relationships would be emerging.

Having said all of this, we would like to suggest that these informal and unstructured forms of sexual interaction are not as new or unique as some have said. At least as far back as the 1960s, hippies (who went against prevailing sex and marital norms) were experimenting with new forms of male-female pair bonding. Libby (1977) described a script for "getting together" as a substitute for the practice of dating. He defined "getting together" as an unstructured activity that allowed men and women to sexually interact without the formal protocols of dating or the expectations of exclusive intimacy. Rather, sexual interaction was a form of friendship or mutual pleasure. Thus, such scripts have existed within American culture for some time. In any event there is a great deal of need for more research in this general area.

In terms of same sex behavior, practically all the research has been conducted with youth who self-identify as lesbian/gay/bisexual, despite the fact that such youth comprise only a small subset of the total number of adolescents with same-sex attraction, fantasies, romances, and/or sexual activity (Savin-Williams, 2001). Furthermore, these various components of same-sex sexuality do not necessarily coincide (Savin-Williams and Diamond, 2002). Quite simply not all adolescents who experience same-sex desires are lesbian, gay or bisexual, and neither are all of those individuals engaging in same-sex activities during adolescence. How many youth are there in these categories? Among respondents to the random, representative, confidential ADD Health survey, over eight per cent of boys and six per cent of girls reported experience either same-sex attractions or a same-sex relationship. Statistics for those reporting actual contact vary tremendously with some report finding from .04 per cent at age 12 to nearly three per cent by age 18 (Remafedi, Resnick, Blum and Harris, 1992). Sometimes it depends on which group is asked. In a Vermont study (DuRant, Krowchuk, & Sinal, 1998), the report of youth reporting same-sex contact in the initial survey rose from 1% to nearly 9% of the young men and 5% of the women when the sample was restricted to youth who had already had heterosexual coitus.

In a retroactive survey of adult data (Laumann, Gagnon, Michael, and Michaels, 1994) found that among male respondents who reported having had same sex contact, 42% of them engaged in such contact only during adolescence. Thus it was more of a youthful experiment rather than an identification. In stark contrast, practically all female respondents with adolescent same-sex contact, pursued such contact into adulthood. It might well be that the women engaging in same-sex contact did so at an older age than the males but in spite of the findings it is not necessarily indicative that youthful experiments with same-sex activity even among girls necessarily lead one to become a lesbian. For the purposes of this book the important thing to note is that those adolescents who identified as gay, lesbian, or bisexual, did so early. For females the age of the first such contact reportedly began at 14 in some studies (Rosario, Meyer-Bahlburg, Hunter, Exner, Gwadz, & Keller, 1996) at 18 in others (Diamond, 1998). For males the range was much narrower, usually averaging between 13-15 years (D'Augelli, in press; Herdt & Boxer, 1993; Rosario, Meyer-Bahlburg, Hunter, Exner, Gwadz and Keller, 1996; 1996; Savin-Williams, 1998). One retrospective study (Savin-Williams, 1998) found pre-pubertal same-sex contact among boys often occurred during play activities with a same-sex friend or relative; if during early adolescence, also with close friends but now less "playful" and more explicitly sexual, and if during the high school years, often with a notably older partner, a stranger, or a dating acquaintance. Among girls, close friends were common first partners at all ages, and young women rarely had their first same-sex contact with a stranger or passing acquaintance but rather within the context of a full fledged love affair (Savin-Williams & Diamond, 2002). Over half of gay bisexual men and about 80% of lesbian/bisexual women also had cross-sex experiences during adolescence. On the whole girls had cross-sex experience before same sexual activity whereas boys had same-sex experience before. What this summary tends to illustrate is that sexuality remains a very important aspect of the life of adolescents in United States today and in the past, and that sexual activity broadly defined began and continue to begin fairly early in the teen age years although actual sexual intercourse was somewhat later.

REFERENCES

Bailey, B (1989) *From Front Porch to Back Seat: Courtship in 20th Century America*. Baltimore: Johns Hopkins University Press.

Bauserman, R. and Davis, C. (1996). Perceptions of early sexual experiences and adult sexual adjustment, *Journal of Psychology and Human Sexuality*, 8, 37-59.

Cassell, C. (1984) *Swept Away: Why Women Confuse Love and Sex*. New York: Simon and Schuster.

Centers for Disease Control (2002, September 27). Trends in sexual risk behavior among high school students–United States, 1991-2001; Morbidity and Morality Weekly Report, 51 (38), 856-859.

D'Augelli, A.R. (2003). Developmental and contextual factors and mental health among lesbian, gay, and bisexual youths. In A. Omoto and H. Kurtzman (Eds)., *Recent Research on Sexual Orientation*. Washington D.C., American Psychological Association Press.

Davos, P. and Lay-Yee, R. (1999). Early sex and its behavioral consequences in New Zealand. *Journal of Sex Research*, 36, 135-44.

Diamond, L.M. (1998). Development of sexual orientation among adolescent and young adult women, *Developmental Psychology*, 234, 2-95-95.

DeLamater, J. And Friedrich, W. N. (2002) Human sexual development. *Journal of Sex Research, 39, 10-14*. DuRant, R.H., Krowchuk, D.P. and Sinal, S.H. (1998). Victimization, use of violence and drug use at school among male adolescents who engage in same-sex sexual behavior. *Journal of Pediatrics*, 132, 113-18.

Gillmore, M.R., Archibald, M.E., Morrison, D.M., Wilsdon, A., Wells, E.A., Hoppe, J. M., Nahom, D. And Murowchick, E. (2002). Teen sexual behavior: Applicability of the theory of reasoned action. *Journal of Marriage and Family*, 64, 885-897.

Glenn, N. And Marquardt, E. (2001) Hooking up, hanging out and hoping for Mr Right: College women on mating and dating today. New York: Institute for American Values: *www.AmericanValues.org*.

Hall, A. (2003, Mary) The mating habits of the suburban high school teenager. Boston Magazine. *Http://www.bostonmagazine.com//ArticleDisplay.php?id-242*.

Halpern, C.T., Joyner, K., and Suchindran, C. (2000). Smart teens don't have sex (or kiss much either). *Journal of Adolescent Health*, 26, 213-225.

Harris, M. (2004, March 3). Casual sex rampant among Canadian teens. Educators rapped for not providing enough information on relationships. *www.Canada..com*

Herdt, G. And Boxer, A.M. (1993). *Children of Horizons: How Gay and Lesbian Teens are Leading a New Way Out of the Closet*. Boston: Beacon Press.

Hoff, T. & Greene, L. (2000). Sex Education in America: Summary of Findings. Menlo Park, CA: Henry J. Kaiser Family Foundation.

Horowitz, S.M., Weis, D.L.,and Laflin, M.T. (2001) Differences between sexual orientation behavior groups and social background, quality of life and health behaviors. *Journal of Sex Research*, 38, 205-18.

Kirby, D. (2002). The impact of schools and school programs upon adolescent sexual behavior. *Journal of Sex Research*, 39, 27-34.

Laumann, E.O., Gagnon, J. H., Michael, R.T. and Michaels, S. (1994). *The Social Organization of Sexuality: Sexual Practices in the United States*. Chicago: University of Chicago Press.

Lawrance, K. And Byers, E.S. (1995). Sexual satisfaction in long-term heterosexual relationships: The interpersonal exchange model of sexual satisfaction. *Personal relationships*, 2, 267-85.

Lewin, T. (2003, May 20). One in Five teenagers has sex before 15, study finds. *New York Times*.

Libby, R.W. (1977) Creative singlehood as a sexual life style. In R.W. Libby and R. N. Whitehurst (Eds), *Marriage and Alternatives: Exploring Intimate Relationships* (pp. 37-61), Glenview, IL Scott Foresman.

Meschke, L.L., Barholomae, S. and Zentall, S.R. (2000). Adolescent sexuality and parent-adolescent processes: Promoting healthy teen choices. *Family Relations*, 49, 143-55.

Moore, M.R. and Chase-Lansdale, P.L. (2001) Sexual intercourse and pregnancy among African American girls in high-poverty neighborhoods: The role of family and perceived community environment. *Journal of Marriage and Family*, 63, 1146-1158.

Newcomer, S. (2002, August). An update of Research on adolescent sexual behavior. Prepared for Office of Adolescent Pregnancy Prevention Grantee's Meeting, San Antonio, TX.

O'Sullivan, L.F. & Meyer-Bahlburg, H.F.L. (2003) African-American and Latina inner-city girls' reports of romantic and sexual development. *Journal of Social and Personal Relationships*. 20, 221-238.

Paul, E. L. and Hayes, K.A. (2002). The casualties of 'casual' sex: A qualitative exploration of the phenomenology of college students' hookups. *Journal of Social and Personal Relationships*, 19, 6:39-661

Raffaelli, M.A. & Green, S. (2003) Parent-adolescent communication about sex: retrospective reports by Latino college students. *Journal of Marriage and the Family*, 65, 474-81.

Rector, Robert E., Johnson, K.A. and Noyes, L.R. (2003, June 2) Sexually active teenagers are more likely to be depressed and to attempt suicide. Washington, D.C.: Heritage Foundation.

Remafedi, G., Resnick, M., Blum, R., and Harris, L. (1992). Demography of sexual orientation in adolescents. *Pediatrics*, 89, 714-21.

Rind, B. (2001) Gay and adolescent boys' sexual experience with men: An empirical examination of psychological correlates in a nonclinical sample. *Archives of Sexual Behavior*, 30, 345-368.

Rodgers, J. L., Billy, J.O.G., and Udry, J. R. (1982) The rescission of behaviors: Inconsistent responses in adolescent sexuality data. *Social Science Research*, 11, 280-96.

Rosario, M., Meyer-Bahlburg, H. F. L., Hunter, J., Exner, T.M., Gwadz, M., and Keller, A.M. (1996) The psychosexual development of urban lesbian, gay, and bisexual youths, *Journal of Sex Research*, 33, 113-126.

Sandfort, T.G.M. (1992). The argument for adult-child sex: A critical appraisal and new data. In W. Donahue and J. H. Geer (Eds). *The sexual abuse of children: Theory and Research*, volume 1, pp. 38-48. Hillside, NJ: Erlbaum.

Savin-Willliams, R..C. (1998) "... and then I became gay"; Young men's stories. New York: Routledge.

Savin-Williams, R.C. (2001). A critique of research on sexual-minority youth. *Journal of Adolescence*, 24, 15-23.

Savin-Williams, F.C. and Diamond, L. M. (2002). *Sexuality*. In Press for *The Handbook of Adolescent Psychology*.

Singh, S. And Darroch, J.E. (1999). Trends in sexual activity among adolescent American women: 1982-1995. *Family Planning Perspectives*, 31, 211-19.

Smith, T.W. (1991). Adult sexual behavior in 1989: Number of partners, frequency of intercourse and risk of AIDS. *Family Planning Perspectives, 23 (3),102-108.*

Stepp, L.S. (2003, January 28) What's love got to do with it? "Buddy sex" and the new dating culture. *Washington Post*, http://www.washingtonpost.com/wp-dyn/articles/A6351-2003Jan17htm/

Weinberg, M.S., Lottes, I. L., and Shaver, F.M. (1995). Swedish or American heterosexual college youth: Who is more permissive? *Archives of Sexual Behavior*, 24, 409-37.

Weis, D. L. (1985). The experience of pain during women's first sexual intercourse: Cultural mythology about female sexual initiation. *Archives of Sexual Behavior*, 14, 421-38.

Whitbeck, L. B., Yoder, I. K. A., Hoyt, D. R. and Conger, R. D. (1999). Early Adolescent sexual activity: A development study. *Journal of Marriage and the Family*, 61, 931-46.

An Empirical Examination of Sexual Relations Between Adolescents and Adults: They Differ from Those Between Children and Adults and Should Be Treated Separately

Bruce Rind, PhD

SUMMARY. The American view that adolescent-adult sexual relations are by definition "child sexual abuse" has spread throughout the Western world and reshaped public policy. This paper, originally presented as a talk, examines the scientific validity of this view. A historical perspective traces the conflation of the adolescent experience with rape, incest, and that of the young, prepubescent child. Biological and cognitive perspectives support the view that adolescents have more in common with adults than children. Sweeping claims that adolescents react as children are said to is critically tested by examining two types of relations–those between heterosexual teenage boys and women and those between gay or bisexual teenage boys and men. Non-clinical empirical data show overwhelmingly that such relations are characterized mostly by positive reactions based on consent if not initiative on the part of the minor, with perceived benefit rather than harm as a correlate. It is concluded that the

---

Bruce Rind is Adjunct Professor, Department of Psychology, Temple University, Philadelphia.

American view is false, and that public policy that heightens official reaction to such relations, such as that currently proposed by the European Union, are either misinformed or disingenuous in alleging to protect when the motive is to control adolescents. *[Article copies available for a fee from The Haworth Document Delivery Service: 1-800-HAWORTH. E-mail address: <docdelivery@haworthpress.com> Website: <http://www.HaworthPress.com> © 2004 by The Haworth Press, Inc. All rights reserved.]*

KEYWORDS. Adolescence, sexual behaviour, adolescent sex life, teenagers, high school students, sex, intercourse, oral sex, orgasm, sexual activity, penetration, United States

How do adolescents react to sexual encounters with adults? In America today, these encounters are referred to as "child sexual abuse," and the widespread view is that such encounters are traumatic and psychologically scarring. This American view has spread to other countries and has re-shaped public policy regarding this issue in both the U.S. and abroad. The purpose of my talk is to examine the scientific validity of this view.

The current heightened concern about child sexual abuse in America can be traced back to the early 1970s. The women's movement campaigned against inadequate social response to the problem of rape, which they characterized as a crime of violence motivated by the need to exert power and control over one's victims. Feminists made dramatic progress in changing public attitudes and social policy. With this success in hand, they next campaigned against incest, using the rape model to characterize it. Mental health professionals incorporated feminist theory in their attempt to deal with these problems. But soon, the 5-year-old girl's suffering at the hands of her step-father through repeated episodes of unwanted sexual abuse became the basis for understanding all sexual interactions between minors and adults. The documented trauma of repeated incestuous rape became the assumed reaction of the adolescent, even if years into puberty and voluntarily, if not enthusiastically, sexually involved with an unrelated adult.

Combining children and adolescents into a single category when it comes to sex with adults is problematic. Adolescents are not children in a biological sense, their cognitive functioning is much more similar to that of adults than children, and they are sexual beings with desires and fantasies. In almost all societies except for the modern West, they have been treated as and have functioned as young adults rather than older children in terms of their activities and responsibilities, which have often included sex and even marriage. Thus, conceptually it seems wrong to call an adolescent's sexual interaction with an adult "child" sexual abuse. Empirically speaking, how an adolescent reacts to sex with an adult should not be assumed to be inferable from how a young child reacts. Yet it is this type of inference that has dominated social, political, and professional discourse over the past few decades.

In order to examine the validity the sweeping view that adolescent-adult sex is traumatizing, in this paper I will focus on two types of adolescent-adult relations–those between heterosexual adolescent boys and women and those between homosexual adolescent boys and men. Studies based on clinical and forensic samples certainly show that such relations can be traumatic for the teenager, but these samples are selective, biased to the more negative episodes. To investigate the nature of these experiences, it is important to examine data from the general population. I now present such data.

HETEROSEXUAL ADOLESCENT MALE SEXUAL RELATIONS WITH WOMEN

The non-clinical empirical data show that heterosexual adolescent boys react predominantly positively to sexual relations with women. For example, in studies in America done by Woods and Dean (1984) and by Condy et al. (1987), half the males reacted positively to sex with women when they were boys, with only a quarter reacting negatively. In a study by Fromuth and Burkhart (1987), 70% of the teens reacted positively and just 10% reacted negatively. In studies by Okami (1991) and by West and Woodhouse (1993), more than 80% reacted positively, and virtually none reacted negatively. These high proportions of positive reactions have to do with the high degree of interest and willingness on the part of the boys involved. For example, in studies done by Coxell et al. (1999) in Britain, Sandfort (1992) in the Netherlands, and Nelson and Oliver (1998) in America, boys saw themselves as consenting to sex with women more than 85% of the time. Negative reactions, as in the Condy et al. study, were associated with incestuous contacts and with feeling coerced, which was relatively rare, as just discussed. In these studies, many youths felt that they benefited from the sexual experiences. In Fromuth and Burkhart's study, 60% of teens felt the effect was positive, while only 3% felt the effect was negative. In Woods and

Dean's study, 37% of the boys thought their sexual functioning was improved by the encounters, while only 13% thought it was harmed.

There has been a genre of coming-of-age films about adolescent boys' sexual awakenings with their interest in and positive experience with women. The best known example in America is *The Summer of 42* in which a 15-year-old boy is initiated into sex by a woman in her mid-20s, whose husband is away at war. The boy's positive and nonproblematic reaction is consistent with the empirical data, and is something that many men recognize as resonating with their own adolescence. This film presents a far superior model for the heterosexual teenage boy's experience than the rape or incest model.

HOMOSEXUAL ADOLESCENT BOYS' SEXUAL EXPERIENCES WITH MEN

The analogue to the heterosexual adolescent boy's experience with a woman is the homosexual adolescent boy's experience with a man. Non-clinical research in this area yields findings quite similar to the research just discussed on heterosexual adolescent boys with women. West and Woodhouse found that most encounters between homosexual adolescent boys and men in their English college sample were positive. Yuill, in a dissertation in preparation, found the same in his English convenience sample. In the 1970s, Spada (1979) examined data on over 1,000 male homosexuals aged 16-77 across the United States through mail questionnaires. He reported that, in the case of the respondent's first youthful experience with an adult, it was usually stressed by the respondent that it was he who made the first advance, he who desired and initiated the encounter, and that coercion was rare. Jay and Young (1977), also in the 1970s, obtained data from over 4,000 gay male respondents aged 14-82. They found that boyhood crushes and fantasies regarding older males were common. When asked whether sexual contacts with adults were helpful or not, most answered positively (69%) or neutrally (12%). The scientific studies are buttressed by a huge literature in autobiographical narrative among gay males in terms of their coming-of-age experiences with older males, which have much more in common with the "Summer of 42" model than the rape or incest models.

To elaborate on psychological research in this area, I next review a study I published a year ago in the *Archives of Sexual Behavior* (Rind, 2001) examining data already collected by Cornell University psychologist Ritch Savin-Williams (1997), who was investigating gay development but in the process gathered data about sexual relations between gay or bisexual male teens and older men. The study included 129 gay and bisexual college-aged men in the state of New York, most of whom were attending college. Each subject was intensively interviewed. Twenty-six of the men (20%), when they were between the ages of 12 and 17, had sexual relations with men involving genital contact.

Savin-Williams measured two factors relevant to psychological adjustment: the subjects' self-esteem and the age at which they achieved a positive sexual identity, if they ever did. Previous research done by researchers at Penn State University showed that these two factors are the best predictors of current mental health for gay and bisexual college-aged men. In the current study, the self-esteem of those who had sex with men as teenage boys was just as high as that of those who did not. Moreover, those who had sex with the men achieved a positive sexual identity earlier than those who did not–the proportion in both groups reaching this milestone was the same. These results indicate that, in this sample, teenage boys' having sex with men was not associated with psychological maladjustment. In fact, in the case of the self-acceptance measure, there was evidence for somewhat better adjustment.

Many Anglophone researchers would refer to these relations as "child sexual abuse." Contrary to the term "child," however, implying naïveté and an unreadiness for sexual experience, in nearly 100% of the cases, before they had sex with the men, the boys had already reached puberty and had already become aware of their own sexual attractions to other males. Often, the subjects in this sample were actually more erotically drawn to men than to same-aged peers. Contrary to the term "sexual abuse," the vast majority of sexual encounters with men were experienced as positive (77%). Only a small minority was experienced as negative (15%). The relations were characterized by consent, not coercion. In almost a quarter of the cases, it was the boy rather than the man who initiated the contact, and in another two-thirds of the cases involvement was by mutual agreement and interest.

Positive reactions were associated with having relations with friends rather than strangers, greater duration of the relationships, and greater frequency of sexual episodes. But reactions were not affected by the boys' ages or the men's ages: younger teenage boys reacted just as positively as older teenage boys, and reactions to sex with older men were the same as reactions to sex with younger men.

In four of the 26 cases the subjects reacted negatively. The interviews reveal that it was the circumstances rather than the sex per se that was behind the negative reaction. For example, an older adolescent felt dirty about engaging in sex in a cemetery with a stranger to whom he was not attracted. A middle adolescent felt accomplishment at first by having anonymous sex with a man in a gay movie theater that he sneaked into, but later felt negative about it because he felt cheap about having sex that way.

But it was positive reactions that predominated. For example, a young adolescent said he "practically had to force sex" on a 22-year-old man with whom he had become friendly, and said it was "great" when it finally occurred. Another young adolescent had a 10 year relationship with a 35-year-old family friend; he described the sex with him as "physically great" and said he fell in love with the man. Still another young adolescent initiated sex with a 38-year-old family friend on a camping trip, which he found "incredibly erotic," "a tremendous release," and "very pleasurable;" the relationship went on for four more years.

Calling these encounters "child sexual abuse," as is so often done in anglophone countries, is scientifically problematic. The subjects were adolescents already with homosexual desires when they had the encounters, rather than naïve children shocked by strange, confusing, and unwelcome events. Savin-Williams (1997), the researcher who did the interviews, noted in his book ". . . And Then I Became Gay" that the subjects usually did not construe their early sexual encounters with men as abusive, but often saw the sex as serving an important function. For example, he noted that one "benefit of many age-discrepant relationships was that they helped a youth feel better about being gay. This was seldom anything but an extremely positive outcome." He added that the youths were often grateful for the experience and its positive influence on their development.

CONCLUSION

An important goal of this paper was to examine the assumption, widespread in anglophone countries, which sex between adolescents and adults is by nature traumatic. To this end, I focused on non-clinical, non-forensic data to avoid biases inherent in the clinical and forensic populations. I focused on male adolescents involved with adults of the gender they preferred. This focus served as a test of the assumption of inevitable and invariant trauma, although it is important to point out that conclusions cannot be extended to other adolescent-adult combinations (e.g., adolescent girl-man) without specific examination of them.

For heterosexual adolescent boys involved with women and for gay/bisexual adolescent boys involved with men, the non-clinical empirical data are strongly at odds with the assumption of trauma. Simply put, the rape and incest models, developed 30 years ago in America to describe the horrors of rape of women by men and incestuous assault of young girls by their male guardians, are inappropriate when applied to adolescent boys sexually involved with adults of the gender they prefer. In these relations, the data point more directly to psychological benefit than harm.

Recently enacted EU-legislation requires all EU member states to criminalize a good deal of contacts of a sexual nature engaged in by persons under 18 years of age (with partners over, and also even under, the age of 18).[1] This proposal has as its aim to prevent the exploitation of children. If this is indeed the true aim, then the proposal is flawed from a scientific, empirical viewpoint, because adolescents are not children, though they are considered children by the proposal, and because adolescents, especially male adolescents, are not at serious risk for the exploitation that the proposal imagines. Either the proposal is misinformed in the ways just discussed, or it is disingenuous in alleging to protect sexually mature persons when in fact it is intending to control them.

NOTE

1. See the Chapters of Graupner in this book for details.

REFERENCES

Condy, S., Templer, D., Brown, R., & Veaco, L. (1987). Parameters of sexual contact of boys with women. *Archives of Sexual Behavior*, 16, 379-394.

Coxell, A., King, M., Mezey, G., & Gordon, D. (1999). Lifetime prevalence, characteristics, and associated problems of non-consensual sex in men: Cross sectional survey. *BMJ*, *318*, 846-850.

Fromuth, M. & Burkhart, B. (1987). Sexual victimization among college men: Definitional and methodological issues. *Violence and Victims*, 2, 241-253.

Jay, K., & Young, A. (1977). *The gay report*. New York: Simon and Schuster.

Nelson, A. & Oliver, O. (1998). Gender and the construction of consent in child-adult sexual contact. *Gender & Society*, *12*, 554-577.

Okami, P. (1991). Self-reports of "positive" childhood and adolescent sexual contacts with older persons: An exploratory study. *Archives of Sexual Behavior*, 20, 437-457.

Rind, B. (2001). Gay and bisexual adolescent boys' sexual experiences with men: An empirical examination of psychological correlates in a nonclinical sample. *Archives of Sexual Behavior, 30,* 345-368.

Sandfort, T. G. (1992). The argument for adult-child sexual contact: A critical appraisal and new data. In O'Donohue, James et al. (eds), *The sexual abuse of children (vol. 1): Theory and research (pp. 38-48).* Hillsdale, NJ: Lawrence Erlbaum Associates.

Savin-Williams, R. C. (1997). *"... And then I became gay:" Young men's stories.* New York: Routledge.

Spada, J. (1979). *The Spada report.* New York: Signet.

West, D. J. & Woodhouse, T. (1993). Sexual encounters between boys and adults. In C. Li, D. West, & T. Woodhouse (eds.), *Children's Sexual Encounters with Adults* (pp. 3-137). New York: Prometheus.

Woods, S. C. & Dean, K. S. (1984). *Sexual abuse of males research project,* Child & Family Services of Knox County, Inc., Knoxville, TN.

Yuill, R. (in preparation). Male age-divergent and intergenerational sexualities. Doctoral dissertation, University of Glasgow.

14 to 18 Year Olds as "Children" by Law? Reflections on Developments in National and European Law

Lilian Hofmeister, JD

SUMMARY. The European Union Council Framework Decision 2004/68/JI of 22.12.2003 "on combating the sexual exploitation of children and child pornography" defines as "child" any person below the

---

The Hon. Justice Dr. Lilian Hofmeister has been a judge in Vienna since 1976. Specializing in commercial law and procedural law, she was nominated as Equal Treatment Representative of female judges in 1993, and President of the Working Group of Equal Treatment and Support of Women at the Federal Ministry of Justice in 1996. Further, she became a member of the federal Equal Treatment Commission (formerly at the Federal Chancellery, later at the Ministry of Social Security) and fulfilled these functions until 2003. In 1998 she was appointed Substitute Judge at the Austrian Constitutional Court.

She was a member of the Austrian government delegation to the UN Women's Conference 1995 in Beijing. Subsequently, as an Austrian delegate, she participated in the human rights dialogue between the European Union and the People's Republic of China (1998 Beijing, 1999 Rowaniemi). She issues publications on questions of human rights and affirmative action. She founded and is president of the Austrian Women Judges Association–AWJA, board member of the Austrian National Committee for UNIFEM, a founding member of the Vienna Circle for Organizational Formations, since 2002 member of the board of trustees of Rechtskomitee LAMBDA, expert in the Austrian Constitutional Convention.

This article is based upon a paper presented at the 1st Forum Sexuality of the Austrian Society for Sexual Research (OeGS), "Sexuality–Threat or Human Right?," 20 January, 2004, in Vienna.

Dr. Hofmeister can be reached at <lilian.hofmeister@justiz.gv.at>.

[Haworth co-indexing entry note]: "14 to 18 Year Olds as 'Children' by Law? Reflections on Developments in National and European Law." Hofmeister, Lilian. Co-published simultaneously in *Journal of Psychology & Human Sexuality* (The Haworth Press, Inc.) Vol. 16, No. 2/3, 2004, pp. 63-70; and: *Adolescence, Sexuality, and the Criminal Law: Multidisciplinary Perspectives* (ed: Helmut Graupner, and Vern L. Bullough) The Haworth Press, Inc., 2004, pp. 63-70. Single or multiple copies of this article are available for a fee from The Haworth Document Delivery Service [1-800-HAWORTH, 9:00 a.m. - 5:00 p.m. (EST). E-mail address: docdelivery@haworthpress.com].

http://www.haworthpress.com/web/JPHS
© 2004 by The Haworth Press, Inc. All rights reserved.
Digital Object Identifier: 10.1300/J056v16n02_06

age of 18. Under Austrian law there are no children between the ages of 7 and 18. The author criticizes that, up to now, the development of age limits in legal history has taken a clearly different way in the various fields of law of the Austrian legal order. The Austrian legislator's tendency, which has evolved in the course of legal history, to grant rights and permits to young people between 14 and 18 years earlier but, at the same time, to impose on them more and more obligations arising from private and public law, to give them the opportunity to grow into adult life with full powers and responsibilities step by step, totally contradicts the Council Framework Decision.

Today, adolescents live in a cultural environment characterized by globalized pop culture and world-wide communication technology. Access to "extreme ideas" is offered everywhere and anytime. It is highly difficult to grow up without any interference and develop one's own personality and sexual orientation according to one's inherent nature under such circumstances of a world society, and this process may be seriously disturbed or even prevented by inappropriate prohibitions imposed by criminal law. However, the aim of any education is to accompany adolescents while they are growing up so that they become self-assured, self-responsible citizens with an understanding of how to work for peace and common welfare who know "how to walk upright" and do so, and who are informed about their civil rights and are able to exercise the same decidedly. We do not need only consumers but also citizens of the world! Repatriarchalization and criminalization are the wrong answers to the urgent questions of world society. The question how to combat child pornography commerce is certainly one of the most important concerns because it is abused children and adolescents for whom it is most difficult to develop their personalities and become citizens of the world.

Legally useful answers can only be expected by those who address precise questions to the law. In this respect Europe failed. Given the fundamental right to respect for one's private life and the prohibition of discrimination on the grounds of age the creation of new offences–involving a definition of the child as a person up to the age of 18, which contradicts well established law and is unrealistic–shoots past the mark in the author's opinion. Such provisions miss the target group of potential offenders, and infantilize and criminalize society instead. With the proposed legal means it will not be possible to attain the actual aims, i.e., to finally destroy the market for child pornography, and to punish its organizers, "wire-pullers" and users as offenders, and to eliminate them once and for all. The legal status of adolescents is weakened or at least serious curtailment of their claims arising from the fact that they have fundamental rights depending on personality and age; and the Council Framework Decision contradicts the equality guarantees in primary law of the European Union that they must not be discriminated on the grounds of age. *[Article copies available for a fee from The Haworth Document Delivery Service: 1-800-HAWORTH. E-mail address: <docdelivery@haworthpress.com> Website: <http://www.HaworthPress.com> © 2004 by The Haworth Press, Inc. All rights reserved.]*

KEYWORDS. Youth protection, youth rights, sexual offences, age of consent, sexual consent, sexual violence, sexual abuse, child sexual abuse, paedophilia, ephebophilia, child pornography, child prostitution, youth pornography, youth prostitution, criminal law, constitutional law, human rights, sexual rights, repatriarchalization, infantilization, age discrimination, European Union, European law, national law

INTRODUCTORY REMARKS AND PERSONAL APPROACH

For many years I have been dealing with affirmative action and equal treatment of women. My approach to this subject is based on law and human rights. Since 1998, I have also been a constitutional judge while my "bread-and-butter" profession is the administration of justice in commercial matters. Further, I am a legistic co-author of the Austrian Act on the Protection Against Violence which has been in force since 1997 and covers situations involving petty acts of domestic violence which are not yet coming under the criminal law. It became a model for other legal orders within and outside Europe.

The reason why this subject is so delicate is because everybody who talks about sexuality is put to the test himself or herself and is questioned not only as an expert, but also as a person with a certain sexual orientation.

HISTORICAL TENDENCIES ON AGE LIMITS IN AUSTRIAN LAW

Austria is a member of the Council of Europe and the European Union. Since 1964 the European Convention on Human Rights and its Protocols have been classified as constitutional law. Austria also figures among the signatories of the UN Convention on the Rights of the

Child–CRC–and ratified the same in 1993 on the level of a simple law–i.e., not constitutional law.

One of the declared aims of the European Union as a legal community is to combat the sexual exploitation of children and child pornography. The relevant Council Framework Decision 2004/68/JI of 22.12.2003 includes the following legal definition in article 1(a): "Child shall mean any person below the age of 18 years." Let us now discuss the Austrian Criminal Law Amendment Act 2004 which seeks to implement the intentions of this framework decision into the national law on sexual offences.

In this context, the question arises how the definition of the child, which is new for Austria, can be harmonized with the national legal order, and in how far criminal law seems suitable to reasonably restrict sexual contacts of adolescents within the framework of the protection of children and adolescents against depictions.

Since 1945 the Austrian legal order has developed into a subtly differentiated democratic order. Looking back in the legal history of the past 50 years, we find that the age limits were gradually and repeatedly lowered in the collective conviction that adolescents, within the framework of well-understood accompanying education to become independent and responsible, are to grow up into adult life with full powers and obligations.

According to the Austrian definition of the term "child," in the legal sense, a child is a person who is younger than seven years. Persons older than 7 years but under 14 are so-called immature minors. Persons between 14 years and 18 are called mature minors or adolescents. This age group has attained the age of criminal responsibility and is subject to juvenile jurisdiction. Within the framework of their economic situation juveniles are able to enter into legally effective obligations arising from private law. Thus, in the legal sense, there are no children between the ages of 7 and 18.

As examples of this tendency observed in the Austrian legal order there may be mentioned: age of majority: gradually lowered from 21 years to presently 18 years; capacity to marry: for both sexes presently 16 years (subject to a court order); right to vote in elections for legislative bodies: presently 18 years on the federal level, in four of the nine states: 16 years; right to stand for election: now 19 years; conscription: 17 years; driver's license: presently 17 years for cars, 16 for motor-bykes and 15 for motor scooters; access to pornography: 16 years; right to smoke cigarettes and to drink alcohol in public: 16 years; right to go out without curfew: 16 years; right to change religious profession: 14 years; right to dispose by will (testamentary capacity): 14 years; criminal and tort responsibility: 14 years; right to decide on abortion: 14 years; right to consent to sex with partners of all age groups (age of consent): 14 years; right to decide on medical treatment: 14 years; legal standing in custody proceedings: 14 years; right of democratic co-ruling in school: 14 years; right to file an application for asylum: 14 years; and many more.

To treat adolescents suddenly as "children" in the legal sense, and to combine this with serious consequences according to criminal law is a clear contradiction. In particular, in case of the so-called protection of adolescents against depictions it may happen that adolescents might be offenders and victims at the same time.

Further, if we bear in mind that Austrian young people today have their first desired sexual contacts at the average age of 15, that they know how to send and receive pictures with mobile phones and other technical equipment without any problems in everyday life, and that it corresponds to the rules of Austrian youth culture to make use of such options without much reflection and just for fun, it is only then that we become aware of the implications of a provision under criminal law generally prohibiting the acquisition or possession of depictions having sexual connotations if persons below the age of 18 years are involved. The inclusion of virtual pornography is questionable, too (Art. 207a Austrian Criminal Code: pornographic depictions involving minors).

INFORMATION SOCIETY IN A GLOBALIZED CULTURAL ENVIRONMENT

Today, young people are living in a cultural environment characterized by globalized pop and fun culture, on the one hand, and world-wide communication technology, on the other hand. Access to "extreme ideas" can be made everywhere and anytime. The diverse impressions created by these aggressively violent and extremely sexist surroundings are difficult to cope with even for adults and, in particular, for children and adolescents. It is hard enough to grow up without interference and to develop one's own personality and sexual orientation according to one's inherent nature under these circumstances of commercialized world society. Personal development–also in view of one's own original inherent orientation–may be seriously disturbed or even prevented by inappropriate prohibitions imposed by criminal law.

And, after all, how do you really become an adult? At first, you are a child, then you are an "old" child, and suddenly–at the age of 18–an adult "breaks out"? Obviously, it is like some people think that democracy or peace "breaks out"?!

"IN THE BEGINNING WAS EDUCATION..."
THE POWER OF DEFINITION
WIELDED BY THE FATHERS AND SEXUALITY

"In the beginning was education...", as Alice Miller wrote in her famous book. The aim of any education is to accompany young people while they are growing up so that they become self-assured, self-responsible adults who are aware of their responsibilities as citizens, and who develop an understanding of how to work for peace and common welfare, and who are informed about their civil rights and are able to exercise the same decidedly. Or, in other words, who know "how to walk upright" and do so. We do not only need manipulated consumers but also citizens of the world!

Together with the great German sociologist Horst Herrmann we regret to find that in Western democracies–among them, also in the "Europe of the *patriots*"–"*Patronomie*," a neologism created by him (Greek: pater = father, nomos = law), i.e., the power of definition, lies with the "fathers." It is therefore not surprising that the law is to serve repatriarchilization and is being defined accordingly. There is no place for the participation of sons and daughters–and no place at all for a personal development following one's inherent sexual orientation. But let us get back to Austria: irrespective of Freud, sexual education here is still seriously neglected. Silence at home and at school, no adult interest in the questions of the young and ignorance characterize today's situation. There are no specialized NGOs for all areas, and their scope is mostly limited. Often, their financing is not guaranteed.

Thus, in total, rather unfavorable findings for Austria.

AGAINST INFANTILIZATION
AND CRIMINALIZATION OF YOUTH
THE BATTLE AGAINST CHILD PORNOGRAPHY FOUGHT
WITH THE WRONG LEGAL MEANS

Repatriarchilization and criminalization of adolescents within the framework of the protection of adolescents against depictions are the wrong answers of law to the urgent questions of world society. One of the most important concerns is certainly the question how to combat child pornography commerce. Because it is abused children and adolescents for whom it is most difficult to develop their personalities and become citizens of the world. However, it is legally wrong to create new provisions under criminal law for the protection of adolescents, and adults "looking like children," against depictions–involving a definition of the child as a person below the age of 18–which contradicts well established law and is unrealistic. The criticized bill started work "at the wrong construction site," so to speak.

However, it is also highly probable that the "wrong" persons–i.e., adolescents as a group who want to find out more about sexuality and try things out–would become punishable to a significantly great extent, which might lead to an infantilization and criminalization of civil society. The criminalization of a great part of one population group, in turn, necessarily causes problems of enforcement since no country is ready for the immediate prosecution of mass phenomena. At least in the medium term, problems will thus arise for the constitutional state. However, due to the history of Europe, the citizens of this continent know what the development into democratic constitutional states has brought them in terms of security and peace. In this respect, the scope of the adopted criminal law provisions on "child" pornography is too narrow and too wide, at the same time: too narrow because it fails to reach the perpetrators of child pornography commerce, too wide because it forces adolescents to leave established society and legality, and subjects their parents and sexual partners to blackmail.

ADOLESCENTS, TOO, HAVE HUMAN RIGHTS DISCRIMINATION ON THE GROUNDS OF AGE

Adolescents growing up, too, are legal subjects and, as such, have Human Rights. In the area of conflict of Article 8 of the European Convention on Human Rights–right to respect for one's private life–and article 13.1 of the EC Treaty–prohibition of discrimination on the grounds of age–as well as in the light of the just described tendencies found within the legal order in legal history, the Council Framework Decision mentioned above as well as the implementation of the Austrian federal government with the creation of new provisions under criminal law relating to the protection of "children" against depictions, if they are older than 14, shoot past the mark and have failed in the legal sense. The actual aims, i.e., to finally destroy the market for child pornography and to convict its organizers, "wire-pullers" and users as offenders, and to eliminate them once and for all, will not be attained with the proposed legal means in any case. The legal status of young people is weakened instead, by violating or at least seriously curtailing their claims arising from the fact that they have fundamental rights depending on personality and age, and the Council Framework Decision contradicts the equality guarantees in primary law of the European Union that they must not be discriminated on the grounds of age.

CONCLUSION AND PERSONAL OPINION

All of us have to pay precise attention as to which questions are addressed to the legal order. If you put the wrong question, you either get no answer at all or a wrong legal answer. In these times which are superficially only orientated to results this is, in my opinion, the most important method of how to deal with the enormous social problems which world society has to face as a system and for which it has to find lasting solutions.

REFERENCES

Adamovich, Ludwig K., Funk, Bernd-Christian & Holzinger, Gerhart. *Österreichisches Staatsrecht, Vol. 3: Grundrechte*, Springer 2003, 3-211-20155-6
Berka, Walter. *Die Grundrechte: Grundfreiheiten und Menschenrechte in Österreich*, Springer 1999, 3-211-83355-2
Chomsky, Noam. *War against people*, Europa 2001, 3-203-76011-8
Dittrich-Tades, Robert Helmuth (Ed.). *Allgemeines Bürgerliches Gesetzbuch und Nebengesetze*, Manz 2003, 3-214-03684-X
Flossmann, Ursula (Ed.), *Probleme bei der Strafverfolgung von Gewalt in Familien*, Trauner 2003, 3-85487-497-9
Gruen, Arno. *Der Verrat am Selbst*, dtv 1992, 3-423-35000-8
Gruen, Arno. *Der Fremde in uns*, Klett-Cotta 2002, 3-608-94282-3
Gruen, Arno. *Der Kampf um die Demokratie*, Klett-Cotta 2002, 3-608-94224-6
Holoubek, Michael & Holoubek, Irmgard (Ed.). *Verfassungsrecht*, Verlag Österreich 2003, 3-7046-4172-3
Horx, Matthias. *Die acht Sphären der Zukunft*, Signum 2002, 3-85436-299-4
Miller, Alice. *Am Anfang war Erziehung*, Suhrkamp 2003, 3-518-03639-4
Rawls, John. *Gerechtigkeit als Fairness–Ein Neuentwurf*, Suhrkamp 2003, 3-518-58366-2
Roth, Jürgen. *Die Gangster aus dem Osten*, Europa 2003, 3-203-81526-5
Sennett, Richard. *Respekt im Zeitalter der Ungleichheit*, Berlin-Verlag 2002, 3-8270-0032-7
Sontag, Susan. *Das Leiden anderer betrachten*, Hanser 2003, 3-446-20396-6
Stiglitz, Joseph. *Die Schatten der Globalisierung*, Siedler 2003, 3-88680-0753-3
Varela, Francisco J. *Kognitionswissenschaft–Kognitionstechnik*, Suhrkamp 1993, 3-518-28482-7
Werner, Klaus & Weiss, Hans, *Das neue Schwarzbuch der Markenfirmen*, Deuticke 2003, 3-216-30715-8
Ziegler, Jean. *Die neuen Herrscher der Welt und ihre globalen Widersacher*, C. Bertelsmann 2003, 3-570-00679-4

Sexuality, Adolescence and the Criminal Law: The Perspective of Criminology

Michael C. Baurmann, PhD

Michael C. Baurmann, Diploma and Doctor in Psychology (University of Mainz), lectures at the Universities of Mainz and Darmstadt.

He is Head of the Section "Criminological Research and Behavioural Analysis (including ViCLAS Database)" within the Research Unit on Criminology and Criminal Investigation at Bundeskriminalamt–BKA (Federal Criminal Police Office) in Wiesbaden (Germany) and is Head of central agency for all German police forces (co-ordination, co-operation, training, and quality standards) in the field of behavioural analysis ("profiling") and for ViCLAS database.

Since 1976 he has been responsible for empirical research in victimology and sexual delinquency, furthermore research on Posttraumatic Stress Disorder. For nine years he has been a member of the Negotiation and Analysing Team of the BKA in cases of serious crime. Since 1995 he has been working on Behavioural Analysis in the field of sexual violence, homicide, extortion and hostage taking, bombing, terrorism, etc.

He has undertaken various empirical studies and has had various publications on sexual delinquency, longitudinal study on sexuality, violence and psychological after-effects on the victim's side, on the situation and needs of crime victims, on victim support and victim rights, on behavioural analysis and on ViCLAS (Violent Crime Linkage Analysis System).

Michael C. Baurmann can be reached at BUNDESKRIMINALAMT, Kriminalistisches Institut–KI 13 D 65 173 Wiesbaden (E-mail: Michael.Baurmann@bka.bund.de).

This essay is based upon a paper presented at the 7th conference of the International Association for the Treatment of Sexual Offenders (IATSO), "Sexual Abuse and Sexual Violence: From Understanding to Protection and Prevention" in connection with the symposium on "Sexuality, Adolescence and the Criminal Law" on 13 September 2002 at the University Hospital in Vienna.

[Haworth co-indexing entry note]: "Sexuality, Adolescence and the Criminal Law: The Perspective of Criminology." Baurmann, Michael C. Co-published simultaneously in *Journal of Psychology & Human Sexuality* (The Haworth Press, Inc.) Vol. 16, No. 2/3, 2004, pp. 71-87; and: *Adolescence, Sexuality, and the Criminal Law: Multidisciplinary Perspectives* (ed: Helmut Graupner, and Vern L. Bullough) The Haworth Press, Inc., 2004, pp. 71-87. Single or multiple copies of this article are available for a fee from The Haworth Document Delivery Service [1-800-HAWORTH, 9:00 a.m. - 5:00 p.m. (EST). E-mail address: docdelivery@haworthpress.com].

SUMMARY. The provisions in the German Criminal Code protecting sexual self-determination–even after several penal law reforms–are still criminologically not yet coherently structured and carry some contradictions. Recent research implies that in the section of the German Criminal Code establishing sexual offences three very divergent forms of deviant behavior are lumped together in an undifferentiated way: violent offences, infractions of moral norms and commercialization of sexuality (the latter in most cases in the form of organised crime). Some offences lack empirical justification in the sense of a concept of protection, for example due to the fact that damage caused to victims is not proven. In addition the establishment of age limits turns out as a difficult task, i.e., when consensual (love) relations of adolescents and of young adults are concerned. International efforts to approximate (sexual) offences legislation carry the risk that reasoned, criminologically analysed and empirically justified regulations are sacrificed to populistic diffused mainstream-thinking. *[Article copies available for a fee from The Haworth Document Delivery Service: 1-800-HAWORTH. E-mail address: <docdelivery@haworthpress.com> Website: <http://www.HaworthPress.com> © 2004 by The Haworth Press, Inc. All rights reserved.]*

KEYWORDS. Youth protection, youth rights, sexual offences, age of consent, sexual consent, sexual violence, sexual abuse, child sexual abuse, pedophilia, ephebophilia, child pornography, child prostitution, youth pornography, youth prostitution, homosexuality, criminal law, sexual crime, victimology, criminal policy, criminology

The German Penal Code came into being in 1871 and was naturally drawn up in accordance with the moral concepts of that time.

In connection with the symposium on "Sexuality, Adolescence and the Criminal Law," it is important to note that the way of thinking about forms of sexuality which prevailed in 1871 found its expression in the structure of Chapter 13 of the German Penal Code as well as in the contents of the individual sections and in many cases has remained unchanged up to the present time. Thus it is also necessary to consider today's criminal law on sexual offences in the light of its historical development. For example, at the time all indecent and criminal acts associated with sexuality in some way were compiled in a single chapter of the Penal Code because it was assumed that a homogeneous phenomenon was involved. However, this was–and continues to be–completely incorrect from a criminological point of view.

The prevailing view today is that criminal law encroaches upon the rights of individual citizens to liberty in an highly intrusive manner and that it should therefore be viewed as the most extreme and harshest means of intervention that can be employed by the state in the case of conflicts. Because strong intervention by means of the criminal law represents the most extreme possibility, the rules and sanctions prescribed there must be repeatedly subjected to careful examination, questioned and brought into line with the most recent knowledge that applies in each case. Just during the 90-year period from 1871 to 1962, German criminal law was amended 65 times before very substantial changes were then made during the 1960s and 1970s, especially with regard to "criminal law on sexual offences."[1] Thus continuous modernization of criminal law is not unusual.

In connection with more recent reforms of the so-called "criminal law on sexual offences" (Sexualstrafrecht), in his 1957 dissertation and during the following years, the Frankfurt criminal law specialist Herbert Jäger explained in a convincing manner on repeated occasions[2] why "criminal law on sexual offences" must have a rational and empirical foundation and why the reasons for stating that an act constitutes an offence must be objectively verifiable. Jäger, along with other criminal law specialists and sexologists, subsequently made a number of demands and raised a variety of critical questions, some of which are still of great significance today.

STRUCTURE OF CHAPTER 13 OF THE PENAL CODE (OFFENCES AGAINST SEXUAL SELF-DETERMINATION)

With regard to offences against sexual self-determination, the subclassifications in the German Penal Code are now considered to be incorrect.

If the original German Penal Code of 1871 is compared with today's version, the following aspect is striking: In addition to the division of the Penal Code into two parts,[3] in many cases the basic structure of the Special Part was preserved[4]–and in particular the structure of Chapter 13 (at the time entitled "Serious and less serious offences against morality," today entitled "Offences against sexual self-determination") has been maintained. Only the old sections on adultery and on sexual intercourse between relatives were integrated into Chapter 12 (Crimes against personal status, marriage and the family) over the course of time which, in view of the current structure, is not really convincing with regard to Section 173 of the Penal Code (Sexual intercourse between relatives).

It should also be noted that, even though the attitude expressed by the heading changed significantly, the contents of the legal provisions to be found under this heading were not fully adapted to this new orientation. For the most part, the range of the normative provisions established at the time has continued to exist up to the present; however, they have been reformulated and their contents altered. Many sections such as Section 175 of the Penal Code, which imposed penalties on "unnatural illicit sexual practices between males or between human beings and animals"[5] were eliminated completely, while others—such as "encouraging prostitution" (Section 180b of the Penal Code), "trafficking in human beings" (Sections 180b and 181 of the Penal Code) as well as "pimping" (Section 181a of the Penal Code)—were added.

If we consider the time when German criminal law came into being, it is not surprising that the organizational concepts which then formed the basis for Chapter 13 with regard to so-called "serious and less serious offences against morality" are no longer convincing.

The offences listed in Section 13 of the Penal Code do not comprise a homogenous offence group, but rather the following subcategories:

a. crimes of *violence* that involve sex (for example, Section 177 of the Penal Code–"Sexual coercion, rape," also Section 176a–"Severe sexual abuse of children" and Section 176b–"Sexual abuse leading to death"[6])
b. acts that tend to represent *violations of norms for sexual morality and decency* (for example, Section 183 of the Penal Code–"Exhibitionist acts" and Section 183a of the Penal Code–"Public indecency" and some kinds of "Sexual abuse of children," when–for example–exhibitionist acts in front children are penalised–Section 176 (2) 1 or Section 182 (2)–"Sexual abuse of Juveniles" without explicit violent behaviour) as well as
c. *offences that commercialise sexual acts*, sometimes in the sense of present-day organised crime (for example, Section 180a of the Penal Code–"Encouraging prostitution," Sections 180b and 181 of the Penal Code–"Trafficking in human beings" and Section 181a of the Penal Code–"Pimping")

From a criminological point of view, the three subcategories listed above do not have much in common. Because these offences have been erroneously grouped together in the Penal Code, for a long time it was incorrectly assumed with almost absolute certainty, and today is still regarded as a matter of course, that the perpetrators of *all* the offences in Chapter 13 commit crimes for the same reasons and have the same motives, and it is also assumed that a criminal career proceeds from relatively harmless to relatively serious offences against sexual self-determination. For this reason, there has been a basic willingness to assume that any perpetrator covered by this chapter of the Penal Code is capable of committing the entire range of sexual offences. If sexual offences are viewed in this way, then *every* offence against sexual self-determination inevitably results in feelings of fear, horror, and dismay, because it is assumed that a potential sexual murderer is terrorising the public who–according to popular opinion–is at the beginning of his criminal career. Such views and assessments are criminologically incorrect and have led to undesirable developments in the fields of sexual and criminal law policy as well as prevention. Thus our most recent empirical study (Straub, Witt et al., 2003[7]) regarding previous police intelligence on more than 400 violent sexual offenders and sexual murderers revealed that only a minute number of these offenders had previous police intelligence on file about them associated *solely* with the field of so-called sexual offences. An overwhelming majority of these offenders had extensive intelligence on file with the police (previous offences and accusations) that concerned *other* fields of crime covered by the Penal Code such as theft, robbery, and bodily injury. The 400 "*violent* sexual offenders" whom we studied (a representative selection was made for Germany) instead tended to be characterised by generally dissocial conduct in more than one area. No evidence of careers characterised by *sexual* crime was found. Instead, a fairly large number of offenders were found to have criminal careers characterised by previous commission of offences whose degree of seriousness continuously fluctuated between "harmless" and "very serious" and who, on the other hand, had committed offences in what appear to be very different areas of crime such as "property crime," "offences against personal freedom," and "offences against sexual self-determination."

Many fashionable theories (for example, that an exhibitionist would turn to rape or sexual murder during the course of his personal criminal career, or that an exhibitionist would be just as likely to commit a rape at any time) therefore lack any sort of empirical foundation. Thus the common characteristic of the multiple offenders we studied was their *dissocial* conduct and not their *sexual* conduct.

THE SCIENTIFIC AND RATIONAL JUSTIFICATION FOR CRIMINAL LAW

Because the encroachment upon civil rights is so significant, criminal offences may only be incorporated into criminal law if their inclusion can be justified beyond all doubt and convincingly with the aid of appropriate and up-to-date scientific methods, on the basis of current expert opinion (for example, based on the results of research involving information and data of legal relevance and on empirical sexology) and in accordance with strictly rational points of view.[8]

THE OBJECT OF LEGAL PROTECTION

In the case of offences against sexual self-determination, with regard to the object of legal protection it is necessary to consider two aspects separately–on the one hand, the interest in maintaining moral standards, traditional concepts of morality and opinions (which tends to be a question of taste) and, on the other hand, the need for protection from exploitation and physical violence. Thus Jäger already discussed this conflict in 1976 using the example of the section on incest: "It would first be necessary to make a decision about the function of criminal law in relation to the concept of morality and the concept of protection. . . . Different types of empirical questions arise in this connection: The concept of morality (insofar as any attempt is made at establishing an empirical basis for it) would try to explain the validity of social norms, while the protection concept would aim at explaining the harm caused by the conduct to be judged."[9] Officially and ostensibly, for the most part the concept of protection has now been established, but the concept of morality often still plays a covert role. Furthermore, thus far the concept of protection has not been subjected to sufficient rational and scientific examination.

DEFINITION OF "VIOLENCE" AND "INJURY"

Inevitably, any attempts at describing the object of legal protection must deal with the problems presented by definition of the concepts "injury" and "violence." Very clearly in the past and to a considerable extent today as well, criminal law has tended to limit the definition of these concepts to freedom from *bodily* harm. Because the taboo on discussing subjects such as "battered wives," "conjugal rape," "general sexual violence," "sexual abuse of children," and "incest" has been lifted during the course of the last decades and these have now actually become popular subjects, a wide variety of interest groups and media have now taken an interest in them and have joined the discussion about corresponding standards. However, this basically desirable democratisation of the discussions about reforming criminal law has often resulted in contributions marred by inadequate knowledge about the subject, contributions which completely ignore systematic aspects of the Penal Code.

For example, many fashionable trends not associated with the professional discussions about the reform of criminal law tend to increasingly broaden, and sometimes dramatically extend, the concept of violence. Thus there are many who think that "something which can have some sort of unpleasant effect on people" (for example, an "obscene word" or "a man's annoying gaze") should be considered "violent" in the sense of criminal law and thus should be penalized. The idea behind this is apparently the hope that criminal law may be able to protect individuals from what are perceived as the difficulties of life. However, this would be asking too much of criminal law–and, to an even greater extent, of the criminal justice authorities. The possible preventive benefit of these proposals is not identifiable. Such proposals grossly neglect the *informal* organs for social control, whose competence with regard to solving such problems is greater.

Punitive law should not–and cannot–protect individuals from the psychological impact of everyday difficulties that are judged by different individuals in varying ways–as serious or as harmless.

PROOF OF HARM AS AN ELEMENT OF THE PROTECTION CONCEPT

In some cases, the justification given for criminal law on sexual offences is the abstract endangerment represented by such offences. It is stated that the mere possibility of causing harm to the victim or *individual* victims is sufficient reason to maintain punitive sanctions. However, several problems are raised by this argumentation. To begin with, even if this argumentation is applied, it is necessary to produce *empirical* proof of harm (including empirically verified causalities) *before* an offence can be subjected to the harsh provisions of criminal law or a penalty can be increased.[10]

With regard to injuries, it is necessary to differentiate between *primary* harm resulting from the conduct of the offender, which is subject to a criminal penalty, and *secondary* harm that may result from the victim's possibly frightening childhood experiences, from the way the victim's family reacted afterwards, or from possible unprofessional conduct by members of the criminal justice authorities. In no single case should the victim who needs protection be subjected to the risk of additional–or initial–harm due to the way the proceedings are handled by the criminal justice authorities. This would constitute a perversion of the victim protection concept. Furthermore, as a matter of principle, investigations and criminal proceedings must be structured and organised in a manner that ensures a child victim does not suffer further harm while serving as a witness.

Modern, generally well-intended, efforts to expand the concept of violence (psychological violence, structural violence) can help to make problems worse, for example when various sexual contacts that a child victim experienced as harmless (this sometimes concerns exhibitionist acts) are inappropriately dramatised and the criminal proceedings are handled in a way that harms the victim.

DEFINITION OF THE CONCEPT "CHILDHOOD"

If children are to be protected from violence and sexual abuse, this becomes more complicated when a consensus on the concept of "childhood" is lacking, when fixed age limits are questioned or when, in individual cases, an age limit is supposed to represent the main basis for an assessment of sexual acts (for example, when children of approximately the same age play "doctor," when there are sexual relationships between young persons of approximately the same age).

My own research has produced astonishing results: With regard to offences involving "sexual abuse of children," males aged 14 to 15 account for the highest number of offences per 100,000 members of this age group in the male population.[11] When we consider the evidently small age difference between the declared victims and the suspects, the following question arises: What types of sexual abuse may have been reported in such cases? It must be feared that these case numbers include conflicts of a different origin as well as cases of "playing doctor," which developmental psychology generally regards as a relatively harmless transitional childhood phase. Because some of the suspects must themselves still be regarded as children, many of these reported sexual acts probably represent awkward expressions of interest by young persons during an experimental phase of their psychosexual development.

The concept of a "childhood" phase that covers a clearly defined period of time is a relatively new idea from a historical point of view and is due in part to the increasing length of time devoted to education and the resulting dependence of young persons in modern societies. While in the past even those under 14 years of age could be gainfully employed, were marriageable, and could be involved in the conduct of war, the respective age limits have risen during the past 100 to 200 years.

Recently, the age limits for those considered to need protection have again been raised in connection with discussions on crime policy and the reform of criminal law. One of two completely different motives plays a role here.

First motive: In connection with the discussion of victim protection, which is certainly most welcome, the age limits for protection are raised in accordance with the following motto: "The more negative sexual self-determination we put into practice, the more potential victims will be protected" or, to put it more simply, "the more sexual contacts we forbid, the less sexual abuse will occur."

CHART 1. "Sexual Abuse of Children" in Germany in 1996: Number of Crime Suspects per 100,000 for the Corresponding Age Group and Sex (based on the Police Crime Statistics) (dark-colored bars–no. of males, light-colored bars–no. of females)

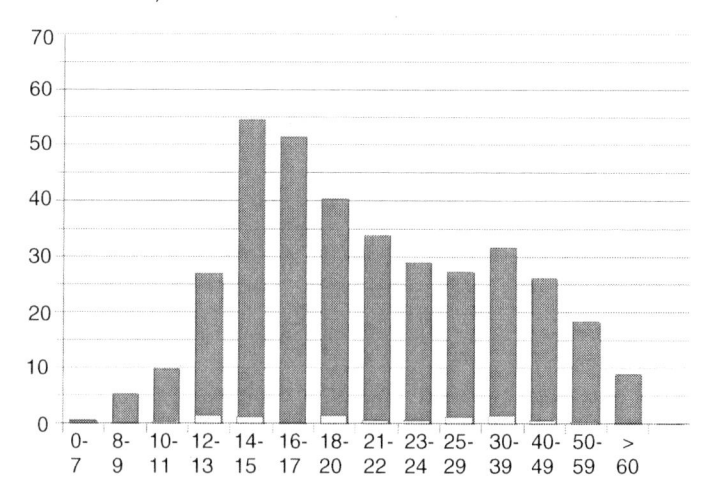

Second motive: In connection with the discussion of equal treatment for men and women, which is also very welcome, sections of the criminal law have now been formulated to make them non-sex-specific. In Germany, one collateral effect has been that the offence "Sexual abuse of juveniles" now can also be used as a basis for punishment of lesbian sexual contacts that were previously exempt from punishment. However, prior to introducing this change in criminal law, no empirical proof was furnished indicating that such lesbian sexual contacts with young people are harmful. At the same time, this section is also intended to ensure that the punishable offences eliminated when the section on homosexuals was deleted would at least continue to apply in the case of young victims. This was also done without scientific examination of the object of such protection.

Some kind of positive–or at least ambivalent–development has been achieved through the most recent reform of German criminal law concerning the age differences between victim and offender, respectively between younger and older sex partners with little age difference. In Section 182 (2)–"Sexual abuse of Juveniles" (victim is 14 or 15 years old) cases without explicit violent behaviour the offender shall only be penalised if he is over 21 years old.[12] Concerning consensual penetrative sex the offender must be over 18, before he can be sentenced under the aggravated offence of "*Severe* sexual abuse of children" (Section 176a [1], victim is under 14 years old).

As a problem remains however that sexual contacts between juveniles and (young) adults (i.e., with little age differences) remain prohibited and that positive sexual self-determination of juveniles is not regarded as a human right.

Today, when generalised references are even made to "*crimes against minors*" in connection with "offences against sexual self-determination," it must be feared that employing this imprecise concept in the field of criminal law is intended to make *all minors* potential victims. If it is actually intended to protect all individuals under 18 from all types of sexual conduct that crosses sexual boundaries and if thereby so-called "seductive situations" are to be targeted as well, then young people and young adults will be denied *positive* sexual self-determination and, at the same time, they will be classified as immature regarding their ability to define negative sexual self-determination for themselves and to ensure this is respected. However, young persons or young adults can certainly be expected to say "no" on their own in the case of *non-violent* situations involving sexual seduction that make them feel uncomfortable. In such cases, we should not refuse to let young persons and young adults take responsibility for their own actions.

The problem with vague concepts regarding the definition of age limits is also evident in the field of science, above all in the case of international comparative studies. When attempts are made to compile figures on the incidence of crime involving "sexual abuse of children" for various countries on the basis of international studies, it is striking to note that the age limits and the elements of the offences defined by those conducting the studies and also the respective national penal codes are so different that comparison of the results is difficult, if not almost impossible.

Despite this, crime incidence rates for the United States are published, for example, in Germany as if they naturally must also apply to Germany, even though the underlying age limits and definitions of abuse are sometimes very different (for example, victims under 18 or older than 18, superficial sexual touching between young people, exhibitionist acts carried out in front of children or young people, etc.).

ACCELERATED PHYSICAL DEVELOPMENT

When German criminal law on sexual offences was introduced in 1871, girls reached sexual maturity (had their first menstrual period) at the age of 16 or 17.[13] In the 1980s, Husslein stated for Germany that almost 77% of girls had their first period by age 13 and that about 61% of boys had experienced their first ejaculation of semen by this time.[14] It is necessary to examine the relationship between the age limits for protection in the case of non-violent sexual acts and the sexual maturity of the groups of victims to be protected. Possibly further empirical research is needed about different ages for maturity in different historical ages.

Furthermore, there is the basic problem that sexual maturity and the desirable ages for protection are highly relative concepts and dimensions when *individual* children and young persons are concerned. While, for reasons of legal certainty and legal economy, it does seem natural to establish age limits for protection with the greatest possible general applicability, in individual cases such provisions can create a disproportionate degree of hardship (for example, sexual relations by mutual agreement between persons of almost the same age, but in a case where the age limit for protection is exceeded for one of the partners).

POSITIVE AND NEGATIVE SEXUAL SELF-DETERMINATION

In connection with the discussion of criminal law reform in Germany in the 1960s and 1970s, the programmatic concept of protecting "sexual self-determination" was consequently introduced as a guiding principle based on a thorough scientific discussion of the subject.[15] This concept is highly suitable for application to adults who may be potential victims, because it is generally assumed that adults are in a position to express their desire for another person (positive self-determination) or their rejection of another person (negative self-determination).

This is more difficult with regard to *children* as potential victims and for some of the *young people* who may be potential victims. Lawmakers assume that, on the one hand, there is such a thing as "undisturbed sexual development" during childhood–this is sometimes understood as development without any exposure to sex, or even asexual development during childhood–and, on the other hand, that children are not able to make independent decisions about their sexual needs or rejection of sex because they lack the necessary "maturity" and experience. Because lawmakers assume that children are not yet able to make these decisions independently, all sexual acts with or in front of children are forbidden, even those of a superficial nature. Thus, at the same time children are denied the possibility of positive sexual self-determination. Approaching the "sexual self-determination" of children in this way means that assistance is provided to ensure that children see *no sexual acts of any kind*, that they do not have active sex with others, and also that they do not have passive sex experiences with others. For example, when children–or children and young people–"play doctor" with each other, intervention by means of a criminal complaint can be problematic. In Germany, efforts have been made to deal with this problem by revising the sections of the law that deal with protecting children and young people from sexual abuse (Sections 176, 176a and 182 of the German Penal Code).

EXAMPLES OF HIDDEN MOTIVES IN CONNECTION WITH ACTS CONSTITUTING CRIMINAL OFFENCES

In the past, parents and educators liked to use the sections on so-called "pandering" and "seduction" to force sexual abstinence on their daughters and sons during their youth. These conflicts generally occurred in connection with the usual problems of children growing up and becoming more independent of their parents. In this context, the threat of intervention under the provisions of criminal law did not serve to protect the sexual self-determination of young people, but rather–from today's point of view–the *positive* sexual self-determination of such young people was *violated*. On the contrary, such legal provisions protected the need of parents and educators to intervene in and determine the conduct of their children as well as the need of parents to ensure that their daughters did not get pregnant too early. Due to modern methods of contraception, the latter motive has become less significant.

ISOLATED REFORM OF THE DEFINITION OF INDIVIDUAL OFFENCES IN THE FIELD OF "OFFENCES AGAINST SEXUAL SELF-DETERMINATION"

During the past years in Germany, the criminal law to be found in individual parts of Chapter 13 of the German Penal Code ("offences against sexual self-determination") has been reformed in isolated cases and in response to specific current incidents. When isolated discussions of individual offences or elements of these offences occur without extensive participation by the appropriate experts, populist proposals may be made that can lead to concentration on the wrong aspects. This then results in a failure to identify comprehensive solutions that would be more suitable.

ENSURING AGREEMENT BETWEEN LEGISLATION AND PUBLIC OPINION AS WELL AS THOSE SPECIFICALLY AFFECTED BY THE LEGISLATION

When the legislative process is handled responsibly, considerable skill is required to achieve a high degree of compatibility between such legislation and the values of the general public, especially those of the groups of persons affected (for example actual and potential victims and offenders). However, such agreement should not be achieved by taking a populist, ingratiating approach (cf. the death penalty), but rather must be accompanied by critical efforts to educate the general population about this subject. Achieving such agreement should also not lead to conflicts with scientific results. On the contrary, efforts must be made to reconcile these different areas of opinion and scientific knowledge to a significant extent. Only then will new criminal laws meet with broad acceptance and thus have a stronger preventive impact.

INTERNATIONAL AGREEMENTS

It makes particular sense to conclude international agreements on offences against sexual self-determination when offences that involve the crossing of international borders are concerned–such as trafficking in human beings (which actually is more closely linked to organized crime) or sex tourism in connection with child prostitution.

However, international agreements and co-operation should not result–for example with regard to setting the age limits for protection (*"crimes against minors"*)–in reduction to the *largest* common denominator (i.e., the upper age limit) in order to avoid possible substantive discussions. With reference to a number of legal systems and for some time to come, reaching agreement on certain subjects will not be easy. Insofar as offences against sexual self-determination in the *narrower* sense are concerned,[16] this does not have to represent a particularly dramatic problem at the present time, because precisely most of these offences *are not international crimes*. Violent sexual offences are generally committed in a narrowly defined geographic and social context.

In the case of any reforms involving offences against sexual self-determination, efforts should be focussed on achieving protection of the potential victims based on careful scientific study. Because primarily child victims are concerned, special care must be taken in this case.

In a constitutional state, the interests of victims and offenders should not be played off against each other to the detriment of the other group. Instead, these interests must be brought into equilibrium with each other, even if such a balance is sometimes difficult to establish and to maintain.

NOTES

1. Regarding the history of criminal law reform up to the 1960s, see Bauer et al., 1963, p. 369 ff.
2. Jäger 1957, Bauer 1963, Jäger 1963, Jäger 1976, Jäger 1981, Jäger 1984 as well as Jäger and Schorsch 1987. (Further literature on the subject in Baurmann 1996)

3. Previously designated as: "Part I: Concerning punishment in general of serious and less serious crimes as well as breaches of regulations" and "Part II: Concerning individual serious and less serious offences as well as breaches of regulations and the punishment for them." Today: "General Part" and "Special Part." (See the 1878 Penal Code and the 1998 Penal Code.)

4. Ibid.

5. 1878 Penal Code, p. 57

6. In the latest revision of the German Penal Code a reasonable differentiation was made between "Sexual abuse of children in general" and "Severe forms of sexual abuse of children," which are mainly cases by using force.

7. In this connection, see the most recent studies of the German Institute of Criminology regarding the field of justice (Egg et al.) as well as the study of the Bundeskriminalamt Research Group regarding the field of police work (Straub, Witt et al.–2003).

8. See also the clear demands made by Baumann et al. (1968) and also by Hanack (1969).

9. Jäger (1976), p. 98 ff. (Translation by the author.)

10. I have established during my own, very extensive studies that there are in fact individual subgroups affected by offences against sexual self-determination in which the declared victims stated to the interviewers six to ten years after the filing of a police complaint that they felt they had never suffered any primary harm. When these declared victims were subjected to psychodiagnostic procedures, many of them also did not show evidence of any psychological damage (Baurmann 1996).

11. See Baurmann 1991, p. 61. In 1988 the rate was 44 per 100,000 male juveniles who were the subject of such complaints. I repeated these calculations for 1996, and the result was 54 offenders per 100,000 persons of this age group in the total population. Thus, in 1996 as well, the incidence of crime for this type of offence was again highest for 14- to 15-year-olds.

12. It should be added however, that the installation of this new law led to the situation in Germany that consensual sexual contacts between lesbians over the age of 14 were penalised for the first time and that the former (and eliminated) Section 175, which, besides others, prohibited consensual male homosexual contacts between a man over 18 and a man between 14 and 18, partly was restored in this new Section 182.

13. Selg et al. (1979), p. 66. It is difficult to judge whether this information from the end of the 19th century is correct as we didn't have empirical sexology at that time.

14. Husslein (1982), p. 117.

15. "Offences against sexual self-determination"–Chapter 13 of the then reformed Penal Code.

16. For example, in contrast to "trafficking in human beings," "sex tourism in connection with child prostitution" and "child abduction."

REFERENCES

Bauer, Fritz, Hans Bürger-Prinz, Hans Giese and Herbert Jäger (eds.) (1963): Sexualität and Verbrechen. Beiträge zur Strafrechtsreform (Sexuality and Crime). Contributions regarding the reform of criminal law. Frankfurt/M.

Baumann, Jürgen et al. (eds.) (1968): Alternativ-Entwurf eines Strafgesetzbuches besonderer Teil–Sexualdelikte. Straftaten gegen Ehe, Familie and Personenstand.

Straftaten gegen den religiösen Frieden and die Totenruhe. (Alternative draft for a Special Part of the Penal Code–Sexual offences, offences against marriage, the family and personal status. Offences against religious peace and the peace of the dead). Tübingen.

Baurmann, Michael C. (1992): Antworten zum Fragenkatalog für die "Öffentliche Anhörung zum Sexualstrafrecht (§§ 175, 182 StGB)" des Ausschusses für Frauen and Jugend des Deutschen Bundesrates am 4. März 1992 in Bonn. (Responses to the list of questions presented for the "Public hearing on criminal law on sexual offences [Sections 175 and 182 of the German Penal Code]" of the upper house of the German parliament's Committee on Women and Young Persons held on 4 March 1992 in Bonn).

Baurmann, Michael C. (1996): Sexualität, Gewalt and psychische Folgen. Eine Längsschnittuntersuchung bei Opfern sexueller Gewalt and sexueller Normverletzungen anhand von angezeigten Sexualkontakten. (Sexuality, violence and the psychological after effects. A longitudinal study of the victims of sexual violence and of violations of sexual norms on the basis of 8,000 reported sexual contacts). (Volume 15 of the BKA Research Series). Wiesbaden.

Federal publication IV/650 of 4 October 1962 (Regierungsentwurf eines Strafgesetzbuches–Government draft of a Penal Code–E 1962). In: Fritz Bauer, Hans Bürger-Prinz, Hans Giese and Herbert Jäger (eds.) (1963): Sexualität and Verbrechen. Beiträge zur Strafrechtsreform. (Sexuality and Crime. Contributions regarding the reform of criminal law). Frankfurt/M., pp. 363–424.

Hanack, Ernst-Walter (1969): Zur Revision des Sexualstrafrechts in der Bundesrepublik. Ein Rechtsgutachten. (Revision of the criminal law on sexual offences in the Federal Republic of Germany. A legal opinion). Reinbek.

Husslein, Adelina (1982): Voreheliche Beziehungen (Premarital relations). Vienna.

Jäger, Herbert (1957): Strafgesetzgebung and Rechtsgüterschutz bei Sittlichkeitsdelikten. (Criminal law and protecting the objects of legal protection in the case of offences against morality). (Sexual research contributions–volume 12). Stuttgart.

Jäger, Herbert (1963): In: Fritz Bauer, Hans Bürger-Prinz, Hans Giese and Herbert Jäger (eds.) (1963): Sexualität and Verbrechen. Beiträge zur Strafrechtsreform. (Sexuality and crime. Contributions regarding the reform of criminal law). Frankfurt/M.

Jäger, Herbert (1976): Veränderung des Strafrechts durch Kriminologie? Ansätze zur Konkretisierung interdisziplinärer Kooperation. (Using criminology to change criminal law? Approaches to concretizing interdisciplinary cooperation) In: Kriminologisches Journal, 2, pp. 98-113.

Jäger, Herbert (1981): Zur Gleichstellung der Homosexualität and Heterosexualität im Strafrecht. (On equal treatment for homosexuality and heterosexuality in criminal law). In: Vorgänge, 4, pp. 18-22.

Jäger, Herbert (1984): Möglichkeiten einer weiteren Reform des Sexualstrafrechts. (Possibilities for further reform of the criminal law on sexual offences) In: Dannecker/Sigusch (eds.): Sexualtheorie and Sexualpolitik. (Sexual theory and sexual policy). (Sexual research contributions–volume 59) Stuttgart, pp. 67-76.

Jäger, Herbert and Eberhard Schorsch (eds.) (1987): Sexualwissenschaft and Strafrecht. (Sexology and criminal law) (Sexual research contributions–volume 62) Stuttgart.

Selg, Herbert et al. (1979): Psychologie des Sexualverhaltens. (The psychology of sexual conduct). Stuttgart et al.

Strafgesetzbuch für das Deutsche Reich. Nebst dem Wortlaut des Einführungsgesetzes und des Ergänzungsgesetzes von 1878 (The Penal Code of the German Reich along with the text of the Introductory Law and of the Supplementary Law of 1878). (Amendment to the Penal Code) Berlin 1878, 10th edition.

Strafgesetzbuch (Penal Code) et al. ('Beck Texts' published by the German paperback publisher "dtv") Munich 1998, 31st edition.

Straub, Ursula, Rainer Witt et al. (October 2003): Prior police records of rapists. A project devoted to optimizing the evaluation of prior police records of rapists for the purpose of developing offender profiles in connection with behavioural analyses. (Bundeskriminalamt–Institute of Law Enforcement Studies and Training) Wiesbaden.

Adolescence, Sexual Aggression and the Criminal Law

Lorenz Böllinger, JD, MA

SUMMARY. Criminal law and criminal policy history is perceived as an evolution of legitimation: from a morality paradigm before the Seventies of last century to a utilitarian concept of interdisciplinary enlightenment and rationality, and on to a factual paradigm of risk containment, security orientation and mere exclusion since the Nineties. However, in the area of sexual crime, and especially as far as "the protection of minors" is concerned, Western law appears to have undergone an additional paradigm change, namely in reverting to moralistic principles in disregard of scientific insight. This process, for which victimology appears to be the door opener, is reflected in legal doctrine and criminal policy, in law enforcement, in populist media and politics. This evolutionary process is interpreted as symptomatic for a post-modern trend in the globalised society where sexual behavior on one hand is blatantly and abusively commercialised, and on the other hand, if deviant, represents the psychologically most expedient object of scapegoating and symbolic policy. The article finishes pleading for a return to the 'project

---

Lorenz Böllinger, born 1944, is tenured Professor of Criminal Law and Criminology, Bremen University Law Dept., a psychoanalyst, and Co-Director of the Bremen Institute for Criminal Policy Research and of the Bremen Institute for Drug Policy Research (BISDRO). His research centers around criminal policy matters with an emphasis on sexual, capital and violent crime, terrorism, and drug problems.

[Haworth co-indexing entry note]: "Adolescence, Sexual Aggression and the Criminal Law." Böllinger, Lorenz. Co-published simultaneously in *Journal of Psychology & Human Sexuality* (The Haworth Press, Inc.) Vol. 16, No. 2/3, 2004, pp. 89-104; and: *Adolescence, Sexuality, and the Criminal Law: Multidisciplinary Perspectives* (ed: Helmut Graupner, and Vern L. Bullough) The Haworth Press, Inc., 2004, pp. 89-104. Single or multiple copies of this article are available for a fee from The Haworth Document Delivery Service [1-800-HAWORTH, 9:00 a.m. - 5:00 p.m. (EST). E-mail address: docdelivery@haworthpress.com].

http://www.haworthpress.com/web/JPHS
© 2004 by The Haworth Press, Inc. All rights reserved.
Digital Object Identifier: 10.1300/J056v16n02_08

of modernity' and to interdisciplinary studies rather than morality as a foundation for criminal policy. *[Article copies available for a fee from The Haworth Document Delivery Service: 1-800-HAWORTH. E-mail address: <docdelivery@haworthpress.com> Website: <http://www.HaworthPress.com> © 2004 by The Haworth Press, Inc. All rights reserved.]*

KEYWORDS. Youth protection, youth rights, sexual offences, age of consent, sexual consent, sexual violence, sexual abuse, child sexual abuse, pedophilia, ephebophilia, child pornography, child prostitution, youth pornography, youth prostitution, homosexuality, criminal law, sexual crime, victimology, criminal policy

INTRODUCTION

Once upon a time–mainly in the Sixties and Seventies of the past century–criminal science aspired to participate in interdisciplinary enlightenment. In Germany several outstanding publications marked this phase (e.g., Jäger, 1957; Bauer et al., 1963; Schorsch, 1993; Lautmann, 1980). Most of the outstanding experts having dealt with matters of sexuality and pertaining criminal policy took part in parliamentary hearings or at least influenced the debate which in 1975 lead to a massive reform and liberalization of criminal statute laws dealing with sexual crime. Only slight residues of mere morality protection were to be found then. However, since the Eighties there seems to have been a 'swing of pendulum' to the other side: a renaissance of morality protection or even a backlash of 'moral entrepreneurs' based on a new assessment of dangers and damages caused by sexual perpetrators. In order to substantiate or refute such assumptions it is necessary to review the state of art in German criminal law theory as well as in the neighbouring sciences.

THE CRIMINAL LAW THEORY DEBATE ABOUT THE 'PROTECTION OF LEGAL GOODS' (RECHTSGÜTERSCHUTZ)

According to modern epistemological thinking the societal 'evil of crime' is not given by nature. It is rather a societal construct: Criminal statutes or precedents define the crime abstractly, law enforcement in implementing the law defines it concretely (Hassemer, 1995; Jäger,

1987). The process of definition is also the expression of a societal power play and must be analysed and differentiated with interdisciplinary methods on two levels, empirically and normatively. The threat and execution of punishment in a democratic rule of law society represents the *ultima ratio* of social policy, the severest kind of intervention into human rights. The label applied by the verdict implies a very strong and emotionally laden value judgement plus an almost total substantial infringement of liberty by imprisonment. Thus, criminal law works both symbolically and instrumentally.

In order to legitimise the depth of infringement of human rights the definition of an 'evil' or a 'social problem' and the attribution of responsibility must not be arbitrary. It must follow strictest normative criteria which in turn imply a number of important empirical assumptions. Even seemingly universal and timeless definitions of 'natural law' have to be, like any state intervention in individual rights, measured normatively along standards of human rights and rule of law (Jäger, 1987).

The German constitution (*Grundgesetz, GG*) and a specific "theory of legislation" provide for a system of criteria and procedures provides for adequate normative and empirical investigation and assessment of substantial values, the need and means to protect them and the proportionality of value to be protected and means of intervention. The aim does not justify any means: the instruments to deal with societal risks have to be compatible with the basic values. The preservation of human dignity is the most essential prerequisite for the attendance of citizens to these norms.

The constitutionality of criminal law as a normative system not only of legitimation but also of limitation of punishment is elaborated and operationalised in the following set of principles (Jäger, 1984; Nestler, 1998).

The question of need to protect certain normatively dignified values, the *Rechtsgüterschutzprinzip* qualitatively substantiates the reasoning and at the same time limitation of state intervention in human rights. It specifies one of three central doctrinal elements specifying the most general constitutional law axiom, the principle of commensurateness: the sub-principle of "necessity" (*Erforderlichkeit*). It is legitimate only to penalize behaviour proven damaging or dangerous for relevant values of others or society. It is not legitimate to penalize behaviour which is part of the right to self-determination or which runs counter to abstract cultural values or individual or sub-cultural morality without substantially damaging others. The damaging or endangering quality of such behaviour has to be proven empirically.[1]

The certainty principle (*Bestimmtheitsprinzip*, Art. *103 II GG*) and the so-called 'theories of punishment' (*Strafzwecke*) aim at grasping the dimension of instrumental aptitude of norm and intervention. They specify the second sub-principle of aptitude or expediency (*Geeignetheit*). Only precisely defined and described damages and dangers resulting from the behaviour in an empirically proven way and substantially justifying the negative social value judgement may be penalized. The management of social problems through criminal law due to its maximally invasive character must remain the extreme means of social policy. Lesser alternatives outside criminal law must be examined and preferred if at all possible. Legislation and judiciary have to balance possible secondary damage inflicted by law enforcement itself against the benefit of instrumental protection of legal goods and symbolic restoration of the legal order. The legislator must, using timely scientific methods and reflecting media manipulation mechanisms, continuously examine whether the definition of 'evil' is still conforming with the changeable value creeds in the population.

Finally the principles of unlawfulness and guilt (*Unrechts-, Schuldprinzip*) provide a third and quantitative touch-stone for normative examination within the constitutional principle of commensurateness: proportionality of any punishment with regard to the weight of a perpetration. The weight must be determined by a generalizing evaluation of the damage and by ascribing guilt as the measure for individual capacity to be motivated by the imperative of the statute law.

Legitimate application of criminal statutes or precedents needs realistic assessment of the perpetration in question and the commensurateness of ascribed guilt and punishment. In the same way when making laws the legislator has to regard and analyse reality through the filter of constitutional principles. Defining a certain crime needs balancing damages and risks both of the behaviour and of the reaction. Only if a positive outcome can realistically be estimated is punishment legitimate, not just for the sake of pursuing a good purpose. Punishing intervention may not be based on assumptions, prejudice, myths, or mere populistic exigencies.

So much for the ideal constitutional background of criminal law. The sociology of law shows, of course, wide discrepancies with respect to the real functioning of law implementation. Always a hidden code contributes to decision making, representing particular or extra-legal interests. But it must remain the aspiration of the criminal law sub-system in a rule of law system to keep tensions between law in the books and law in action low. The definition and interpretation of law has to be continuously confronted with scientific research and the analysis of normative agreement in the society (Hassemer, 1995). There should be regular evaluation measures to examine whether a law fulfils its purpose. The legislator is comparable to a producer having to take responsibility for his product toward the consumer. When in doubt about any of the listed criteria the option should be against criminalizing and looking for functional alternatives.

Cum grano salis in the Seventies and Eighties some progress was made to meet the ideals sketched out above. However, the reached state was instable and prone to relapse (Jäger, 1987). It appears as though only the strict rule of law façade stays while the rest of the building behind has been torn down–especially in the area of sexual crimes. Some indicators for this thesis will be shown in the following.

Evolution of the Principle of Protection of Legal Goods

In criminal law theory the pervasive interpretation of the principle of protection of legal goods had a substantial, essentialist foundation: the original definition was: "Human interest needing protection" (Hassemer, 1995). This definition expresses the need for societal reasons, for objective and standardised categories of normatively defined values. Thus the definition of a "legal good" was the fundamental element of criminalization by law. On the level of application of laws this same definition was the basis for interpretation. This approach accommodated the criminal law transition from protection of a certain morality to protection of substantially represented values.

However, there was always danger of interpreting and abstracting the term "legal good," to make it flexible with respect to state and particular vested interests. In legal doctrine the acceptance for "universal" and "collective legal goods" has grown, thus loosening the tie to the essential human interest.

Now another phase of erosion of the substantial definition of "legal good" can be observed: the so-called victim doctrine (*Victimodogmatik*) attempts to introduce victims' interests immediately into the application of criminal statutes. This method is alien to classical criminal law doctrine as it introduces a high amount of individual subjectivity and partiality into a procedure devised to digest social conflict normatively and in a generalizing way, not giving the victim a lot of say in the concrete court case.

This loss of rule of law orientation cannot, in my opinion, be legitimised by a stronger consideration of victims' interests. It is another question that victims should be provided adequate compensation for their damages and suffering through society. Also criminal law provides for means of restitution, compensation, and mediation between perpetrator and victim. But the socio-ethical reproach and the power of inflicting pain and humiliation by punishment must strictly be reserved to the state in order not to fall back into historical phases of self-justice. The state cannot let himself become the representative of individual retribution, the "dignity of punishment" lies on another level.

Also with respect to the second, procedural aspect of the principle of commensurateness, the determination of criminal law intervention aptitude, a controversial development can be observed. On one side the theories of punishment, especially the so-called positive special prevention or rehabilitation principle, are increasingly being regarded as a necessary corollary of the substantial "legal good" principle. Subsequently a steady decrease of empirically dysfunctional and counter-productive imprisonment and an increase of less invasive sanctions can be observed–e.g., diversion, public work, ban orders, mediation, restitution, treatment, etc.

But on the other hand, under the impression of dramatisation in the media and in politics in the area of sexual crime, legislation, and jurisdiction have vastly widened the realm of threat and implementation of imprisonment.

Victims may be satisfied to receive acceptance as symbolized by criminal procedure. Research shows, however, that imprisonment is not necessarily part of victims' compensation needs. In most cases the victim is more satisfied with functional and instrumental reactions like restitution, public work, treatment.

With respect to the third, constitutional law aspect of unlawfulness and adequateness of guilt it can be observed that, both in legislation and in criminal justice, it is attempted to regard the complex socio-genetic background both of the perpetrator and the victim.

The decrease in procedural guarantees and the increasing subjectivity in interpreting the term "legal good" therefore lead to a re-moralisation of sexual crime statutes, to strengthening of arbitrary and populistic definitions pushed forward by medial and political power. The theoretical progress of the legal reform of the Seventies, of differentiating morality and the term "legal good" appears to have been revoked.

Diffusion of Doctrine and Contradictory Valuations

Both on the level of legislation and higher court jurisdiction there is a tendency toward increasingly vague and global terminology and to extensive and aim-oriented interpretations, allowing to subsume a broad array of circumstances under the statute. Drastic example for this tendency is the area of drug delicts, but it can also be observed in the area of sexual crimes. The constitutional certainty principle is being undermined. Only in few cases the supreme constitutional court has stopped such erosion processes.

The phenomenon of parliamentary "deals" is also increasing, resulting in weak compromises, e.g., the insisting on abstract determination of unlawfulness while de-penalising on the procedural level.

Enhancing Punishability

All around the world criminal law is increasingly being used as a populistic means of suggesting state activity while the actual socio-structural causes and determinants remain untouched. Such 'symbolic policy' seems to have become the instrument of choice for modern 'risk society.' It is overlooked that practically all defined risks are created by societal mechanisms and cannot be successfully reduced on the symptom level. So more and more "risk behaviour" which should be dealt with in terms of civil or administrative law, e.g., in the logic of an insurance system or with fines as sanctions, is becoming the object of criminal law intervention. Increasingly not only the damage of legal goods is put under the threat of punishment but also even any slight endangerment of such values. This concept of criminal law used to be reserved to very severe kinds of risks. Furthermore, on the procedural level law enforcement is increasingly entitled to intervene even without concrete suspicion of a criminal act, merely legitimised by what is actually a policing task of preventing dangers. In Germany the separation between policing and criminal law enforcement used to be taken very seriously as the amalgamation of both was part of the NAZI outrages. All this results in a loss of democratic rule of law substance.

Inconsistency of Sanctions

In a remarkable ignorance of clinical findings about sexual perversions and delinquency both legislation and courts count on imprisoning sexual delinquents rather than committing them to treatment–just like before the law reform of the Seventies. They are once again being implicitly supported by forensic psychiatrists who are increasingly diagnosing them as fully accountable and not as mentally disturbed. It seems the whole system is bowing to public pressure while actually in the last 30 years statistics show a steady decrease in sexual delinquency.

INTERPRETATION OF CRIMINAL LAW DEVELOPMENTS

Developments as sketched out above appear symptomatic. They seem to signify a general tendency of the state away from strict rule of law principles toward pragmatic action oriented by functionality and efficiency. This *'Zweckrationalität'* (in the sense of Max Weber) does not primarily serve the purpose of the defined problem, but rather the purpose of symbolizing and demonstrating seemingly effective state action in view of voters' perception, but without cost. Part of this is the dramatization of relatively non-dramatic situations and even the construction of pseudo-problems.

Paradoxically and cynically, in an epoch of socially constructed mass and mega dangers, criminal law has been chosen to be the means of choice, denying the fact that the substantial risks cannot really be fought on the symptom level.

Substantial reasoning, empirical investigation, and diligent balancing with respect to preconditions and effectiveness of criminal law have become obsolete. The decision to make criminal law is determined merely politically, either 'demand oriented', based on surveys, or 'supply oriented', based on pre-calculated resources and assumptions. The aggregated risks are only being administered, not addressed in a substantial way. The problems and human problem groups are increasingly contained or excluded from the rest of society rather that integrated.

All this may have been the basic disposition in a post-industrialist rule-of-law society. However, in my opinion it is the globalisation, monopolisation and power concentration process that has caused a qualitative leap. There seems to be a new bluntness and brazenness which could be paralleled to the brazenness of today's public sexuality. This is not meant in the sense of a new morality. I want to express that sexual delinquency in a way is only the negative of this sexualisation of public life: Those who cannot keep the superficial rules are excluded. The common feature of both is what can be called an increasing collective borderline structure: alienation, the absence of meaningful and emotionally lasting relationships, solidarity and empathy, the psychological splitting mechanism of the good-and-bad dichotomy, exploiting, abusing, and manipulating the other.

This interpretation, in my opinion, does not refute the view that there are also reasonable developments in criminal law. Partially criminal law makers establish intervention methods that seem human and effective at the same time. In Germany, for example, all sexual perpetrators have to be diagnosed and treated. If they refuse they lose the right to parole. This progress, however, proves to be a façade as the implementation does not work: firstly there are not enough trained psychotherapists in prison and the state has no money to finance them; secondly, the psychotherapists are forced by law to report about the contents of their work with the patient–which in many cases will result in pseudo-therapy, since only favourable statements will help the prisoner to get early release.

LAW AND MORALITY, LAW AND SEXUALITY

How then are criminal law in the books and in action influencing the problem of sexual aggression and child abuse today. My thesis: Criminal law and its actual judicial, political, and medial implementation cannot absorb or cope with what remains of the central problem of sexual aggression and child abuse. They even aggravate the problem.

Criminal law is presently, at least in the professional and political mainstream, constructed as a timely instrument of societal risk prevention and risk management. In that form it tends to define sexual crimes as risk and does this in a gross and undifferentiating way. In the professional areas profiting from this definition–especially the therapy 'business' and the media–differential symptomatology and the social context are being ignored, everything is being valued along dichotomous lines and with the aim of "adapting to normality." This lack of understanding the complex interactive development of sexual disturbances secretly leads back to un-reflected morality as we had before.

More than in the area of general property and assets crimes the agencies of populistic political and commercial presentation can target the deeply rooted fantasies and affects that have been suppressed, denied, projected, and externalised. This constitutes what can, somewhat superficially, be called 'hysterisation' of public opinion. One aspect of this projection process is represented by 'fear of crime' as surveyed and largely manipulated by the media and politics.

Steered by market interests, but also by a certain element of drive and lust, politics and the media have become agents in a construction process in which, largely unhampered by reality, in the perception of people a drama is being staged. For example, 1971: 77 Sexual murders, 80 reports about sexual child abuse; 1996: 22 Sexual murders, 800 reports about sexual child abuse (Rüther, 1998). This kind of easy vicarious drive fulfillment in the form of voyeurism does not remain without effect on perpetrators and victims of sexual crimes.

In a mechanism, macroscopically and sociologically called 'labeling', societal actors metaphorically speaking pull over their roles. That is not a simple mechanism but rather the role-players' self-attribution result of a lengthy interaction process. The micro-structure of this process can be cleared up psychoanalytically, both on a social and individual level. We are dealing with the basic, though collectivised defence mechanism of splitting and the pertaining syndrome of denial, projection, externalisation, and isolation of affects.

The more sexual crimes become subject of dramatising, demand oriented and profitable reports, the larger the echo of published opinion. The concordance of both results in demand-oriented populistic campaigns of politicians, in sharper legislation and jurisdiction. In a circular, self-enhancing process this in turn influences simplification and dramatisation in the public media and mass perception. The more political and medial simplification results in dichotomy, the more such construction seeps into the life world of individuals and into their mental set. There the result is again polarisation and splitting, a pervasive tendency to uniform perception and identification with the conforming ideal, even to a compulsion to confess. The price: elimination, disintegration, and dissociation of conscious residues of fantasy and ambivalence which could normally be integrated. The adverse images of good and evil are being purified, the negative ideal is projected onto apt individuals. In the sense of what in psychoanalysis is called 'projective identification' such individuals cognitively and affectively take over the negative ideal. They feel 'bad', 'worthless' indeed, and react even more aggressively and destructively. On the other hand, the conformity ideal becomes even more purified: every single spot must be erased due to the fear of it signalising the break-through of evil.

CIRCULAR DEVELOPMENTS

There is a dialectic development in the sense of the civilisation process as described by N. Elias: the reduction of violence in society and its monopolisation by the state. Reflexivity and enlightenment about human psyche, about ubiquitousness of aggression and sexuality, of their destructive and positive variants, about ambivalence. All this obviously and paradoxically tends to produce norms and education which in turn create unrealistic ideals and anti-ideals without ambivalence.

Today there is a normative and pedagogic advocacy for implementing enlightenment and experience about sexuality in a new ideal or even morality of treating sexual behaviour as a matter of civil discourse (Schmidt, 1998). This may be a 'project of modernity', but it also bears the danger of defending against the essence and reality of sexual and aggressive drives. The term 'drive' as used in this context can be viewed as a symbolic analogy or even an essentialist expression for archetypical forces of nature within man: they will never be totally civilised or controlled. Human violence and sexuality contain a universal, archaic, natural residue which expresses itself in omnipresent tensions and conflicts and is controllable only under certain social circumstances and only to a certain degree.

There seems to be a fundamental misunderstanding in equally applying the phantasmatic drive civilisation ideal to youths, young adults and youths with developmental disturbances and retardations. The formation of ideals as well as the definition of criminal sexual behaviour also represent a psychological splitting process, defending against ambivalence and insecurity. It contributes to the societal process of denying specific developmental tensions, conflicts and regressions in youths and refusal to empathize.

Avoiding violence, ability to communicate and understand, consensual sexuality, capacities to love, enjoy, work and suffer, the internalisation of societal norms–all these need long-term development of insight based on inter-human relationship experiences, conscious emotionality, and sensible reflection. This process cannot be short-cut by mere pedagogy. Society has to provide framework institutions enabling those processes and developments to take place. However, a residue of un-calculable sexuality will always remain. Sociological insight into the dichotomous process should also be appreciated: on one hand prolongation of the juvenile developmental phase, on the other hand acceleration into a pseudo-status of adulthood.

The loss of empathy for adolescents and their imperfection is accompanied by a process of over-sensitisation with respect to violence and non-conforming sexuality. This can be interpreted from exaggerated, hysterical and un-differential perceptions, depictions and exaggerations of violence in school and sexual child abuse (Habenicht, 2002). At the same time we observe a relapse into ideological patterns which seemed long overcome: minors are constructed as asexual beings–ignoring a century of psychological enlightenment. A salient example for this is the 2002 EU commission framework decision about the fight against sexual exploitation of children and child pornography. The legal term 'child' in the framework decision means any person under the age of eighteen (Art. 1 a EU draft). Also many other legal terms are so vague that many works of art and literature could easily be indicted. In January 2003 the German government has followed suit by passing a draft law about "The protection of children and youths from sexual violence and exploitation." There are some abstract formulations about social policy and prevention measures. But by and large the draft relies on widening and toughening criminal punishment.

When the European Union introduces criminal law binding 20 member states and over 350 million citizens it must be remembered what has been said in the beginning of this paper: criminal punishment represents the severest intervention into human rights and therefore has to be scrutinized maximally with respect to necessity, expediency, and commensurateness. Criminal law must not be abused to protect particular moralities if there is no proven violation of legal goods, of inter-individual damage.

In the area of sexual crimes the law rightly aims at protecting sexual self-determination and undisturbed development of personality and, there-in, sexuality. In this respect the German and most European legislatives in setting the protection age limit at 14 years were wise to refer to the insights of developmental psychology, sexuology, and youth sociology.

The EU draft grotesquely defies these well-founded standards in defining as "child" any person under the age of 18. Theoretically perpetrations involving "victims" of almost 18 or 4 years of age could be treated alike. This kind of criminal law is bound to loose credibility and denounces itself. Furthermore the EU draft violates the subsidiarity principle in exceeding its competence for supra-national crime. By German constitutional law standards it also violates the criminal law principles of certainty, equality, and commensurateness by extremely wide and weak statute formulations and by the threat of extremely harsh punishments.

Sexual perpetrators not having passed the vital youth status experiences mentioned above should be perceived as individuals retarded in their maturation and socialization process. In consequence functional rehabilitation programmes would replace threatening harsh punishment. But in today's populistic politics it seems more expedient for society to label them either evil in a moralistic sense or deviant in a biological sense, thus promoting the societal mechanism of splitting and exclusion (Lautmann, 1987).

The same mechanisms apply to victims: societal dramatisation and ostracism with respect to perpetrators induce the victims as well as law enforcement and treatment institutions to deny any interactive component and co-responsibility in the victimization process. Due to those the victim may have conscious or subconscious guilt feelings but has to project those in order not be caught in the process of guilt ascription. The intensity of the victim trauma is thus being increased instead of reduced.

Violence and sexuality in the relatively integrated and civilized forms of 'paraphilic mechanisms' or 'perversions' cannot be extinguished (Berner, 1996). They can only be channelled as long as their real and projected potentials are not being ignored and denied. Ex-communication of such contents is not only counterproductive, it is even destructive. Their tension and projected explosive force should be made conscious and positively integrated through social rituals of experience, reflection and moderated acting-out. The S/M subcultures can be seen as an example for this. At the same time the realm of paedophilic urges and cravings will have to be dealt with differently as children are really not equal partners (Dannecker, 2001).

As mentioned before criminal law in itself is contradictory: official criminal policy provides for socially integrative concepts, especially treatment. But forced treatment in this case bears the risk of abstract normativism and hidden punishment without understanding–especially when therapists are obliged to report about 'progress or failure' (Böllinger, 1995).

It remains to be asked: How can such societal relapses happen? As mentioned above the statistical reality of sexual crimes in Germany is very un-dramatic: continuous reduction over the last thirty years in the major categories (Bundesminister, 2002; Egg, 1999). Even in the area of violent crime it can be seen that only a small segment of very dissocial youths accounts for the bulk of increase (Bundesminister, 2002). Also the relapse figures after intramural treatment, empirically proven to amount to about 20%, are excessively exaggerated in the media (Egg, 2000; Elz, 2001, 2002; Nowara, 2001).

What has not changed seems to be the over-determinedness and ambiguity of sexuality on both the individual and social levels. On one hand the problematic exigencies of individualisation, the diversification of life-styles and the dispersion of relationships (Sigusch, 2001). On the other hand, the increased collective de-sublimation of sexuality implying certain norms of conformity and fears of non-conformity. The modern evolution of alienation and loss of bonding, superficially labelled as the process of individualisation and globalisation are being represented intra-psychically, thus revitalizing archaic fear. This fear is then defended against individually and collectively by mechanisms of splitting, projection, and denial—as the "invention" of taboos, gods, and dichotomous moralities has always been the predominant means of defending against fear and exerting power.

ADVOCATING THE RETURN TO INTERDISCIPLINARITY IN LEGAL SCIENCE

In view of the insights sketched out here there should be a return to the principles and tendencies of the Seventies and, at the same time, a look forward to timely modernisation. Given the social and global problems of today the present techniques of making positive law are less sufficient than ever. It seems vital to include social, psychological, and sexual sciences in the legislative procedure in order to better estimate the reality of social problems involved, the need for state control, the instrumental or symbolic expediency as well as proportionality of criminal law and criminal sanctions to solve or reduce the problem.

To sum up, there are normative "clues" for scientifically enlightened criminal law legislation:

- Acceptance of ambivalence of "normal," "sane" sexuality in view of aggressive components and inter-individual as well as intra-psychic conflict.

- Consideration of sexuality as a discourse between mature adults on one hand and specific juvenile status conflicts in modern society (prolongation of youth, acceleration, etc.).

- Intensification of complexity and pertaining discourse about "damage" to the individual and to society done by sexual acts, including interactive aspects.

- Reducing populistic dramatisation and the functionality as symbolic politics of 'sexual crime'; furthering re-integration of projected components of violent and sexual fantasies through societal discourse.

Criminal law should totally retreat from any moralistic definition in the area of sexuality. It should limit itself strictly to sanctioning clearly defined acts damaging relevant others. As far as the protection of children and minors is concerned a scientific research agenda and renewed social discourse should be started, abstaining from dramatizing and populistic notions.

NOTE

1. The German supreme constitutional court (Bundesverfassungsgericht) has so judicated in a pornography case (BVerfGE 23, 40ff.–'Fanny Hill'); for comprehensive analyses see: Jäger 1957 and Hassemer 1995.

REFERENCES

Bauer, Fritz/Bürger-Prinz, Hans/Giese, Hans/Jäger, Herbert: Sexualität und Strafrecht. Frankfurt 1963 (Fischer-Verlag)

Berner, Wolfgang: Wann ist das Begehren krank? Vom Perversionsbegriff zur Paraphilie. ZSexualfosch. 1996, pp. 62-75,

Böllinger, Lorenz: Ambulante Psychotherapie mit Sexualstraftätern. In: ZSexualforsch. 1995, pp. 199-221.

Bundesminister (2002): Bundesminister des Innern u. Bundesminister der Justiz (Ed.): Erster Periodischer Sicherheitsbericht der Bundesregierung. Berlin 2002.

Dannecker, Martin: Sexueller Mißbrauch und Pädosexualität. In: Sigusch, Volkmar (Ed.): Sexuelle Störungen und ihre Behandlung. Stuttgart 2001, pp. 465-474.

Egg u.a. (Eds.): Sexualstraftäter und Maßregelvollzug. Schriftenreihe Kriminologie u. Praxis, Bd.29, 2000, Kriminologische Zentralstelle e.V. (Eigenverlag).

Egg u.a. (Eds.): Sexueller Mißbrauch von Kindern. Täter und Opfer. Schriftenreihe Kriminologie u. Praxis, Bd.27, 1999, Kriminologische Zentralstelle e.V. (Eigenverlag).

Elz, Jutta: Legalbewährung und kriminelle Karrieren von Sexualstraftätern–Sexuelle Missbrauchsdelikte. Wiesbaden 2001. Schriftenreihe Kriminologie u. Praxis, Bd.33, Kriminologische Zentralstelle e.V. (Eigenverlag).

Elz, Jutta: Legalbewährung und kriminelle Karrieren von Sexualstraftätern–Sexuelle Gewaltdelikte. Wiesbaden 2002. Schriftenreihe Kriminologie u. Praxis, Bd. 34, Kriminologische Zentralstelle e.V. (Eigenverlag).

Habenicht, Arne: Gründe für eine veränderte Sichtbarkeit sexueller Gewalt. Neue Kriminalpolitik 2002, 100-5.

Hassemer, Winfried: Vorbemerkungen zu § 1 StGB. In: Nomos Kommentar zum Strafrecht. Loseblattsammlung, Stand: 1995, Baden-Baden (Nomos), Anm. 255ff.

Jäger, Herbert: Entkriminalisierungspolitik im Strafrecht. In: Jäger/Schorsch (Ed.): Sexualwissenschaft und Strafrecht. Beitr. z. Sexualf. 62. Stuttgart 1987 (Enke), pp. 1-9.

Jäger, Herbert: Möglichkeiten einer weiteren Reform des Sexualstrafrechts. In: Dannecker, M./Sigusch, V. (Eds.): Sexualtheorie und Sexualpolitik. Stuttgart (Enke), 1984. pp. 68-79.

Jäger, Herbert: Rechtsgüterschutz und Strafgesetzgebung. Beitr. z. Sexualf. 12. Stuttgart 1957 (Enke).

Lautmann, Rüdiger: Die heterosexuelle Verführung-sexuelle Interaktion und Kriminalisierung bei § 182 StGB. In: Jäger/Schorsch (Eds.): Sexualwissenschaft und Strafrecht. Beitr. z. Sexualf. 62. Stuttgart 1987 (Enke), pp. 54-70.

Lautmann, Rüdiger: Straftaten ohne Opfer. In: Zeitschrift für Rechtspolitik 1980, pp. 178-182.

Nestler, Cornelius: Betäubungsmittelstrafrecht. Bürgerautonomie und Drogenkontrolle durch Strafrecht. In: Kreuzer, Arthur (Ed.): Handbuch des Betäubungsmittelstrafrechts. München 1998, pp. 697-860.

Quensel, Stefan: Zur kulturellen Konstruktion von Gewalt. In: Monatsschrift für Kriminologie 1998, pp. 426-432.

Rüther, Werner: Internationale Erfahrungen bei der Behandlung von Sexualstraftätern. MSchrKrim 1998, pp. 246-262.

Schmidt, Gunter/Strauß, Bernhard. Sexualität und Spätmoderne. Beitr. z. Sexualf. 76. Stuttgart 1998 (Enke).

Schorsch, Eberhard: Perversion, Liebe, Gewalt. Beitr. z. Sexualf. 68. Stuttgart 1993 (Enke).

Sigusch, Volkmar (Ed.): Sexuelle Störungen und ihre Behandlung. 3. Aufl. Stuttgart 2001 (Thieme).

Prostitution of Young Persons: A Topic of Social Work and/or Penal Legislation

Thomas Moebius, MA

SUMMARY. Juvenile prostitution in the German welfare work is being interpreted as a peculiar behaviour which cannot be influenced by criminal law but by psychodynamic and social condition factors and motives. The public prostitution of adolescents largely takes place unaffected by criminal persecution. In view of the legislation in Germany, the regulations of criminal law have not had any decisive influence at juvenile prostitution. In Germany there exists a sufficient protection of children and adolescents. The current discussion about the expansion of the childhood definition of young people up to 18 years, and a de-legalization of agreed sexual actions between people under and over 18 years, ignores a typical juvenile behaviour. A change in the situation of life of juvenile prostitutes by a legal intensification, as well as a change in be-

---

Thomas Moebius has academic degrees in Psychology (Diplom) and Special Education (MA) and is experienced in outreach programmes for male prostitutes and streetkids. He is Director of a sociological institution in Hamburg, Germany, and has done research work about delinquent adolescents/streetkids and methods of welfare work. In 1992 he served as an expert heard by the second chamber of German parliament ("Bundesrat") on the issue of youth-prostitution and the criminal law.

Address correspondence to: Institut des Rauhen Hauses für Soziale Praxis (isp), D–20148 Hamburg, Germany (E-mail: moebius.isp@rauheshaus.de).

[Haworth co-indexing entry note]: "Prostitution of Young Persons: A Topic of Social Work and/or Penal Legislation." Moebius, Thomas. Co-published simultaneously in *Journal of Psychology & Human Sexuality* (The Haworth Press, Inc.) Vol. 16, No. 2/3, 2004, pp. 105-110; and: *Adolescence, Sexuality, and the Criminal Law: Multidisciplinary Perspectives* (ed: Helmut Graupner and Vern L. Bullough) The Haworth Press, Inc., 2004, pp. 105-110. Single or multiple copies of this article are available for a fee from The Haworth Document Delivery Service [1-800-HAWORTH, 9:00 a.m. - 5:00 p.m. (EST). E-mail address: docdelivery@haworthpress.com].

http://www.haworthpress.com/web/JPHS
© 2004 by The Haworth Press, Inc. All rights reserved.
Digital Object Identifier: 10.1300/J056v16n02_09

haviour through an anonymous sanction system like that of legislation, cannot be expected. *[Article copies available for a fee from The Haworth Document Delivery Service: 1-800-HAWORTH. E-mail address: <docdelivery@haworthpress.com> Website: <http://www.HaworthPress.com> © 2004 by The Haworth Press, Inc. All rights reserved.]*

KEYWORDS. Youth protection, youth rights, sexual offences, age of consent, sexual consent, sexual violence, sexual abuse, paedophilia, ephebophilia, child prostitution, youth prostitution, juvenile prostitution, homosexuality, criminal law, social work, street work

Young people of both sexes prostitute themselves in different sociocultural and economic contexts and out of a variety of reasons. In the following under 'prostitution' shall not be understood the sexual exploitation of children (in Germany the age limit lies at 14 years) nor the sexual abuse of young persons under use or threat of bodily or mental violence. The subject is rather the prostitution of adolescents and young adults, which occurs in public–mostly in the station districts of the big cities–on the basis of a barter deal "sex against money."

The extent and the consequences of the prostitution, as well as the reactions of the societal authorities, differ in dependency above all from the economic and social conditions under which prostitution of young people takes place. Adolescents "in the street" prostitute themselves in Latin America or in East Europe above all out of material need, in order to safe-guard their own survival or also the existence of whole families. To the contrary, adolescents in Germany prostitute themselves in order to satisfy their desires of consumer goods, for the procurement of drugs, or even on quest for social and emotional closeness and recognition. An additional motive for male youths is the experimenting with their own more or less accepted homosexuality (Bader/Moebius, 1991). I would like to restrict the following to the public prostitution in Germany and in this context to point out the possibilities for action in the German juvenile welfare and justice.

INITIAL FASCINATION

Youths, who prostitute themselves, often live "in the street" and are a traditional part of the downtown area scene of German Cities. They expose themselves to health risks like an HIV infection and the consumption of hard drugs. Physical decay, as well as changes in social behaviour and psychiatric peculiarities may be the result (Moebius, 1996). The family background oftentimes is being marked by violence and experience in abuse, social deprivation, and material poverty. Many youths have lived in hostels of the juvenile welfare service, or still live there, and are "swinging" between the street and the hostel. They do not feel understood or accepted in the hostels. The social ostracism and the making taboo by the social environment, as well in the institutions of the social works themselves, intensifies the process of being socially excluded and thus encourages the withdrawal of the youths into the sub-cultural scenery like the prostitution-milieu. These marginalized youths leave more and more their original environment and shift their centre of life "into the street" (Permien/Zink, 1998). With young male prostitutes the experienced and also anticipated exclusion is being made stronger once more by the taboo of homosexuality still existing in social work.

The prospects of a (re)integration of the youths into a stable social environment outside of the prostitution-milieu decreases the longer the youths have been living in the scenarios of the street. Youngsters are just at the time of the entry situation fascinated by the possibilities of earning and consumption, the attentiveness of the "suitors," and the action at the central meeting points of the scene. A regular attendance at school or work and educational programmes with low earning possibilities can not compete. Most of the youngsters change their point of view when remaining at the scene. Drug dependency, social isolation, and a physical and psychical destabilization, however, are aggravating the exit from the prostitution at this time. Only very few young people "of the street" develop a professional identity and position themselves open and self-assuredly with their occupation (Bader/Moebius, 1991).

EFFICIENT ACCEPTING SOCIAL WELFARE AND INEFFICIENT CRIMINALIZATION

Juvenile prostitution in the German welfare work is being interpreted as a peculiar behaviour which can not be influenced by criminal law but by psychodynamic and social condition factors and motives. The prostitution of male and female adolescents differs in view of the motives, approach and progress which in this context can be referred to only marginally. The juvenile welfare service tries to contact the young people "in the street" through special offers of the social welfare like shelters and overnight accommodation or street-work projects. Streetworkers offer, apart from help to escape and AIDS prevention, assistance for survival in the prostitution scenario (recreation rooms, conflict counselling, food, clothing, etc.). The target of the social work in the prostitution scenario is to strengthen the youngsters "in the street," to give them confidence in the help system again and to keep open options for their escape (Hansbauer, 1998, Permien/Zink, 1998, Pfennig, 1996). However, social welfare has no mission to prevent juvenile prostitution or to stop the contact between the suitors and the youngsters.

The public prostitution of adolescents largely takes (and took) place unaffected by criminal persecution. In view of the post war legislation in Germany, the regulations of criminal law effective at the time, have not had any decisive influence on juvenile prostitution. In West-Germany neither the article (§) 175 of the penal code (abolished in the meantime) which put under penalty the homosexual contact between adults and adolescents under 18 years, nor the article (§) 182 of the penal code, which has been implemented to strengthen the protection of adolescents by penalizing sexual contact between adults and adolescents between 14 and 16 years, i.e., in exchange of remuneration, could prevent public adolescent prostitution or even embank it.

The penal legislation can assume a protective function only–and here I would like to point out explicitly again to a difference in the situation of children under 14 years–if it is oriented on the reality of life and does not run counter to an executed societal liberalization. This is valid for the prostitution of young people, as well as for common typical juvenile sexual behaviour, where the contact with adults is not out of the way. In Germany there exists a sufficient protection of children and young people. A change in the situation of life of juvenile prostitutes by a legal intensification, as well as a change in behaviour through an anonymous sanction system like that of legislation, can not be expected. Adolescents who prostitute themselves should be contacted by accepting and not sanctioning offers of the welfare work and be supported by individual help for escape. A criminalization of sexual contacts in the prostitution, as was executed by the § 182, involves to the contrary the danger that the prostitution shifts to private scenarios which are no longer accessible for the social work and health prevention, and adolescent prostitutes take advantage of the criminal prosecution of their suitors for their own offending actions (blackmail). Old-fashioned protective regulations can then even take a counterproductive effect and rather aid the criminalization of the youths than have a protective function.

THREATENED AUTONOMY

The current discussion about the expansion of the childhood definition of young people up to 18 years, and a de-legalization of agreed sexual actions between people under and over 18 years ignores both, a typical juvenile behaviour which includes sexual contacts between adolescents and adults, as well as psychological development processes. The sexual behaviour of children and youths changes also like other forms of social behaviour with the transition from childhood to youth. The current separation between child and youth, namely by the age of 14, as it is enshrined in the German penal code, but as well under the law for infantile and juvenile welfare, takes this into account in an appropriate manner. This separation stands the test also with the work in juvenile welfare. Probably juvenile prostitutes would disapprove of an expansion of the childhood definition up to 18 years. The autonomy against societal socialization authorities reached by "living in the street" would be threatened by an expansion of the protected age, as this new definition would involve also a strengthening of the protection and intervention functions of the socialization authorities, if it should have any practicable impact.

COUNTERPRODUCTIVE REPRESSION

As a closing remark let me point out a development in the German social work, which will have far more impact on the situation of the juvenile prostitutes than the change in the penal legislation. Up to now the social work with youths was based on the maxims to act of "voluntariness instead of force" and "support instead of sanctions" (Wolf, 1993). These guidelines are based on reform processes in the education at hostels, which, as a consequence, involved principally an abolishment of closed hostels in Germany. During the coming months the city state of Hamburg, known for its advanced juvenile welfare, will introduce again places in closed institutions for difficult young people. This will happen against all scientific knowledge and experience about the negative effect of such an implement of sanctions on the course of life of young people. Youngsters, who may count as especially difficult for social work, may then by resolution of a domestic relations court be retained again in such a closed institution (Koettgen, 2003). Especially youths in the public prostitution are frequently considered as particularly tough at social welfare, as they ever and anon shuffle off the offers of the juvenile welfare and live a life full of risks for themselves and for others. It is to be expected that a high quota of the youths in closed institutions have been prostituting themselves in public (and will do so again the moment they have been released from the closed institution, as all previous experience has shown). In the past, particularly girls who prostituted themselves, were affected by this sanction. The contacts of the social workers to the juvenile prostitutes, based on voluntariness and acceptance, are extremely threatened. As a result the youths will again in an amplified manner submerge into the sub-milieu and break their contacts to the shelters. The help for survival which led, at least, to a physical and psychical stabilization of many juvenile prostitutes, will, with this, no longer be possible to be offered in the current form. The consequence will be a further impoverishment of the youngsters and a further aggravation of their perspectives of escape.

The current separation of juvenile welfare and justice when treating the young prostitutes stood the test and should be kept in this form. A transfer of the responsibility for difficult youths from the social welfare to the domestic relation courts–and thus to the justice–is, with the re-implementation of accommodation in the closed institutes, no acceptable solution concept. Juvenile prostitution contains socially problematic situations for the young people, which have to be solved by educational means and not by sanctions through the justice.

REFERENCES

Bader, B., Moebius, Th., 1991: Thesen zur männlichen Prostitution. In: Bader, B., Lang, E., (Hg.): Stricherleben. Hamburg
Hansbauer, P. (Hg.), 1998: Kinder und Jugendliche auf der Straße. Muenster
Moebius, Th., 1996: Lebensort Straße–Hamburg, der lokale Kontext, in: Institut für soziale Arbeit (Hg.), Heft 17. Muenster
Koettgen, C., 2003: Kriminalpolitik auf Irrwegen. Zur Wiedereinführung der geschlossenen Unterbingung in Hamburg, in: ZJJ 3/2003
Permien, H., Zink, G., 1998: Endstation Straße? Deutsches Jugendinstitut Muenchen, Muenchen
Pfennig, G., 1996: Lebenswelt Bahnhof. Neuwied, Kriftel, Berlin
Wolf, K., (Hg.), 1993: Entwicklungen in der Heimerziehung, Muenster

Sexual Consent: The Criminal Law in Europe and Outside of Europe

Helmut Graupner, JD

Helmut Graupner (www.graupner.at), Doctor in Law (University of Vienna), is *Rechtsanwalt* (attorney-at-law), admitted to the bar in Austria and in the Czech Republic. He is Vice President of the Austrian Society for Sex Research (ÖGS); and President of the Austrian lesbian and gay rights organisation Rechtskomitee LAMBDA (RKL); Vice President for Europe, International Lesbian and Gay Law Association (ILGLaw); Austrian member, European Group of Experts on Combating Sexual Orientation Discrimination working for the Commission of the European Union; member, Scientific Committee of the Center for Research and Comparative Legal Studies on Sexual Orientation and Gender Identity (CERSGOSIG), Turin; member, Editorial Board of the *Journal of Homosexuality*; member, World Association for Sexology (WAS); member, Expert Committee for the Revision of the Law on Sexual Offences, appointed by the Austrian Minister of Justice in 1996; 1996 and 2003, expert, Justice Committee of the Austrian Federal Parliament; 2002, lecturer, University of Innsbruck ("Sexuality & the Law"); 2001, winner of the Gay and Lesbian Award (G.A.L.A.) of the Austrian Lesbian and Gay Movement.

This essay is an update of a study previously published in German (*Sexuelle Mündigkeit–Die Strafgesetzgebung in europäischen und außereuropäischen Ländern*, Zeitschrift für Sexualforschung, 10, 4, 281-310, Dec 1997) and English language (*Sexual Consent: The Criminal Law in Europe and Overseas*, Archives of Sexual Behavior (Plenum), Vol. 29, No. 5, 415-461, 2000). It has been presented as keynote-lecture at the 7th International Conference of the International Association for the Treatment of Sexual Offenders (IATSO), "Sexual Abuse and Sexual Violence–From Understanding to Protection and Prevention" (Vienna, September 11th-14th 2002), http://www.medacad.org/iatso; Last update: 15.01.2004.

Address correspondence to: Rechtskomitee LAMBDA, Linke Wienzeile 102, A-1160 Vienna, Austria (E-mail: hg@graupner.at).

[Haworth co-indexing entry note]: "Sexual Consent: The Criminal Law in Europe and Outside of Europe." Graupner, Helmut. Co-published simultaneously in *Journal of Psychology & Human Sexuality* (The Haworth Press, Inc.) Vol. 16, No. 2/3, 2004, pp. 111-171; and: *Adolescence, Sexuality, and the Criminal Law: Multidisciplinary Perspectives* (ed: Helmut Graupner, and Vern L. Bullough) The Haworth Press, Inc., 2004, pp. 111-171. Single or multiple copies of this article are available for a fee from The Haworth Document Delivery Service [1-800-HAWORTH, 9:00 a.m. - 5:00 p.m. (EST). E-mail address: docdelivery@haworthpress.com].

http://www.haworthpress.com/web/JPHS
© 2004 by The Haworth Press, Inc. All rights reserved.
Digital Object Identifier: 10.1300/J056v16n02_10

SUMMARY. What role can the criminal law play in the battle against child sexual abuse? Should sexual relations of, and with, persons under a certain age be criminalized regardless of the circumstances, even if they are consensual ("age of consent", "minimum age")? Where should such a minimum age-limit be fixed? Should there be a special, higher age-limit for particular conditions (e.g., "seduction", "corruption")? Should sexual contacts with minors within a relationship of authority be criminalized generally or just if authority is abused? Should criminal proceedings be instituted ex officio or upon complaint only? Should authorities be provided with a power of discretion or should they be obliged to prosecute and sentence in each case? In answering these important questions, it is highly beneficial to have a look across the borders to the solutions other countries have reached in this area.

This analysis will provide an overview on the criminal law governing the sexual behavior of, and with, children and adolescents in all European jurisdictions and in selected jurisdictions outside of Europe. It will show which categories of offenses exist and from which age onward young people can effectively consent to various kinds of sexual behavior and relations in the different countries. It turns out that all states in Europe and all of the studied jurisdictions overseas do have minimum age limits for sexual relations, do punish sexual relations with persons under a certain age. Nowhere is this age set lower than 12 years. In Europe in one-half of the jurisdictions, consensual sexual relations with 14-year-old adolescents are legal; in two-thirds with 15-year-olds; in a majority, this is also the case when the older partner has started the initiative (and also when the initiative contains an offer of remuneration). In nearly all jurisdictions, such relations are legal from the age of 16 onwards. Nearly all European jurisdictions set the same age limit in the criminal law for depicting sexual activity as for the sexual activity itself. Most states apply a higher age limit for contacts in relationships of authority. If the authority is not misused the age limit in most jurisdictions is set between 14 and 16; if it is misused between 16 and 18. Most states make no difference between heterosexual and homosexual relations. *[Article copies available for a fee from The Haworth Document Delivery Service: 1-800-HAWORTH. E-mail address: <docdelivery@haworthpress.com> Website: <http://www.HaworthPress.com> © 2004 by The Haworth Press, Inc. All rights reserved.]*

KEYWORDS. Youth protection, youth rights, sexual offenses, age of consent, sexual consent, sexual violence, sexual abuse, child sexual abuse, statutory rape, pedophilia, ephebophilia-child pornography, child prostitution, youth pornography, youth prostitution, juvenile prostitution, homosexuality, criminal law, human rights, sexual rights, comparative law, sex laws

INTRODUCTION[1]

It is not the intention of this study to provide final answers to the two questions posed below. It should rather present a factual comparative law basis for the further discussion of these problems. Comparing national law has become a crucial element in the European Court on Human Rights' scrutiny of domestic legal regulations on their compatibility with human rights law. The Court held that laws which regulate (i.e., criminalize) sexual behavior in private do interfere with the right to respect for private life[2] and that they are justified only if they can be considered necessary in a democratic society for the protection of certain legitimate aims.[3] In determining the "necessity" of a regulation the Court frequently turns to a comparative analysis of the domestic laws. The more jurisdictions do not penalize a certain behavior the less necessary the norm does appear and the stricter the review by the Court will be.[4] So it is the intention of this study to present such a comparative analysis and not a final answer to the two questions posed below. The author, however, in the final section will comment on what he thinks to be the most desirable answer.

Criminal law is the strongest weapon the state has in combating socially dangerous behavior and society always has used it to fight child sexual abuse. Today, according to the case-law of the European Court of Human Rights, states are even in an obligation to use the criminal law if effective deterrence cannot be achieved otherwise.[5] But while there is a basic consensus about the effectiveness and the necessity of the criminal law in this area there is a good deal of controversy about the exact construction of offenses.[6]

This controversy mainly centers around two questions:

1. *Should the laws be enforced without reserving the possibility to screen out cases of minor importance and cases where no harm has been done?* This question, on the one hand, arises out of the negative experience victims of sexual abuse have made with the criminal justice system and from the fear that in some cases criminal proceedings would do more harm than good; on the other hand the question arises out of the fact that each age limit–where ever it may be fixed–is arbitrary and that there always will be cases which do not require punishment.

2. Up to which age should the special protection reach? It is easy to hold that a sexual contact with a 5-year-old always is abuse, but it is much harder to hold that a sexual relation with a 12-year-old in each and every case is abusive and it is definitely impossible to hold that a sexual contact with a 16-year-old is abuse in each and every case. If the age limit is set too high the law easily can come into conflict with the need of adolescents to sexual liberty and it could easily turn from a mean of protection to a threat itself for the sexual self-determination of juveniles. So legislators have to find a reasonable and fair balance between the need of adolescents to protection from unwanted sex and their equally needed freedom to engage into self-determined sexual relationships.

Aware of the problems most jurisdictions have developed a multistage system consisting of 3 kinds of provisions in this area:

1. Minimum age limits
2. "Seduction" provisions and
3. Provisions on sexual contact in relations of authority

This multistage system reduces the protection with the decreasing need to protection and the increasing capacity to self-determination.[7] A majority of jurisdictions stick to this multi-stage system. Only a minority to a single-stage system, which sets only one single minimum age limit. Below this limit all sexual contact is illegal; so once youths have reached this age limit they are treated the same way as adults. This system can be found mainly in the common-law countries and the jurisdictions on the territory of the former Soviet-Union.

It is this division into a multi-stage and a single-stage system of youth protection which makes many differences between the several countries understandable.

MINIMUM AGE LIMITS

Minimum age provisions are provisions which generally declare sexual contact of and with persons under a certain age criminal.

Such minimum age limits are an invention of the past 200-300 years. The time before individual biological sexual maturity was the decisive factor. Sexual contact with immature children–consensual or not–always has been punished under the offenses against (sexual) violence but consensual (heterosexual) relations with mature adolescents have been legal. With the exception of England and Wales[8] and the German state of Saxony[9] a fixed minimum age had not been introduced before the 18th/19th century. These limits have been set very low, around the age of 10 to 12. In the 1920s the age limit in most European states still had been at 12 or 13 (as was the case with for instance Denmark, France, Finland, Greece, Ireland,[10] Italy, Spain, UK,[11] and in 11 Swiss cantons). The same is true for the U.S. and Australia, where the age limits have been raised only as late as in the 50s, 60s or 70s of 20th century. In South Africa it was not until 1988 when the age limit for sexual relations between women and boys was raised from 7 (!) to 16 (and the one for lesbians from 12 to 19). In the beginning the minimum age limits just covered vaginal intercourse with girls. Only later these offenses have been extended to cover (heterosexual) relations with boys as well. Girls traditionally have been seen more vulnerable than boys. Behind this historical background it is understable why Estonia, Cyprus, and Scotland have different age limits for girls and for boys (Table I).

Today all states in Europe and all of the studied jurisdictions overseas do have minimum age limits (Tables I & VIII). When "no limit" is indicated on the table it must be said that in these countries there is no age limit only at first sight. If one studies the respective jurisdictions one can see that in all these states there are age limits, just for some kinds of sexual conduct there are none. For such conduct individual capacity to give informed consent is the decisive factor or "depravation," and the courts often look to the explicitly established limits for the other kinds of contact in determining if such a capacity is already given or if the conduct did "deprave." So the explicitly set limit (for some kinds of contact) is used analogously (for the other kinds of contact for which there is no expressed limit on the books). In addition in some of the jurisdictions on the territory of the former Soviet Union the law enshrines the criterion "individual sexual maturity"; the courts, however, elaborated the rule that it is irrebuttably presumed that under 14 everyone is immature. So the minimum age in these countries in fact is at 14, since adolescents over 14 seldom are still biologically sexually immature.

The lowest age limit is set at 12 and the highest one at 17 (Table I).[12] In most jurisdictions the limit is set at 14, 15, or 16. The following table shows in how many states consensual sexual relations (without "seduction" and out of a relationship of authority) are legal in a certain age-group:

14	48% (28-59)
15	70% (41-59)
16	98% (58-59)

So about 1/2 of the jurisdictions do not generally criminalize consensual sexual relations with 14 year olds. And more than 2/3 do not with 15 year olds. Only a minority established a general age limit of 16 and just one jurisdiction in Europe a higher one (namely Northern Ireland with 17).

When we have a look at which countries fixed the limit at 16 and which ones lower we are confronted with the two systems mentioned in the beginning. As one can see from Table I the jurisdictions which established the age at 16 in most cases have a single-stage system (common-law countries, Belgium, Luxemburg, Latvia, Moldova). They do not have special provisions on authority-relations. So their general minimum age limit has to be valid for these–more problematic–relations as well. Once a juvenile has reached the age limit in these countries he is put on the same footing with adults, he enjoys no special protection against the misuse of authority. That's why in these countries the minimum age limit has to be higher than in countries with a multi-stage system. Besides this there are a few countries with a multi-stage system and nevertheless an age limit of 16. The characteristics of these is however that they allow for extensive screening, so that the law need not be and is not enforced in each and every case (that is so in the NL–where about 2/3 of the cases are dropped–Andorra, Finland, and Norway). So jurisdictions with an age limit of 16 either established a single-stage system or allow for extensive screening or both.[13]

Nearly all states allow for *screening* out of cases which do not require prosecution and punishment. That means that either authorities have a power of discretion not to instigate proceedings and to judge each case on its merits or that criminal proceedings can only be instituted upon a complaint by the juvenile or his/her legal guardian. Remarkably those jurisdictions without any possibility to screen out cases did set the age limit low, in most cases at 14 (Table I), and countries with an age limit of 16 do grant wide-ranging possibilities for screening.[14] The only exception is Switzerland which combines an age limit of 16 with the principle of legality[15] and proceedings (always) ex officio.[16] No other state has a legislation as strict as this.

TABLE I. Minimum Age Limits for Sexual Relations (Europe)

I.: No Minimum Age Limits

CIS[1]: Belorus
     Ucraine
Cyprus[2]
Finland[3]
France[4]
Guernsey[5]
Latvia[6]

II.: Minimum Age Limits–screening possible[7]

	MA Mf	MA Fm
Albania	14	14
Andorra	16	16
Armenia	16	16
Azerbaijan	16	16
Belgium	16	16
Bosnia-Herzegovina	14	14
Bulgaria	14	14
CIS: Belorus Georgia Moldova Russian Federation Ucraine	–/MT[8] 16 14 14 –/MT[9]	–/MT[10] 16 14 14 –/MT[11]
Croatia	14	14
Cyprus	–/13/16[12]	–/13[13]
Czechia	15	15
Denmark	15/18[14]	15/18[15]
Estonia	14	14
Färöer	15	15
Finland	–/16[16]	–/16[17]
FR Jugoslavia: (Cosovo Montenegro Serbia Vojvodina)	14 14 14 14	14) 14 14 14)
France	–/15[18]	–/15[19]
Germany	14	14
Gibraltar	16[20]	16[21]
Greece	15	15
Greenland	15	15
Guernsey	16[22]	16[23]
Hungary	14	14
Ireland	15/17[24]	15/17[25]

118 Adolescence, Sexuality, and the Criminal Law: Multidisciplinary Perpectives

TABLE I (continued)

	MA Mf	MA Fm
Isle of Man	16/21[26]	16/21[27]
Italy	13/14[28]	13/14[29]
Jersey	16[30]	16[31]
Latvia	–/14/16[32]	–/14/16[33]
Lithuania	14	14
Luxembourg	16	16
Macedonia	14	14
Malta	12	12
Monaco	15	15
Netherlands	16	16
Norway	16	16
Poland	15	15
Portugal	14	14
Romania	15	15
San Marino	14	14
Slovakia	15	15
Slovenia	14	14
Spain	12	12
Sweden	15	15
UK: E & W Northern Ireland Scotland	16 17[34] 16	16 17[35] MT
Vatican	12	12

III. Minimum Age Limits–No Screening Possible

	MA Mf	MA Fm
Austria	12/13/14[36]	12/13/14[37]
Iceland	12/14[38]	12/14
Liechtenstein	14[39]	14[40]
Switzerland	16[41]	16[42]
Turkey	15/18[43]	15/18[44]

Abbreviations:
MT: individual (biological) sexual maturity
MA Mf: Minimum age limit for sexual relations between a man and a girl
MA Fm: Minimum age limit for sexual relations between a woman and a boy

Notes:
[1] These countries set an age limit for certain sexual contacts only (mostly for vaginal, anal and oral intercourse). There is no fix age limit for other kinds of sexual contact. Such contacts (up to a certain age) however can be prosecuted if considered "depraving acts" (cf II. below).
[2] In Cyprus an age limit exists for vaginal intercourse with girls (16) and for anal intercourse (with boys and girls) only. For other sexual contacts individual capacity to give informed consent is decisive.
[3] The limit for sexual penetration (which is penetration by a sexual organ or directed at a sexual organ, Chapter 20 § 10 CC as amended by law EV 60/1998vp) is set at 16 (Ch. 20 § 6 CC as amended 1998). Other kinds of sexual relations with persons under 16 are outlawed only if the contact is "conducive to impairing his/her development" (ch. 20 § 6 CC as amended 1998). There is no fix minimum age for such sexual contacts not considered being "conducive to impairing his/her development".
[4] The age limit (of 15) applies to partners over 18 only. Persons under 18 having sexual contacts with other persons under 18 are not covered.

[5] Express minimum age limit for vaginal intercourse with girls only.

[6] There is no express age limit for sexual contacts not "imitating natural" sexual intercourse (as mutal masturbation, touching etc.). Such contacts can however be prosecuted, if considered "depraving", when the young person is under 14 or his/her partner is over 18 (Art. 162 CC).

[7] These jurisdictions allow for screening of cases which do not require prosecution. This means that either prosecution authorities are being granted power of discretion to prosecute or not and to judge each case on its merits or that prosecution does require a complaint (mostly by the minor, his legal representative or a youth protection authority).

[8] For "sexual intercourse" (presumably vaginal, anal, oral sex) (with persons of 16 or older) the limit is individual biological maturity. For sexual contacts not deemed to constitute "sexual intercourse" (with persons of 16 or older) there is no fix age limit. Such contacts (up to the age of 18) however can be prosecuted if deemed "depraving acts". (Persons under 16 can never be prosecuted under these offences).

[9] For "sexual intercourse" (presumably vaginal, anal, oral sex) with persons of 16 or older the limit is individual biological maturity (Art. 120 CC). For "sexual intercourse" with persons younger than 16 and for sexual contacts not deemed to constitute "sexual intercourse" there is no fix age limit. These contacts, if committed by a person of 16 or over, however can be prosecuted if deemed "depraving acts" (Art. 121 CC) (Ministry of Justice 1997).

[10] For "sexual intercourse" (presumably vaginal, anal, oral sex) (with persons of 16 or older) the limit is individual biological maturity. For sexual contacts not deemed to constitute "sexual intercourse" (with persons of 16 or older) there is no fix age limit. Such contacts (up to the age 18) however can be prosecuted if deemed "depraving acts". (Persons under 16 can never be prosecuted under these offences).

[11] For "sexual intercourse" (presumably vaginal, anal, oral sex) with persons of 16 or older the limit is individual biological maturity (Art. 120 CC). For "sexual intercourse" with persons younger than 16 and for sexual contacts not deemed to constitute "sexual intercourse" there is no fix age limit. These contacts, if committed by a person of 16 or over, however can be prosecuted if deemed "depraving acts" (Art. 121 CC) (Ministry of Justice 1997).

[12] In Cyprus an age limit exists for vaginal intercourse with girls (16) only. This limit is set at 16. There is no fix minimum age for other kinds of sexual contact save anal intercourse. Before 1998 Art. 171 CC outlawed anal intercourse without reference to the age of the partners (life imprisonment). On 21st May 1998 parliament passed a law abolishing this ban on anal intercourse (Criminal Law Amendment Law 40(1) of 1998). While the minimum age limit for homosexual anal acts has been set at 18 (Art. 171 CC) the limit for heterosexual anal intercourse has been chosen to be 13 (Art. 174 CC).

[13] In Cyprus an age limit exists for vaginal intercourse with girls (16) and for anal intercourse (with boys and girls) (13) only.

[14] The age-limit of 18 applies only to persons, who fully or in part make a living through prostitution (Art. 223a.CC). Contacts with such persons under 18 are completely illegal, even if non-commercial and not related to prostitution.

[15] The age-limit of 18 applies only to persons, who fully or in part make a living through prostitution (Art. 223a CC). Contacts with such persons under 18 are completely illegal, even if non-commercial and not related to prostitution.

[16] see note 4

[17] see note 4

[18] The age limit (of 15) applies to partners over 18 only. Persons under 18 having sexual contacts with other persons under 18 are not covered.

[19] The age limit (of 15) applies to partners over 18 only. Persons under 18 having sexual contacts with other persons under 18 are not covered.

[20] Anal intercourse is punishable with life-imprisonment whatever the age of the partners may be.

[21] Anal intercourse is punishable with life-imprisonment whatever the age of the partners may be.

[22] Anal intercourse is punishable with life-imprisonment whatever the age of the partners may be. Express minimum age limit for vaginal intercourse with girls only.

[23] Anal intercourse is punishable with life-imprisonment whatever the age of the partners may be. Express minimum age limit for vaginal intercourse with girls only.

[24] The limit for vaginal intercourse with girls and for anal intercourse (with boys and girls) is set at 17. For other kinds of sexual contact the age limit is 15.

[25] The limit for anal intercourse is set at 17. For other kinds of sexual contact the age limit is 15.

[26] The limit for anal intercourse is set at 21. For other kinds of sexual contact the age limit is 16.

[27] The limit for anal intercourse is set at 21. For other kinds of sexual contact the age limit is 16.

[28] The age limit is 13 when the older partner is not more than 16. In all other cases it is 14.

[29] The age limit is 13 when the older partner is not more than 16. In all other cases it is 14.

[30] Anal intercourse is punishable with life-imprisonment whatever the age of the partners may be.

[31] Anal intercourse is punishable with life-imprisonment whatever the age of the partners may be.

TABLE I (continued)

[32] There is no express age limit for sexual contacts not "imitating natural" sexual intercourse (as mutal masturbation, touching, etc.). Such contacts can however be prosecuted, if considered "depraving", when the young person is under 14 or his/her partner is over 18 (Art. 162 CC). For "natural" sexual intercourse and for sexual contacts "imitating natural" sexual intercourse (as oral and anal sex, interfemora intercourse, etc.), the minimum age limit is 16, if the partner is 18 or older (Art. 161 CC 1998), it is 14, if the partner is under 18 (Art. 160 CC 1998).

[33] There is no express age limit for sexual contacts not "imitating natural" sexual intercourse (as mutal masturbation, touching, etc.). Such contacts can however be prosecuted, if considered "depraving", when the young person is under 14 or his/her partner is over 18 (Art. 162 CC). For "natural" sexual intercourse and for sexual contacts "imitating natural" sexual intercourse (as oral and anal sex, interfemora intercourse, etc.) the minimum age limit is 16, if the partner is 18 or older (Art. 161 CC 1998), it is 14, if the partner is under 18 (Art. 160 CC 1998).

[34] Anal intercourse is punishable with life-imprisonment whatever the age of the partners may be.

[35] Anal intercourse is punishable with life-imprisonment whatever the age of the partners may be.

[36] The three limits apply to various kinds of contacts as follows:
   Age limit 12: applies to non-penetrative sexual contact when disparity in age between the partners is not more than four years.
   Age limit 13: applies to penetrative sexual contact when disparity in age is not more than three years (but only in case of penetration with a part of the body not in case of penetration with an object)
   Age limit 14: applies (a) to non-penetrative sexual contact when disparity in age is more than four years, (b) to penetrative sexual contact with parts of the body when disparity in age is more than three years and (c) to penetrative sexual contact with objects whatever the age of the partners may be. (Art. 206, 207 CC as amended by the Criminal Law Amendment Act 1998 (BGBl. 153/1998)).

[37] The three limits apply to various kinds of contacts as follows:
   Age limit 12: applies to non-penetrative sexual contact when disparity in age between the partners is not more than four years.
   Age limit 13: applies to penetrative sexual contact when disparity in age is not more than three years
   Age limit 14: applies (a) to non-penetrative sexual contact when disparity in age is more than four years, (b) to penetrative sexual contact with parts of the body when disparity in age is more than three years and (c) to penetrative sexual contact with objects whatever the age of the partners may be. (Art. 206, 207 CC as amended by the Criminal Law Amendment Act 1998 (BGBl. 153/1998)).

[38] Age limit is 12 when disparity in age is not more than three years, and 14 in all other cases.

[39] Sexual contact (save vaginal intercourse) is not punishable if the age difference is no more than two years.

[40] Sexual contact (save vaginal intercourse) is not punishable if the age difference is no more than two years.

[41] Sexual contact is not punishable if the age difference is no more than three years.

[42] Sexual contact is not punishable if the age difference is no more than three years.

[43] The age limit of 18 covers vaginal and anal intercourse only. The minimum age for all other kinds of sexual contact is set at 15.

[44] The age limit of 18 covers vaginal and anal intercourse only. The minimum age for all other kinds of sexual contact is set at 15.

In some countries (as for instance Germany, Austria, Switzerland) the minimum age limit covers also (non-public) sexual acts in front of children and youths (*private exhibition*) and *incitement to masturbation*. Most jurisdictions however do not have such offenses. Private exhibition is not criminal in 2/3 of the European jurisdictions and incitement to masturbation not in 80%. Recently, Portugal (1995) and Italy (1996) decriminalized incitement of children and youths (under 16) to masturbation.[17]

Error about the age (if honest, not negligent) removes liability in nearly all European countries, with the only exceptions of the U.K., Ireland, Italy, and Norway. In the majority of jurisdictions also negligent error removes liability; mens rea (criminal intent) is afforded.

The *penalties* established are very diverse. They reach from 2 years in the U.K. (for vaginal intercourse with a girl between 13 and 16) to 21 years in Norway.

HOMOSEXUAL RELATIONS

As we turn to homosexual relations we can establish a clear international trend towards equality of lesbians and gay men. The European Court of Human Rights repeatedly ruled that a total ban on homosexual behaviour violates the European Convention on Human Rights,[18] that also when more than two persons are involved,[19] and in 1997 the now defunct European Commission on Human Rights held that a higher minimum age limit for homosexual conduct than for heterosexual violates the European Convention on Human Rights (Art. 8 and 14).[20] The Commission rejected the arguments put forward in favor of a special age limit. It stated that current medical opinion is to the effect that sexual orientation is fixed in both sexes before the age of puberty,[21] that the risk posed by predatory older men would appear to be as serious whether the victim is a man or woman and it denied that "society's claimed entitlement to indicate disapproval of homosexual conduct and its preference for a heterosexual lifestyle . . . could in any event constitute an objective and reasonable justification for inequality of treatment under the criminal law."[22] In 2003 the European Court of Human Rights followed that path[23] and awarded a juvenile considerable compensation payments for–between the ages of 14 and 18–for not having been allowed by the law to engage in intimate relations with (adult) partners of his choice.[24]

Also the United Nations Human Rights Committee held that a total ban on homosexual behavior violates the fundamental right to privacy (*Toonen v. Commonwealth of Australia,* 1994). And in its concluding observations on the report of Austria under the International Convenant on Civil and Political Rights (ICCPR) the Committee declared higher age limits for homosexual conduct, as compared to heterosexual, as violating international human rights law and called on Austria to repeal its respective law: (quote) "The Committee considers that existing legislation on the minimum age of consent for sexual relations in respect of male homosexuals is discriminatory on grounds of sex and sexual orientation. It requests that the law be revised to remove such discriminatory provisions" (Human Rights Committee 1998, par. 13).[25] The *Committee on the Rights of the Child* repeatedly called for the repeal of higher ages of consent for homosexual conduct[26] and expressed its concern "that homosexual and transsexual young people do not have access to the appropriate information, support, and necessary protection to enable them to live their sexual orientation."[27]

The World Health Organisation (WHO) deleted homosexuality from its International Classification of Diseases (ICD) in 1993.

The parliamentary bodies of the Organisation for Security and Cooperation in Europe (OSCE),[28] the Coun{il of Europe (COE) and the Euqopean Union (EU) all demanded the end of discrimination of homosexuals with the COE- and EU-bodies calling on their member states to fully equalize homo- and bisexuals with heterosexuals before the law.[29] The Parliamentary Assembly of the Council of Europe repeatedly condemned discrimination on the basis of sexual orientation as "especially odious" and "one of the most odious forms of discrimination."[30]

More and more states not only have repealed special offenses against homosexual conduct but even further have enacted anti-discrimination laws, outlawing discrimination of homo- and bisexuals,[31] and legally recognized same-sex partnerships (cf. for extensive survey in Graupner 1998a, 1998c, 1999a, 2003). The Scandinavian countries (Denmark; Greenland; Norway; Sweden; Iceland; Finland) and Germany even introduced de facto (not de iure) marriage of same-sex couples, so-called "registered partnership," (cf. for details in Graupner 1998a, 1998c, 1999a, 2003). The Netherlands in 2001 and Belgium 2003 opened up civil marriage and more and more jurisdictions now also do allow for joint adoption by same-sex couples. The European Parliament repeatedly declared that it will not allow the accession of states to the European Union which in their legislation discriminate against lesbians and gay men (European Parliament 1998b, 1998c, 2000). The Parliamentary Assembly of the Council of Europe did the same for accession to the Council of Europe.[32]

Since 1998 Art. 13 of the *Treaty on the Foundation of the European Community (EC-Treaty)*, as amended by the Treaty of Amsterdam,[33] expressly empowers the Council of Ministers of the European Union to act against discrimination on the basis of "sexual orientation."[34] In 2000 the Council of Ministers availed itself of this power by issuing a directive obliging the member states of the European Union to comprehensively ban sexual-orientation-based (direct and indirect) discrimination in employment and occupation.[35] The Charter of Fundamental Rights of the European Union also outlaws discrimination on the basis of sexual orientation (Art. 21).[36]

The European Court of Human Rights today explicitly considers discrimination on the basis of sexual orientation as unacceptable[37] and as serious as discrimination on the basis of race, colour, religion and sex.[38] For distinctions on the basis of sexual orientation to be justified the Court requires particularly serious reasons,[39] which make such a distinction necessary.[40] Predisposed bias on the part of a heterosexual majority against a homosexual minority cannot, as the Court has repeatedly held, amount to sufficient justification for interference with the rights of homo- and bisexual women and men, any more than similar negative attitudes towards those of a different race, origin, or colour.[41] Society could be expected to tolerate a certain inconvenience to enable individuals to live in dignity and worth "in accordance with the sexual identity chosen by them."[42]

In our field 2/3 of the jurisdictions in Europe today set equal age limits (Table II).[43,44] In addition most of the countries with unequal limits are states from the former Communist bloc. In the Eastern bloc only Poland (since 1932), the GDR (since 1988) and Slovenia (since 1977) treated homo- and heterosexuality equally in their criminal law. All the other states had special provisions against homosexual conduct, often a total ban. Disintegration of the Communist bloc has been the starting point for a remarkably rapid development towards equality and decriminalization in these countries. So the picture given in Table II. in some way just reflects a snapshot of this development.

Among the member states of the Council of Europe a vast majority (37 out of 44) has set equal age limits and only 2 of the 15 EU-states (Ireland and Portugal[45]) still have a higher age limit for homosexual conduct.

SEDUCTION

Most jurisdictions don't have a provision on "seduction" of youths (Table III). The states which do have mostly set lower minimum age limits: at 12, 14, or 15. Just three states combine an age limit of 16 with an additional provision on "seduction" (Andorra, Finland, and the NL). As can be seen from Table III in most jurisdictions the offense is restricted to certain forms of "seduction," certain means are afforded.

Generally we can speak of two types of "seduction-provisions," an older one and a more modern type. The older type covers all kinds of "seduction," regardless of the means employed (see Greece, Iceland, Germany before 1994). Under such laws each sexual contact with an

TABLE II. Minimum Age Limits for Homosexual Relations (Europe)

I: Uniform Age Limits for Hetero- and Homosexual Relations:

	R DMA	HTS	HSF	HSM
Andorra	n.k.	16	16	16
Armenia		16	16	16
Austria	2002	12/13/14[1]	12/13/14[2]	12/13/14[3]
Azerbaijan	2001	16	16	16
Belgium	1985	16	16	16
CIS: Georgia Moldova Russian Federation Ucraine	 2003 1997 1991	 16 14 14 –/MT[4]	 16 14 14 –/MT[5]	 16 14 14 –/MT[6]
Czech Republic	1990	15	15	15
Croatia	1998	14	14	14
Denmark	1976	15/18[7]	15/18[8]	15/18[9]
Germany	1994	14	14	14
Estonia	2002	14	14	14
Finland	1998	–/16[10]	–/16[11]	–/16[12]
France	1982	–/15[13]	–/15[14]	–/15[15]
FR Yugoslavia: Montenegro (Vojvodina	 1977 1977	 14 14	 14 14	 14 14)
Greece	1951	15	15	15
Greenland	1978	15	15	15
Hungary	2002	14	14	14
Iceland	1992	14	14	14
Italy	1889	13/14[16]	13/14[17]	13/14[18]
Latvia	1998	–/14/16[19]	–/14/16[20]	–/14/16[21]
Liechtenstein	2001	12/14[22]	12/14[23]	12/14[24]
Lithuania	2003	14	14	14
Luxembourg	1992	16	16	16
Macedonia	1996	14	14	14
Malta	1973	12	12	12
Monaco	n.k.	15	15	15
Netherlands	1971	16	16	16
Norway	1972	16	16	16
Poland	1932	15	15	15
Romania	2001	15	15	15
San Marino	1865	14	14	14
Slovakia	1990	15	15	15
Slovenia	1977	14	14	14
Spain	1822	12	12	12
Sweden	1978	15	15	15
Switzerland	1942	16[25]	16[26]	16[27]
Turkey	1858	15/18[28]	15	15/18[29]
UK: **England & Wales** **Northern Ireland**	 2000 2000	 16 17[30]	 16 17[31]	 16 17[32]
Vatican	1929	12	12	12

II. Different Age Limits–screening possible[33]

	R TB	HTS	HSF	HSM
Albania	1995	14	18[34]	18[35]
Bulgaria	1968	14	16/18[36]	16/18[37]
CIS: Belorus	1994	–/MT[38]	–/MT[39]	–/18[40]
Cyprus	1998	–/13/16[41]	–[42]	–/18[43]
Färöer	1930	15	18	18
Gibraltar	1993	16[44]	16	18[45]
Guernsey	1983	–/16[46]	–[47]	18[48]
Ireland	1993	15/17[49]	15	17
Isle of Man	1992	16/21[50]	16	21[51]
Jersey	1990	–/16[52]	–[53]	16/21[54]
Portugal	1945	14	14/16[55]	14/16[56]
Serbia	1994	14	14	14/18[57]
UK: **Scotland**	1980 (2000)[58]	16/MT[59]	16	16

III. Different Age Limits–no screening possible
No jurisdiction.

IV. Total Ban on Homosexuality

	HTS	HSF	HSM
Bosnia-Herzegovina (M)[60]	14	14	–/14[61]
FR Yugoslavia: (Cosovo (M)	14	14	–/14[62])

Abbreviations:
R DMA: year of the repeal of the different age limit. In states where a different limit never existed the year of the repeal of the total ban on homosexual behaviour is given.[63]
R TB: year of the repeal of the total ban on homosexual behaviour.
MT: individual (biological) sexual maturity
HTS: Minimum age for heterosexual relations
HSF: Minimum age for homosexual relations between females
HSM: Minimum age for homosexual relations between males
(M): the total ban covers male homosexual relations only
(MF): the total ban covers male and female homosexual relations
n.k.: not known

Bold Member states of the European Union
Italics Member states of the Council of Europe

Notes:

[1] The three limits apply to various kinds of contacts as follows:
Age limit 12: applies to non-penetrative sexual contact when disparity in age between the partners is not more than four years.
Age limit 13: applies to penetrative sexual contact when disparity in age is not more than three years (but only in case of penetration with a part of the body not in case of penetration with an object)
Age limit 14: applies (a) to non-penetrative sexual contact when disparity in age is more than four years, (b) to penetrative sexual contact with parts of the body when disparity in age is more than three years and (c) to penetrative sexual contact with objects whatever the age of the partners may be. (Art. 206, 207 CC as amended by the Criminal Law Amendment Act 1998 (BGBl. 153/1998)).

TABLE II (continued)

[2] The three limits apply to various kinds of contacts as follows:
Age limit 12: applies to non-penetrative sexual contact when disparity in age between the partners is not more than four years.
Age limit 13: applies to penetrative sexual contact when disparity in age is not more than three years (but only in case of penetration with a part of the body not in case of penetration with an object)
Age limit 14: applies (a) to non-penetrative sexual contact when disparity in age is more than four years, (b) to penetrative sexual contact with parts of the body when disparity in age is more than three years and (c) to penetrative sexual contact with objects whatever the age of the partners may be. (Art. 206, 207 CC as amended by the Criminal Law Amendment Act 1998 (BGBl. 153/1998)).

[3] The three limits apply to various kinds of contacts as follows:
Age limit 12: applies to non-penetrative sexual contact when disparity in age between the partners is not more than four years.
Age limit 13: applies to penetrative sexual contact when disparity in age is not more than three years (but only in case of penetration with a part of the body not in case of penetration with an object)
Age limit 14: applies (a) to non-penetrative sexual contact when disparity in age is more than four years, (b) to penetrative sexual contact with parts of the body when disparity in age is more than three years and (c) to penetrative sexual contact with objects whatever the age of the partners may be.
(Art. 206, 207 CC as amended by the Criminal Law Amendment Act 1998 (BGBl. 153/1998)).

[4] For "sexual intercourse" (presumably vaginal, anal, oral sex) with persons of 16 or older the limit is individual biological maturity (Art. 120 CC). For "sexual intercourse" with persons younger than 16 and for sexual contacts not deemed to constitute "sexual intercourse" there is no fix age limit. Such contacts, if committed by a person of 16 or over, however can be prosecuted if deemed "depraving acts" (Art. 121 CC) (Ministry of Justice 1997).

[5] For "sexual intercourse" (presumably vaginal, anal, oral sex) with persons of 16 or older the limit is individual biological maturity (Art. 120 CC). For "sexual intercourse" with persons younger than 16 and for sexual contacts not deemed to constitute "sexual intercourse" there is no fix age limit. Such contacts, if committed by a person of 16 or over, however can be prosecuted if deemed "depraving acts" (Art. 121 CC) (Ministry of Justice 1997).

[6] For "sexual intercourse" (presumably vaginal, anal, oral sex) with persons of 16 or older the limit is individual biological maturity (Art. 120 CC). For "sexual intercourse" with persons younger than 16 and for sexual contacts not deemed to constitute "sexual intercourse" there is no fix age limit. Such contacts, if committed by a person of 16 or over, however can be prosecuted if deemed "depraving acts" (Art. 121 CC) (Ministry of Justice 1997).

[7] The age-limit of 18 applies only to persons, who fully or in part make a living through prostitution (Art. 223a CC). Contacts with such persons under 18 are completely illegal, even if non-commercial and not related to prostitution.

[8] The age-limit of 18 applies only to persons, who fully or in part make a living through prostitution (Art. 223a CC). Contacts with such persons under 18 are completely illegal, even if non-commercial and not related to prostitution.

[9] The age-limit of 18 applies only to persons, who fully or in part make a living through prostitution (Art. 223a CC). Contacts with such persons under 18 are completely illegal, even if non-commercial and not related to prostitution.

[10] The limit for sexual penetration (which is penetration by a sexual organ or directed at a sexual organ, Chapter 20 § 10 CC as amended by law EV 60/1998vp) is set at 16 (Ch. 20 § 6 CC as amended 1998). Other kinds of sexual relations with persons under 16 are outlawed only if the contact is "conducive to impairing his/her development" (ch. 20 § 6 CC as amended 1998). There is no fix minimum age for such sexual contacts not considered being "conducive to impairing his/her development".

[11] See note 7

[12] See note 7

[13] The age limit (of 15) applies to partners over 18 only. Persons under 18 having sexual contacts with other persons under 18 are not covered.

[14] The age limit (of 15) applies to partners over 18 only. Persons under 18 having sexual contacts with other persons under 18 are not covered.

[15] The age limit (of 15) applies to partners over 18 only. Persons under 18 having sexual contacts with other persons under 18 are not covered.

[16] The minimum age is 13 when the older partner is not more than 13. In all the other cases it is 14.

[17] The minimum age is 13 when the older partner is not more than 13. In all the other cases it is 14.

[18] The minimum age is 13 when the older partner is not more than 13. In all the other cases it is 14.

[19] There is no express age limit for sexual contacts not "imitating natural" sexual intercourse (as mutal masturbation, touching, etc.). For "natural" sexual intercourse and for sexual contacts "imitating natural" sexual intercourse (as oral and anal sex, interfemora intercourse, etc.), the minimum age limit is 16, if the partner is 18 or older (Art. 161 CC 1998), it is 14, if the partner is under 18 (Art. 160 CC 1998).

[20] There is no express age limit for sexual contacts not "imitating natural" sexual intercourse (as mutal masturbation, touching, etc.). For "natural" sexual intercourse and for sexual contacts "imitating natural" sexual intercourse (as oral and anal sex, interfemora intercourse etc.), the minimum age limit is 16, if the partner is 18 or older (Art. 161 CC 1998), it is 14, if the partner is under 18 (Art. 160 CC 1998).

[21] There is no express age limit for sexual contacts not "imitating natural" sexual intercourse (as mutal masturbation, touching, etc.). For "natural" sexual intercourse and for sexual contacts "imitating natural" sexual intercourse (as oral and anal sex, interfemora intercourse, etc.), the minimum age limit is 16, if the partner is 18 or older (Art. 161 CC 1998), it is 14, if the partner is under 18 (Art. 160 CC 1998).

[22] The three limits apply to various kinds of contacts as follows:
Age limit 12: applies to non-penetrative sexual contact when disparity in age between the partners is not more than four years.
Age limit 13: applies to penetrative sexual contact when disparity in age is not more than three years (but only in case of penetration with a part of the body not in case of penetration with an object).
Age limit 14: applies (a) to non-penetrative sexual contact when disparity in age is more than four years, (b) to penetrative sexual contact with parts of the body when disparity in age is more than three years and (c) to penetrative sexual contact with objects whatever the age of the partners may be. (Art. 206, 207 CC as amended by the Criminal Law Amendment Act 1998 (BGBl. 153/1998)).

[23] The three limits apply to various kinds of contacts as follows:
Age limit 12: applies to non-penetrative sexual contact when disparity in age between the partners is not more than four years.
Age limit 13: applies to penetrative sexual contact when disparity in age is not more than three years (but only in case of penetration with a part of the body not in case of penetration with an object).
Age limit 14: applies (a) to non-penetrative sexual contact when disparity in age is more than four years, (b) to penetrative sexual contact with parts of the body when disparity in age is more than three years and (c) to penetrative sexual contact with objects whatever the age of the partners may be. (Art. 206, 207 CC as amended by the Criminal Law Amendment Act 1998 (BGBl. 153/1998)).

[24] The three limits apply to various kinds of contacts as follows:
Age limit 12: applies to non-penetrative sexual contact when disparity in age between the partners is not more than four years.
Age limit 13: applies to penetrative sexual contact when disparity in age is not more than three years (but only in case of penetration with a part of the body not in case of penetration with an object).
Age limit 14: applies (a) to non-penetrative sexual contact when disparity in age is more than four years, (b) to penetrative sexual contact with parts of the body when disparity in age is more than three years and (c) to penetrative sexual contact with objects whatever the age of the partners may be. (Art. 206, 207 CC as amended by the Criminal Law Amendment Act 1998 (BGBl. 153/1998)).

[25] Sexual contact is not punishable if the age difference is no more than three years.

[26] Sexual contact is not punishable if the age difference is no more than three years.

[27] Sexual contact is not punishable if the age difference is no more than three years.

[28] The higher age limit of 18 covers vaginal and anal intercourse only.

[29] The higher age limit of 18 covers vaginal and anal intercourse only.

[30] Anal intercourse is punishable with life imprisonment regardless of the age of the partners.

[31] Anal intercourse is punishable with life imprisonment regardless of the age of the partners.

[32] Anal intercourse is punishable with life imprisonment regardless of the age of the partners.

[33] These jurisdictions allow for screening of cases which do not require prosecution. This means that either prosecution authorities are being granted power of discretion to prosecute or not and to judge each case on its merits or that prosecution does require a complaint (mostly by the minor, his legal representative or a youth protection authority).

[34] "Homosexual Intercourse"

[35] "Homosexual Intercourse"

[36] 16 applies when the older person is under 18, 18 applies when the older person is 18 or above (Art. 157 CC as amended by Criminal Law Amendment Act 1997 (Official Gazette 62/1997)).

[37] 16 applies when the older person is under 18, 18 applies when the older person is 18 or above (Art. 157 CC as amended by Criminal Law Amendment Act 1997 (Official Gazette 62/1997)).

[38] In Belorus there is a minimum age limit (MT) for certain kinds of sexual contact (vaginal, oral, anal) only. For other sexual contacts there is no minimum age limit. Such contacts (up to the age of 18) can be prosecuted if considered "depraving".

[39] See note 24

[40] The limit of 18 covers anal and oral intercourse between men only. For other male homosexual contact there is no minimum age. Such contacts (up to age 18) can (only) be prosecuted if considered "depraving" (Art. 119 CC as amended 01.03.1994).

TABLE II (continued)

[41] In Cyprus there is a minimum age for vaginal intercourse with girls (16) and for anal intercourse (heterosexual: 13; homosexual: 18) only. For other sexual acts individual capacity to give informed consent is decisive.

[42] In Cyprus there is a minimum age for vaginal (penile) intercourse with girls and for anal intercourse only. For other sexual acts individual capacity to give informed consent is decisive.

[43] The European Court on Human Rights in 1993 held that the total ban on anal intercourse ("carnal knowledge against the order of nature") violates the right to respect for private life (Modinos vs. Cyprus). In 1998 parliament repealed the total ban but kept a special age limit of 18 for anal intercourse between males (Art. 171 CC as amended by the Criminal Code (Amendment) Law 40 (I) of 1998). For male homosexual acts not constituting anal intercourse there is no fix minimum age limit. Individual capacity to give informed consent is decisive in these cases.

[44] Hetersosexual anal intercourse is punishable with life-imprisonment whatever the age of the partners may be.

[45] Also male homosexual relations between persons over 18 are an offence if more than two persons are present.

[46] There is a total ban on heterosexual anal intercourse regardless of the age of the partners. Express minimum age limit for vaginal intercourse with girls only.

[47] Express minimum age limit for vaginal intercourse with girls only.

[48] Also male homosexual relations between persons over 18 are an offence if more than two persons are present.

[49] The minimum age limit of 17 covers vaginal intercourse with girls and anal intercourse with girls and boys. For all other kinds of (heterosexual and lesbian) contact there is an minimum age limit of 15.

[50] On the Isle of Man the age limit for anal intercourse is fixed at 21; for all other kinds of heterosexual contact at 16.

[51] Also male homosexual relations between persons over 21 are an offence if more than two persons are present.

[52] Heterosexual anal intercourse is punishable with life imprisonment regardless of the age of the partners. Express minimum age limit for vaginal intercourse with girls only.

[53] Express minimum age limit for vaginal intercourse with girls only.

[54] The age limit of 21 covers anal intercourse only. For other male homosexual contact the limit is 16. Also male homosexual relations between persons over these limites are an offence if more than two persons are present.

[55] 14 applies when the older person is under 18 (Art. 172 CP 1995), 16 applies when the older person is 18 or above (Art. 175 CP 1995).

[56] 14 applies when the older person is under 18 (Art. 172 CP 1995), 16 applies when the older person is 18 or above (Art. 175 CP 1995).

[57] The age limit of 18 covers anal intercourse; the limit of 14 all other kinds of sexual contact.

[58] In 2000 the higher age limit of 18 for male homosexual acts was repealed. Since then the only unequality lies in the fact that for sexual relations of women with boys the limit is individual biological maturity, not 16.

[59] For man/girl relations there is a minimum age of 16; for woman/boy relations the individual (biological) sexual maturity of the boy is decisive.

[60] The International Lesbian and Gay Association (ILGA) reports that the total ban would have been repealed. This report however could not yet be confirmed.

[61] The total ban covers anal intercourse between men only. For other male homosexual contact the minimum age is 14.

[62] The total ban covers anal intercourse between men only. For other male homosexual contact the minimum age is 14.

[63] Following the French Revolution numerous European countries decriminalized homosexual relations and did establish uniform minimum age limits for hetero- and homosexual relations (mostly the age of individual maturity or 12 to 14). With the exception of Italy and Turkey only all of these jurisdictions (which decriminalized homosexuality in the 18th or 19th century) did (for some time) reintroduce discriminatory legislation in the 20th century (for details see Graupner 1998; 1997b, 2, 359ff). The years shown in the table therefore do indicate the year, from which on uniform age limits (without interruption) have been in force until today (that is the year, when a total ban has been repealed and uniform age limits established or when prior unequal limits have been equalized).

adolescent is rendered criminal if the older partner has taken the initiative to the contact. Relations, however, are complex and in most cases it is not clearly discernible who took the initiative to which sexual contact. Moreover the quality of a relationship does not really depend on who started the initiative to a contact. So those general seduction-provisions emphasizing just on who took the initiative often lead to a "moralizing" case-law that protects more traditional moral norms than self-determination and autonomy of young people. "Seduction"-provisions which focus on the mean "false promise of marriage" also belong to this type of offenses.

The more modern type of "seduction"-provisions is restricted to certain constellations and certain kinds of behaviour. These type of offenses aim to protect adolescents over the general age limit against certain inferences with their sexual self-determination. Inferences which do not reach the intensity needed for the enforcement of the offenses on sexual violence. An example for this more modern type of seduction provisions is the German law with its three constellations *"practising on a position of constraint,"* *"against remuneration"* and *"practising on lacking capacity to sexual self-determination"* (Art. 182 CC).[46]

Also this law of the modern type however mainly is based on the convictions of lawyers. During the hearings in both chambers of the German parliament experts of all other areas of science (physicians, psychologists, psychotherapists, criminologists, sexologists, and social workers) did oppose the law. They expressed the opinion that in the case of adolescents over 14 years of age the law can not contribute to the solution of the problems involved and they expressed the fear that the law would do more harm than good to the adolescents involved. While the lawyers focused on the "immaturity" of 14- and 15-year-old adolescents and their need for protection against undue influences, the other experts pointed out that adolescents of 14 and over generally are sufficiently able to cope with such influences and emphasized their right to sexual self-determination. They took the view that this age group requires protection of the criminal law only against the use of force and coercion and against misuse of a relationship of authority and they feared that criminalization beyond that would endanger the sexual self-determination of adolescents. While they acknowledged that problematic situations could occur which bear the potential of leading to negative experiences they were of the opinion that neither does the (attempted) eradication of all negative experiences further a positive psychosexual development nor are the criminal law and criminal investigations a positive means to solve the problems connected with such problematic situations.

The non-legal experts did accept the concerns of the lawyers but they pointed out that the criminal law, as being not only the strongest but also the bluntest weapon of the state, would not be suited to solve the problems and to enable adolescents to a self-determined sexual life; instead the employment of the criminal law would create serious problems and dangers for the youths it intends to protect.[47] In reaction to this opposition by the non-legal experts heard by parliament, somewhat as a compromise a clause has been included into the law obliging the courts to drop a case if the wrong-doing was minor, whereby special consideration should be given to the behavior of the younger partner (Art. 182 par. 4 CC). This clause according to the case-law primarily is applied when the younger one starts the initiative or when he/she readily agrees to the initiative.[48] Moreover prosecution based on the alternative "practising on lacking capacity to sexual self-determination" (Art. 182 par. 2 CC) has been bound to a complaint by the legal guardian of the juvenile.[49] Also in Austria, recently a similar provision could only be passed against considerable resistance from experts, youth organisations, and the public at large.[50]

Table III. does not supply information, from which age onwards a minor can legally consent to "seduction"; since also in states which do not have special provisions on seduction, seduction of course can be prosecuted under the minimum age provisions, which do cover all sexual contacts, regardless of the means employed. Table IV shows in how many states consensual sexual relations (with "seduction" but out of a relationship of authority) are legal in a certain age-group:

14	41% (24-59)
15	58% (34-59)
16	88% (52-59)

So in almost 1/2 of the jurisdictions a 14-year-old can legally consent to "seduction"; and in a majority a 15-year-old can. The countries which do allow this as of 16 only again are those with a single-stage system or with extensive possibilities to screen out.[51,52]

RELATIONS OF AUTHORITY

Most jurisdictions do have special higher age limits for contact within relations of authority (Table V); mainly those with a minimum age limit of under 16. Only a minority does not have such provisions; e.g., mainly common-law countries and former soviet-union-jurisdiction. In most jurisdictions it does not suffice that a relationship of authority exists but it is afforded that the authority is misused in order to gain consent to the sexual contact. With one regular exception: contacts

TABLE III. "Seduction" (Europe)

I.: No Laws Against "Seduction"

Albania
Armenia
Azerbaijan
Belgium
CIS:
    Belorus
    Georgia
    Moldova
    Russia
    Ucraine
Czechia
Former Yugoslavia:
    (3 jurisdictions additional to Slovenia)
France
Gibraltar
Greece (heterosexual and lesbian relations)
Guernsey
Hungary
Isle of Man
Jersey
Latvia
Lithuania
Luxemburg
Malta
Norway
Poland
Slovakia
Slovenia
Switzerland
UK: E & W
    Northern Ireland
    Scotland
Vatican

II. Laws Against "Seduction"–screening possible[1]

	Age	G	Sex. Cont	Means Afforded
Andorra	18	MF	All	"Deception"; "Abuse of a superiority based on authority or situation";
Austria	16	MF	All	"Practising on a position of constraint"; "Practising upon lacking maturity[2] and upon a superiority based on a considerable difference in age" "Seduction immediately against remuneration"
	18	MF	All	
Bulgaria	–	Mm	All	"against payment", "incitement to perversion"
Cyprus[3]	18	Mm	Al	"indecent behaviour, incitment, or provocation or advertising"
Denmark[4]	18	MF	All	"Gross abuse of a superiority based on age and experience"
Färöer	18/21[5]	MF	All	"(Gross) Abuse[6] of a superiority based on age and experience"
Finland	18	MF	All	"promising or giving remuneration"[7] "taking advantage of immaturity"[8]

TABLE III (continued)

	Age	G	Sex. Cont	Means Afforded
Former Yugoslavia: 4 jurisdictions	18	Mf	VI	"false promise of marriage"
Germany	16	MF	all	"Practising on a position of constraint"; "Against remuneration"; "Practising on lacking capacity to sexual self-determination"
Greenland	18	MF	all	"Gross abuse of a superiority based on age and experience"
Ireland	17	MF	all	"using for the purpose of prostitution"
Italy	16	MF	all	"against remuneration"[9]
Monaco	21	F	all	"false promise of marriage or deceitful acts"
Netherlands[10]	18	bMF	all	"money and goods"; "abuse of superiority"; "deception"
Portugal	16	MF	VV	"practising on inexperience"
Romania	18	Mf	VI	"false promise of marriage"
San Marino	21	Mf	all	"promise of marriage under deception over one's marital status"
Spain	– 16	MF MF	all all	"abusing a manifest situation of superiority which restricts the victims sexual liberty" "Deception"
Sweden	– 18	MF MF	All All	"to the participation in pornographic productions" "casual relations against remuneration";
Turkey	"girls"[11]	Mf	"defloration"	"false promise of marriage"

III. Laws Against Seduction–no screening possible

	Age	G	Sex. Cont.	Means afforded
Greece	17	Mm	all	–
Iceland	16	MF	all	"Deception, gifts or other ways"
Liechtenstein	16	MF	All	"Practising on a position of distress"; "Against remuneration"; "Practising on lacking capacity to sexual self-determination"

Abbreviations:
Age: "Seduction" is punishable up to the age of
G: "protected" gender:
M: Law covers "seduction" of males only
F: Law covers "seduction" of females only
MF: Law covers "seduction" of males and females
Mf: Law covers "seduction" of females by males only
Mm: Law covers "seduction" of males by males only
Mf: Law covers "seduction" of females by females only
bMF: Law covers "seduction" of "blameless" males and females only
Means afforded: Only "seduction" by the mentioned means is punishable
Sex, Cont,: Punishable is only "seduction" to
    AI: anal intercourse
    OI: oral intercourse
    VI: vaginal intercourse
    all: all sexual contacts

Remarks:

[1] These jurisdictions allow for screening of cases which do not require prosecution. This means that either prosecution authorities are being granted power of discretion to prosecute or not and to judge each case on its merits or that prosecution does require a complaint (mostly by the minor, his legal representative or a youth protection authority).
[2] "Lacking maturity" means an inability to understand the nature of a sexual act or to act according to such an understanding. Such a lack has to be the result of delayed development and to be established on the basis of specified facts.
[3] Art. 174A CC as amended by the Criminal Code (Amendment) Law 40 (I) of 1998.
[4] The law is hardly ever enforced. The offence of having sexual contact with a prostitute, which is under 18, (Art. 223a CC) has not been included in the table since it hardly can be seen as a "seduction"-provision. It seems to outlaw all, even non-commercial, sexual contacts of persons under 18, who prostitute themselves.
[5] Heterosexual "seduction": 18; Homosexual "seduction": 21;
[6] Heterosexual "seduction": the abuse must be "gross"; Homosexual "seduction": the abuse need not be "gross".
[7] Art. 20:8 CC (as amended by law EV 60/1998 vp-HE 6 ja 117/1997 vp)
[8] 1998 the following provision has been introduced: "Section 5 *Sexual* Abuse (1) A Person who abuses his/her position and entices one of the following into sexual intercourse, into another sexual act essentially violating his/her right of sexual self-determination, or into submission to such an act, ... 2. a person younger than eighteen years of age, whose capacity to independently decide on his/her sexual acting is essentially weaker than that of offender's owing to his/her immaturity and the age difference between the parties, where the offender blatantly takes advantage of that immaturity ... shall be sentenced for sexual abuse to a fine or to imprisonment for at most four years" (Ch. 20 CC).
[9] Art. 600bis CP as amended by law 269 (02.08.99)
[10] The law is hardly ever enforced.
[11] The law does not set a fix age limit. It just speaks of the defloration of "girls".

between ascendents and their descendents always are criminal regardless if authority has been misused or not. Therefore two different situations must be separated:

a. *Authority has not been misused* (for instance a love relationship between a student and his/her teacher)

Table VI shows in how many states such relations are legal in a certain age-group:

14	39% (23-59)
15	54% (32-59)
16	83% (49-59)

(This table does not cover sexual relations between ascendents and their descendents!)

b. *Authority has been misused* (but the misuse does not arise to intimidation, coercion, or force covered by the offenses on sexual violence)

Table VII shows in how many states such relations are no criminal offence in a certain age-group:

14	17% (10-59)
15	25% (15-59)

16   46% (27-59)

18   93% (55-59)

(This table does not cover sexual relations between ascendents and their descendents!)

Accordingly if authority has been misused the age limit mostly is set at 16 or 18, and if it is not misused at 14, 15 or 16.

OVERSEAS[53]

Remarkably common-law countries (or countries having been under their influence) set the age limit in most cases at 16 and sometimes even today they still do have a total ban on homosexuality or on certain kinds of sexual contact; or a special higher age limit for certain sexual practices.

Countries with French or Spanish influence or which never have been a colony in most cases set the minimum age low, with the notable exception of countries which have been a prime target of Western sex tourism: Thailand raised from 13 to 15 in 1987 and in 1996 (for contacts "in the place of prostitution") to 18; and the Philippines, while leaving the minimum age at 12, passed a law criminalizing sexual contact with under 18-year-olds, if the contact occurred for money, gift, or any other consideration or due to any influence of an adult. Apart from these cases seduction-provisions however are very rare outside of Europe.

In the *USA* legislation in our field is up to the several states. The various states did establish very divergent regulations and there are minimum age limits from 14 up to even 18 in some states. It is striking that in the U.S. the age limits go a lot higher than in the rest of the world.[54] A specialty of the U.S.-system is that many states have established different age limits for different kinds of sexual practices (vaginal, anal, oral intercourse, mutual masturbation, etc.)[55] often combined with different limits for different age breaks between the partners. This leads to very complex legal situations which hardly can be understood by ordinary people without the help of a specialized lawyer.

There is only one Federal Law in our field.[56] In 1994 a provision was introduced against sextourism into the Federal Criminal Code. This law is worded in a way that can produce obscure results. The law makes it an offence to travel in interstate or international commerce with the intent to engage in sexual contact with someone under 16 (§§ 2423, 2243 Fed-

TABLE IV. "Seduction" (without coercion and out of relationships of authority) Legal from the Age of[1] (Europe)

individual sexual maturity	from 12	from 13	from 14	from 15	from 16	from 17	from 18	from 21
Belorus Scotland[2] Ucraine	Malta Vatican	Cyprus[3]	Albania Bosnia-Herzegovina Bulgaria Croatia Estonia FR Yugoslavia (Cosovo) Serbia Montenegro (Vojvodina) Hungary Italy[4] Latvia[5] Lithuania Macedonia Moldova Portugal[6] Russia San Marino Slovenia	Czech Republic France[7] Greece Ireland[8] Monaco[9] Poland Romania Slovakia Sweden[10] Turkey	Armenia Azerbaijan Austria[11] Belgium Cyprus[12] Germany England & Wales Georgia Gibraltar[13] Guernsey[14] Iceland Isle of Man[15] Italy[16] Jersey[17] Latvia[18] Liechtenstein Luxemburg Norway Portugal[19] Scotland[20] Spain Switzerland	Ireland[21] Northern Ireland[22]	Andorra Austria[23] Denmark Färöer Finland Greenland Netherland Sweden[24]	Isle of Man[25] Monaco[26]

From the individual capacity to give informed consent: Cyprus,[27] France[28]
General ban on "seduction": Sweden ("against remuneration"), Spain (cf. Table III.)

Remarks:

[1] Some jurisdictions (*Czech Republic, Malta, Romania, Slovak Republic, the Vatican and jurisdictions on the territory of the former Soviet Union*) have laws against "corruption" or "depravation" of youths or against "seduction" to an "idle or indecent life". But these provisions have in common that they are intended to protect the "orderly life" of the youths. Therefore often a more intensive and repeated influence on the youth is afforded, so that he (or she) as a result of the offence is led into a "disorderly" life. A single contact, for instance against remuneration, normally does not invoke criminal liability. Likewise it is not punishable to "seduce" a juvenile (for instance by offering money for sexual contact) who already does lead a "disorderly" life. Such offences therefore have not been counted as "seduction"-provisions for the purpose of this table.
Four jurisdictions on the territory of the former Yugoslavia and Monaco, Romania, San Marino and Turkey have laws against "seduction of minor girls under false promise of marriage". This offence however is intended to protect virginity of the girls. The intention of these laws therefore is so narrow that they have not been counted as "seduction"-provisions for the purpose of this table. In addition these laws (with the exception of Monaco and San Marino) do cover vaginal intercourse with girls only and they are seldom enforced and of no practical importance. In *Austria, Finland, Germany, Italy, Liechtenstein* and *Sweden*, there is a higher age limit for "sexual acts with a minor against remuneration." Contacts with minors against remuneration in many cases do not constitute "seduction" (in many cases the adolescents offer themselves or readily agree to such an offer); the intention of legislators for such provisions however mostly are based upon the suggestion that the offer of remuneration contains an element of "seduction". Therefore such provisions have been included here. *Special offenses for homosexual "seduction"* (only in Greece still on the books) have been excluded from this table to keep it clear and legible. Moreover they are based upon very special reasoning making it unapposite to mix them together with general seduction provisions.

TABLE IV (continued)

[2] In the case of heterosexual "seduction" of boys
[3] In the case of seduction to heterosexual anal intercourse.
[4] Seduction is legal from 13 onwards, if the older partner is not older than 16 and 14 if he is older than 16. Except "against remuneration".
[5] If the "seducer" is not 18 or older.
[6] For all contacts but vaginal intercourse with boys and girls
[7] For partners over 18 only.
[8] For all contacts save anal intercourse and penile vaginal intercourse with girls and not for using for the purposes of prostitution
[9] For "seduction" of boys
[10] Except "against remuneration" and "seduction" to the participation in pornographic productions.
[11] Except "against immediate remuneration"
[12] For vaginal intercourse with girls
[13] Heterosexual anal intercourse is a criminal offense regardless of the age of the partners.
[14] Heterosexual anal intercourse is a criminal offense regardless of the age of the partners.
[15] For anal intercourse there is a special limit of 21
[16] "Against remuneration"
[17] Heterosexual anal intercourse is a criminal offense regardless of the age of the partners.
[18] If the "seducer" is 18 or older.
[19] For vaginal intercourse with boys and girls
[20] In the case of "seduction" of girls
[21] For anal intercourse and penile vaginal intercourse with girls as well as for using a person (under 17) for the purposes of prostitution
[22] Anal intercourse is a criminal offense regardless of the age of the partners.
[23] "Seduction immediately against remuneration"
[24] "Seduction" to the participation in pornographic productions.
[25] For anal intercourse
[26] For "seduction" of girls
[27] Valid for all sexual contact except vaginal intercourse and anal intercourse with girls and boys.
[28] The minimum age limit of 15 applies not to partners under 18.

eral Criminal Code). The minimum age limit is set at 14 in Puerto Rico for instance. A couple consisting of a 15- and a 21-year-old therefore can legally have sex there. But when both travel to another U.S.-state or to another country their relation becomes a criminal offence and the older partner is liable to imprisonment of up to 10 years, even if the relation also is legal in the other U.S.-state (e.g., Florida) or in the other country (e.g., Canada).

In Europe in the recent years several countries (Austria,[57] Belgium, Finland,[58] Germany,[59] France,[60] and Norway[61]) have passed legislation making their citizens liable to prosecution under their laws on sexual minimum age regardless where the contact occurred, even when the contact has been completely legal in the country where it occurred.[62] These laws also can produce obscure situations. A 19-year-old Belgian for instance who travels to Spain and there has sex with his 15-year-old Spanish summer-love commits a criminal offense (under Belgian law). But he is the only one who does so. All the other people making holidays there, from Britain, Italy, Denmark or elsewhere, could legally engage in a relation with the 15-year-old without getting a problem

TABLE V. Sexual Relations with Juveniles in Relations of Authority (Europe)

I.: No Laws

Albania (I)
Armenia
Azerbaijan
Bulgaria (I)
CIS:
    Belorus
    Georgia
    Moldova
    Ucraine
Cyprus (I)
Estonia
Gibraltar (I)
Greenland
Guernsey (I)
Ireland (I)
Isle of Man (I)
Jersey (I)
Latvia
Lithuania
Luxembourg
Malta
Monaco (for boys; for girls see II. below)
San Marino (I)
Turkey
UK:

    E & W (I)[1]
    Northern Ireland (I)[2]

II. Laws–screening possible[3]

		Age	G	Sex Cont	Abuse of Authority
Andorra	Asc	18		all	–
	other	18		all	afforded
Austria	Asc	–		VI	–
		18		other contacts than VI	–
	other	18		all	afforded
Belgium	Asc	18		all	–
	other			no provisions	–
Bosnia-Herzegovina	Asc	–		VI	–
	other	18		all	afforded
Croatia	Asc	–		VI	–
	other	18		all	afforded
Czechia	Asc	–		VI	–
	other	18		all	afforded
Denmark	Asc	–		all	–
	other	18		all	–
Färöer	Asc	–		all	–
	other	18		all	–
Finland	Asc	18		All	–
	Other	18		All	afforded

TABLE V (continued)

		Age	G	Sex Cont	Abuse of Authority
FR Yugoslavia:					
(Cosovo	Asc	–		VI	–
	other	18		all	afforded)
Montenegro	Asc	–		VI	–
	other	18		all	afforded
Serbia	Asc	–		VI	–
	other	18		all	afforded
(Vojvodina	Asc	–		VI	–
	other	18		all	afforded)
France	Asc	18		all	–
	other	18		all	afforded, if the authority is based upon a public office (teacher, educator, etc.)
Germany	Asc	–		VI	–
	other	18		all	up to 16 not afforded; from 16 onwards afforded
Greece	other	18		all	–
Hungary	Asc	–		all	–
	other	18		all	"Endangering of the moral development" afforded
Lithuania	Asc	–		all	afforded
	other	–[4]		all	afforded
Macedonia	Asc	–		VI	–
	other	18		all	afforded
Monaco	Asc	18		all	–
	other	21	F	all	afforded
Netherlands	Asc	18		all	–
	other	18		all	–
Norway	Asc	–		all	–
	other	18		all	–
Poland	Asc	–		all	afforded
	other	–[5]		all	afforded
Portugal	other	16		all	–
		18		all	up to 16 not afforded; from 16 onwards afforded
Romania	Asc	–		VI	–
	other	18		all	afforded
Russia	other	–[6]		all	afforded
Slovakia	Asc	–		VI	–
	other	18		all	afforded
Slovenia	Asc	18		VI	–
	other	18		all	afforded
Spain	Asc	–[7]		all	afforded
	other	–[8]		all	afforded
Sweden	Asc	–		all	–
	other	18		all	–
UK: Scotland	Asc	–		VI	–
	other	16		VI	"common household" afforded
Vatican[9]	other	15		all	–

III. Laws–no screening possible

		Age	G	Sex Cont	Abuse of Authority
Greece	Asc	18		all	–
Iceland	Asc	–		all	–
	other	18		all	–
Italy	Asc	–[10]		all	–
	other	16		all	–
Liechtenstein	Asc	–		VI	--
		18		other contacts than VI	–
	other	18		all	afforded
Switzerland	Asc	–		VI	–
	other	20		all	afforded
Vatican	Asc	–[11]		all	–

Abbreviations:
Age: Sexual relations in relations of authority are punishable with persons up to the age of other: relations of authority which are not ascendent/descendent-relations (e.g., education, care, supervision, etc.)
Asc: Ascendents/Descendents-Relations
Abuse of Authority:
–: abuse of authority is not afforded for prosecution afforded: not all sexual contacts in relations of authority are punishable but only if the authority has been abused
G: "protected" gender (where nothing is indicated the law covers males and females):
F: law covers authority relations over females only
(I): there is a general offence of incest regardless of the age of the partners
Sex Cont: punishable is only
AV: anal intercourse
OV: oral intercourse
VI: vaginal intercourse
all: all sexual acts
all HTS: all heterosexual acts
all HS: all homosexual acts

Remarks:
[1] In 2000 sexual contact with persons under 18 has been outlawed which are kept in certain institutions (children's home, hospital, penitentiaries, etc.) Due to the very limited nature of this offence it has not been included for the purpose of this table.
[2] In 2000 sexual contact with persons under 18 has been outlawed which are kept in certain institutions (children's home, hospital, penitentiaries, etc.) Due to the very limited nature of this offence it has not been included for the purpose of this table.
[3] These jurisdictions allow for screening of cases which do not require prosecution. This means that either prosecution authorities are being granted power of discretion to prosecute or not and to judge each case on its merits or that prosecution does require a complaint (mostly by the minor, his legal representative or a youth protection authority).
[4] In Lithuania there is a general law against the abuse of dependency for sexual purposes regardless of the age of the partners.
[5] In Poland there is a general law against the abuse of dependency for sexual purposes regardless of the age of the partners.
[6] In Russia it is an offence (irrespective of age) to practise upon a financial or other dependency to gain sexual contact.
[7] In Spain there is a general law against the abuse of authority for sexual purposes regardless of the age of the partners.
[8] In Spain there is a general law against the abuse of authority for sexual purposes regardless of the age of the partners.
[9] No screening possible if the offence is committed by abuse of parental power or of the power of a guardian
[10] Sexual relations between ascendents and descendents (over 16 years of age) are punishable only if they are held in a way that invokes a public scandal.
[11] Sexual relations between ascendents and descendents (over 15 years of age) are punishable only if they are held in a way that invokes a public scandal.

when returning home. While in Germany and Austria the respective laws address only the citizens of their countries going abroad,[63] Belgium criminalizes everyone who is caught on its territory.[64] As a result, for example, a 20-year-old German (or Austrian, French, etc.) can be prosecuted in Belgium for sexual relations with his 15-year-old girlfriend in his homecountry, which are legal there. In the UK such a law-project has been rejected.[65] The Council of the European Union recommended to introduce the principle of exterritoriality but expressly left it open to the member states to bind prosecution on the requirement that an act constitutes a criminal offence in the country itself and abroad (Council of Ministers of the European Union 1997, 4). The Council of Europe generally recommends to "introduce rules on exterritorial jurisdiction in order to allow the prosecution and punishment of nationals who have committed offenses concerning sexual exploitation of children outside the national territory" (Committee of Ministers 1993, 12, 42), also leaving it open to the member states to afford double punishability.

DEPICTIONS OF LEGAL SEXUALITY

Federal U.S.-legislation from 1984 renders all visual depiction of sexual acts by and with persons under 18 years of age criminal.[66] Also visual depictions representing "lascivious exposure" of the "genitals or the pubic area" of a person under 18, even if this person is fully clothed and when the outlines of these areas are not discernible through clothing.[67] Since the minimum age limits in most states are lower than 18, this law renders depictions of legal sexual activity a criminal offence. *Canada* passed a similar law in 1993[68] and the European Union followed that suite ten years later.

Recently enacted EU-legislation[69] will effect interferences with the sexual lifes of adolescents across Europe in an intensity so far not known in any of the European states.[70] The "Framework-Directive on combating sexual exploitation of children and child-pornography" will oblige all member States of the European Union to create extensive offenses of *"child"-pornography* and *"child"-prostitution*,[71] defining as "child" every person up to 18 years of age, without differentiating between five-year-old children and 17-year-old juveniles.

These offenses go far beyond combating child pornography and child prostitution, thus making a wide variety of adolescent sexual behaviour, hitherto completely legal in the overwhelming majority of jurisdictions

TABLE VI. Sexual Relations with Juveniles in Relations of Authority *without coercion* and *without misuse of authority*[1] (Europe)[2]

Legal from the age of

individual maturity	12	13	14	15	16	17	18	21
Belorus Scotland[3] Ucraine	Austria[4] Liechtenstein[5] Malta Spain	Austria[6] Cyprus[7]	Albania Austria[8] Bosnia-Herzegovina Bulgaria Croatia Estonia FR Yugoslavia: (Cosovo) Montenegro Serbia (Vojvodina) Latvia[9] Liechtenstein[10] Lithuania Macedonia Moldova Russia San Marino Slovenia	Czechia Greenland Ireland[11] Monaco Poland Romania Slovakia Turkey Vatican	Andorra Armenia Azerbaijan Belgium Cyprus[12] England & Wales Finland Georgia Germany Gibraltar[13] Guernsey[14] Isle of Man[15] Italy Jersey[16] Latvia[17] Luxemburg Portugal Scotland[18] Switzerland	Ireland[19] Northern Ireland[20]	Denmark Färöer France Greece Hungary Iceland Netherlands Norway Sweden	Isle of Man[21]

From the individual capacity to give informed consent: Cyprus[22]

Remarks:

[1] Excluding relations between ascendents with their descendents.

[2] *Special offenses for homosexual relations* have been excluded from this table to keep it clear and legible. Moreover they are based upon very special reasoning making it unapposite to mix them together with general provisions.

[3] For other contacts with boys than vaginal intercourse

[4] Non-penetrative sexual contact with a partner not more than four years older

[5] If the partner is not more than three years older

[6] For penetrative sexual contact (with parts of the body), if the partner is not more than three years older.

[7] In the case of heterosexual anal intercourse.

[8] The limit is 12 in the case of non-penetrative sexual contact with a partner not more than four years older, and it is 13 in the case of penetrative sexual contact (with parts of the body), if the partner is not more than three years older. In other cases it is 14.

[9] If the partner is under 18

[10] If the partner is more than three years older

[11] For all contacts save anal intercourse and penile vaginal intercourse with girls

[12] For vaginal intercourse with girls

[13] Heterosexual anal intercourse is a criminal offense regardless of the age of the partners.

[14] Heterosexual anal intercourse is a criminal offense regardless of the age of the partners.

[15] For anal intercourse there is a special limit of 21.

[16] Heterosexual anal intercourse is a criminal offense regardless of the age of the partners.

[17] If the partner is over 18

[18] For sexual contacts with girls and for vaginal intercourse with boys

[19] For anal intercourse and penile vaginal intercourse with girls

[20] Anal is a criminal offense regardless of the age of the partners.

[21] For anal intercourse

[22] Not for vaginal intercourse with girls, and not for heterosexual anal intercourse

in Europe, serious crimes; for instance: sex between 16-year olds for "remuneration" or "consideration," which includes invitations to cinema or to a dinner; "lascivious" drawings of a 17-year-old girl possessed by a 15-year-old boy; photographs of a 16 year-old girl in her bikini "lasciviously" exposing her pubic area, taken by her 17 year-old boyfriend on the beach and used for his bedside-table; standard pornography involving younger looking 20-year-old adults or "webcam-sex" between 17-year-old-adolescents; even pictures of one's own adult spouse in "lascivious" poses, if this spouse looks younger than 18.

No European jurisdiction so far has such a restrictive law.[72] The massive criminalisation and the equation of adolescents with children caused heavy criticisms among experts but this criticism could not prevent this plan from becoming law.[73,74]

GOVERNMENTAL EXPERT COMMISSIONS

National governments frequently appointed expert commissions to scrutinize the law on sexual offenses and to make recommendations.

Most of these commissions in Europe recommended a minimum age limit of 14;[75] the Dutch "Melai-Commission" even of 12.[76] Also the experts heard by both chambers of the German parliament and by the Austrian parliament favoured an age limit of 14.[77] Three commissions suggested 15[78] and only one 16.[79] Nearly all of them called for effective screening of cases where criminal proceedings would do more harm than good to the child and made concrete proposals in this respect (as a necessity of a complaint, power of discretion for prosecution authorities and the courts, power for the victim to veto criminal proceedings, etc.) (Graupner 1995, 2, 26ff; 1997b, Vol. 2, 26ff).

Just one of the commissions proposed a special age limit for "seduction": the Dutch "Melai-Commission," which recommended a minimum age limit of 12 suggested to criminalize sexual contacts with 12 to 16 year olds, if the older partner initiated the contact.[80] Most of the European commissions proposed not to criminalize "seduction" over the age of 14.[81] Three set this limit at 15[82] and one at 16.[83] No European commission recommended a special provision for sex against remuneration. The Swedish Commission explicitly called for the repeal of the respective provision in the Swedish law.[84] The non-legal experts heard by both chambers of the German parliament opposed "seduction"-provisions (see above).[85]

TABLE VII. Sexual Relations with Juveniles in Relations of Authority *without coercion* but *under misuse of authority*[1] (Europe)[2]

Legal from the age of

individual maturity	12	13	14	15	16	17	18	21
	Belorus Scotland[3] Ucraine	Malta	Cyprus[4]	Albania Bulgaria Estonia Latvia[5] Moldova San Marino	Greenland Ireland[6] Monaco[7] Turkey Vatican	Armeinia Azerbaijan Belgium Cyprus[8] England & Wales Georgia Gibraltar[9] Guernsey[10] Isle of Man[11] Italy Jersey[12] Latvia[13] Luxemburg Scotland[14]	Ireland[15] Northern Ireland[16]	Andorra Austria Bosnia-Herzegovina Croatia Czechia Denmark Färöer Finland FR Jugoslavia: Cosovo Montenegro Serbia Vojvodina France Germany Greece Hungary Iceland Liechtenstein Macedonia Netherlands Norway Portugal Romania Slovakia Slovenia Sweden Switzerland	Isle of Man[17] Monaco[18]

No Age Limit: Lithuania,[19] Poland,[20] Russia,[21] Spain[22]
From the individual capacity to give informed consent: Cyprus[23]

Remarks:
[1] Excluding relations between ascendents with their descendents
[2] *Special offenses for homosexual behaviour* have been excluded from this table to keep it clear and legible. Moreover they are based upon very special reasoning making it unapposite to mix them together with general provisions.
[3] For other contacts with boys than vaginal intercourse
[4] For heterosexual anal intercourse
[5] If the partner is under 18
[6] For all contacts save anal intercourse and penile vaginal intercourse with girls
[7] For contacts with boys
[8] For vaginal intercourse with girls
[9] Heterosexual anal intercourse is a criminal offence regardless of the age of the partners.
[10] Heterosexual anal intercourse is a criminal offence regardless of the age of the partners.
[11] For anal intercourse there is a special age limit of 21.
[12] Heterosexual anal intercourse is a criminal offence regardless of the age of the partners.
[13] If the partner is 18 or older

TABLE VII (continued)

[14] For sexual contacts with girls and for vaginal intercourse with boys
[15] For anal intercourse and penile vaginal intercourse with girls
[16] Anal intercourse is a criminal offence regardless of the age of the partners.
[17] For anal intercourse
[18] For sexual contacts with girls
[19] In Lithuania it is an offence regardless of the age of the partners to gain consent to a sexual contact by abusing a dependency
[20] In Poland it is an offence regardless of the age of the partners to gain consent to a sexual contact by abusing a dependency
[21] In Russia it is an offence (irrespective of age) to practise upon financial or other dependency to gain sexual contact.
[22] In Spain it is an offence regardless of the age of the partners to gain consent to sexual acts by abusing a relationship of superiority which restricts the victim's sexual liberty.
[23] For sexual contacts save vaginal intercourse with girls and anal intercourse with girls and boys.

No European commission recommended an age limit in the criminal law for depicting sexual activity that is higher than the general age-limit for sex. In a public hearing of experts in the *Austrian parliament* the experts (in law, child psychiatry, psychotherapy, and child sexual exploitation) unanimously rejected such an indiscriminate criminalization.[86]

Since the late sixties, only one of the European commissions proposed a special (higher) age limit for homosexual contacts.[87] All other commissions advocated uniform provisions.[88] The same is true for almost all of the experts heard by the German parliament[89] and by the Austrian parliament.[90]

The European commissions did not find to uniform conclusions in the area of *relations of authority*. The English *Policy Advisory Committee* (1981) and based upon its findings *the Criminal Law Revision Committee* (1984) opposed a special provision on contacts in relationships of authority. Sixteen- and 17-year-old adolescents, they argued, don't require special protection against teachers, employers, youthclub-leaders, and other persons in authority over them. Disciplinary law would suffice.[91] Moreover, such a law would be contradictionary since the partners could even marry in this age group. The other commissions advocated a special higher age limit for relationships of authority. As age limit the Dutch *Melai-Commission* (1980) recommended 16, the *Law Reform Commission of Ireland* (1990) 17 and the *Swedish Commission on Sexual Offenses* as well as the *Swiss Law Reform Commission* (1977) 18. In Germany four of the experts heard by parliament advocated 16, two 18 Deutscher Bundestag (1970).[92]

Helmut Graupner

TABLE VIII. Sexual Consent (Overseas)

I. Age Limits for Sexual Relations:

	Mf	Fm	Ff	Mm	Sed	Auth	FRO	MST	R TB
Australia									
Australian Capital Territory	10/16				–	–	10/16	–	1976
New South Wales	16	16	16	18	–	17	16	16	1987/90
Northern Territory	16	14	16	18	–	–	–/16		1983
Queensland	16/18[2]	16/18[3]	16	16/18[4]	–	–	16	16	1990
South Australia	16/17				–	18	16	16	1972
Tasmania	–/12/15/17				–	–	–	–	1997
Victoria	–/10/16				–	17/18	–/16		1980
Western Australia	16	16	16	21	–	17	(A)	16	1989
Brasilia	14	14	14	14	18	–	n.k.	–	n.k.
Canada	–/14/18[5]				18	18	–/14		1969
Chile	20	20	20	20	–	–	–	–	1998[6]
Ghana	14	–	–	–	–	–	–	–	–
India	15/16	–	–	–	–	–	–	–	–
Japan	13	13	13	13	18[7]	–	–	–	1880[8]
New Zealand	12/16	–	–/12/16	16	–	–/20	–	–	1986
Papua New Guinea	–/16	–/14	–/16	–	–	–	–	–	–
Philippines	12	12	12	12	18[9]	18	–	–	–
South Africa	–/16	–/16	19	–	–	–	16/19	16/19	1998[10]
South Korea	13	13	13	13	–	–	–	–	–
Taiwan	16	16	16	16	–	–	–	–	1912/30
Thailand	15/18[11]	15/18[12]	15/18[13]	15/18[14]	–	–	[?]	[?]	1957[15]
Tuvalu	–/15	–	–/15	–	–	–	–	–	–
USA[16,17,18]	Mf	Fm	Ff	Mm	sed	AV	VOR	MST	RTB
Alabama	–/12/16				–	–	(A)	–	–
Alaska	16	16	16	16	–	18	(A)	–	1980
American Samoa	14	14	14	14	–	–	n.k.	n.k.	n.k.
Arizona	–/15/18				–	–	(A)	–	2001
Arkansas	–/14/16				–	–	–	–	2001[19]
California	14/16/18[20]				18	–	(?)		–/1976
Colorado	–/15				–	18	(A)	–	1972
Connecticut	–/15/16				–	18	–	–	1971
D.C.	16	16	16	16	–	–	(A)	–	1992
Delaware	14/16				–	–	(A)	–	1973
Florida[21]	16/18[22]	16/18[23]	16/18[24]	16/18[25]	–	18	n.k.	n.k.	–
Georgia	14	14	14	14	–	–	14	14	1998[26]
Guam	16	16	16	16	–	–	n.k.	n.k.	n.k.
Hawaii	14/16	14/16	14/16	14/16	–	–	–	–	1973
Idaho	18				–	–	–	–	–

TABLE VIII (continued)

	Mf	Fm	Ff	Mm	Sed	Auth	FRO	MST	R TB
Illinois	16	16	16	16	–	18	–	–	1962
Indiana	–/16				–	–	–	–	1977
Iowa	–/14/16				–	16	(A)	–	1976/1978[27]
Kansas	16	16	16	16	–	–	(A)	–	–
Kentucky	14/16				–	–	(A)	–	1992[28]
Louisiana	–/12/15/17				–	–	–/17	–/17	–
Maine	–/14/16				–	–	–	–	1976
Maryland	–/14/16				–	–	–	–	1999[29]
Massachusetts	14/16				–	–	–	–	1974[30]
Michigan	13/16				–	16	–	–	–
Minnesota	13/16				–/15[31]	16/18	–	–	–
Mississippi	–/14/18[32]				–	18	–	–	–
Missouri	14/17				–	–	–	–	1999[33]
Montana	16				–	–	–	–	1996[34]
Nebraska	–/14/16				17	–	–	–	1978
Nevada	14/16[35]	14/16[36]	14	14	–	–	14	–	1993
New Hampshire	13/16				–	16	16[37]	–	1975
New Jersey	–/13/16				–	16/18	–	–	1978/1979[38]
New Mexico	13/16				–	16	–	–	1975
New York	14/17				–	–	–	–	1980[39]
North Carolina	–/13/16				–	18	16	16	–
North Dakota	15/18				–	18	(A)	15	1973
Ohio	13/16				–	–	(A)	–	1974
Oklahoma	–/14[40]/16/18	–	–	–	–	16	16	–
Oregon	14/18				–	–	–	–	1972
Pennsylvania	13/16[41]				18[42]	–	(A)	–	1980/1995[43]
Puerto Rico	14	14	14	14	–	–	n.k.	n.k.	–
Rhode Island	15[44]/16				–	–	(A)	–	1998
South Carolina	–/14/15[45]				–	16	(A)	–	–
South Dakota	16[46]				–	–	(A)	–	1977
Tennessee	13/18				18	–	–	–	1996[47]
Texas	–/14/17				–	–	(A)&14	–	–[48]
Utah	14	14	14	14	18	18	(A)	–	–
Vermont	16	16	16	16	–	–	–	–	1977
Virgin Islands	–/16				–	–	n.k.	n.k.	–
Virginia	13/14/15	13/14/15	13/14	13/14	14	–	14	13	–
Washington	–/12/14/16				–	18	(A)	–	1976
West Virginia	–/11/16				–	–	–	–	1976
Wisconsin	15/18[49]				–	–	"child"[50]	"child"[51]	1983
Wyoming[52]	19	19	19	19	–	–	–	–	1977
People's Republic of China	–/14	–	–	–	–	–	–	–	1912/30
Vietnam	16	16	16	16	–	–	n.k.	n.k.	n.k.

II. Total Ban on (Certain) Homosexual Contacts
Australia: Northern Territory (HSM)[53]
Chile (HSM,HSF)
USA:[54] Kansas (AnI,F,C,PA)
      Oklahoma (HSF, HSM)
      Texas (AnV,F,C,PV,PA,PP,Va/An)[55]

III. Total Ban on (Hetero- and Homosexual) Anal and Oral Intercourse
Canada (AnI)[56]
USA;[57] Alabama (AnI,F,C)
      California (AnI, F, C)[58]
      Minnesota [M] (AnI,F,C)[59]
      Utah [M] (AnI,F,C,Va/An)
      Virginia [M] (AnI,F,C a.o.)
      Virgin Islands (AnI,F,C)

IV. Total Ban on Heterosexual Anal and Oral Intercourse and on (All) Kinds of Homosexual Contact
Papua Newguinea [M] (AnI,HSM)
Tuvalu [M] (AnI,HSM)
USA:[60] Puerto Rico ("Sodomy", "Homosexual Intercourse")

V. Total Ban on "Unnatural and Perverse Acts"[61]
Ghana [M] (AnI,HS a.o.)
India [M] (AnI,F,HSPV a.o.)[62]
USA:[63] Florida (AnI, F, C a.o.)
      Idaho [M] (AnI,F a.o.)
      Louisiana [M] (AnI,F,C a.o.)
      Michigan [M] (AnI,GI)
      Mississippi [M] (AnI,F,C a.o.)
      North Carolina [M] (AnI,F,C a.o.)
      South Carolina [M] (AnI a.o.)

VI. "Fornication"[66] & Cohabitation[67]
USA: D.C. (FORN)
      Florida (FORN, COH)
      Georgia (FORN)
      Idaho (FORN)
      Illinois (FORN)
      Massachusetts (FORN)[68]
      Michigan (FORN, COH)
      Minnesota (FORN)
      Mississipi (FORN)
      New Mexico (COH)
      North Carolina (FORN, COH)
      North Dakota (COH)
      Oklahoma (FORN)[69]
      South Carolina (FORN, COH)
      Utah (FORN)
      Virginia (FORN, COH)
      West Virginia (FORN, COH)

Abbreviations:
(G): There does exist a general offence covering exhibition in private regardless of the age of the persons involved
RTB: Year in which the total ban on certain sexual relations (e.g., homosexual contacts, anal intercourse, etc.) has been lifted (if such a total ban ever existed in this country)
Auth: Sexual Relations within certain relations of authority are punishable up to the age (of the juvenile) of
AnI: Anal intercourse
C: Cunnilingus
COH: Cohabitation

TABLE VIII (continued)

Abbreviations (continued):

D.C.: District of Columbia
F: Fellatio
Ff: Minimum age for sexual relations of a girl with a woman
Fm: Minimum age for sexual relations of a boy with a woman
FORN: Fornication
GI: "Gross Indecency"
HSF: Homosexual relations between females
HSM: Homosexual relations between males
HSMAST: mutual masturbation between persons of the same sex
HSPV: Homosexual penetration of the vagina
[M]: The total ban of the listed kinds of sexual contact does also cover contact between married partners
MAST: Mutual masturbation
Mf: Minimum age for sexual relations of a girl with a man
Mm: Minimum age for sexual relations of a boy with a man
MST: Incitement to masturbation punishable up to age (of the juvenile) of
n.k.: not known
PA: Penetration of the anus
PP: Penetration of the penis
PV: Penetration of the vagina
Va/An: Vagina/anus-contacts
Sed: Provisions on "seduction" of youths up to the age (of the adolescent) of–mostly restricted to certain means of seduction
FRO: Sexual contacts in front of children or adolescents (without bodily contact) punishable up to age (of the juvenile) of

Remarks:

[1] Where in this table different age limits are indicated this means that there are established different limits for different kinds of sexual acts and/or for different kinds of age difference between the partners. The respective regulations are too complex to represent them here in detail. A detailed representation is given in H. Graupner (*Sexualität, jugendschutz und Menschenrechte*, Fft./M. et al.: Peter Lang, 1997, Vol. 2, 324-357).

[2] The age limit of 18 applies to anal intercourse.

[3] The age limit of 18 applies to anal intercourse.

[4] The age limit of 18 applies to anal intercourse.

[5] The age limit of 18 applies to anal intercourse between unmarried persons. In the recent years, however, several (superior) courts have invalidated this higher age limit as unjustified discrimination on the basis of age, sexual orientation and marital status (R. v. C.M. (1995), Henry Halms v. The Minister of Employment and Immigration (1995), R. v. Roy (1998); for more decisions cf. R.v.Roy (1998)).

[6] Law 1047 (Official Gazette 23.12.1998)

[7] "Giving or promising to give a remuneration" (Art. 2, 4 Law for Punishing Acts Related to Child Prostitution and Child Pornography, and for Protecting Children of 18th May 1999, published 26th May 1999, entered into force 1st November 1999)

[8] In Japan just one time there was a law outlawing some sexual acts generally. At the beginning of the Meiye restauration in 1873 - in the course of the reform of the Japanese criminal law under western influence - homosexual acts have been criminalized. This law however has not been adopted to the first Criminal Code of the year 1880.

[9] "Seduction" of "well-reputed" unmarried women under 18 by "deception". In addition in 1992 the Philippines outlawed sexual contacts indulged by minors (under 18) for money, profit or other consideration or due to the coercion, or influence of any adult, syndicate or group (Sec. 5 RA 7610, approved 17th June 1992).

[10] The total ban on male homosexual acts has been declared unconstitutional by the High Court and the Constitutional Court of South Africa (National Coalition for Gay and Lesbian Equality v. Minister of Justice (08.05.1998 & 09.10.1998: with the declaration having been granted effect even back to 27.04.1998)). Heterosexual intercourse interfemora and heterosexual oral sex has been decriminalized in 1932 (R v. K & F); heterosexual anal intercourse in 1961 (R v N).

[11] The age limit of 18 (introduced with the Suppression of Prostitution Act 1996) applies to (extra-marital) sexual contacts "in the place of prostitution" only (Sec. 4, 8 Prevention & Suppression of Prostitution Act B.E. 2539 (1996)).

[12] The age limit of 18 (introduced with the Suppression of Prostitution Act 1996) applies to (extra-marital) sexual contacts "in the place of prostitution" only (Sec. 4, 8 Prevention & Suppression of Prostitution Act B.E. 2539 (1996)).

[13] The age limit of 18 (introduced with the Suppression of Prostitution Act 1996) applies to (extra-marital) sexual contacts "in the place of prostitution" only (Sec. 4, 8 Prevention & Suppression of Prostitution Act B.E. 2539 (1996)).

[14] The age limit of 18 (introduced with the Suppression of Prostitution Act 1996) applies to (extra-marital) sexual contacts "in the place of prostitution" only (Sec. 4, 8 Prevention & Suppression of Prostitution Act B.E. 2539 (1996)).

[15] The Criminal Code of 1908 - the first one - made "carnal knowledge of man or woman against the order of nature" an offence (incarceration of three months up to 3 years and a fine). The adoption of this provisions seems to have been the result of influence of Western advisers in elaborating Thailand's first Criminal Code and seems to have found its way into Thailand's law from English law over the Indian Criminal Code 1860 and the Egyptian Criminal Code 1904 since all other Criminal Codes used as a model (France 1810, German Empire 1870, Hungary 1878, Netherlands 1886, Japan 1907) did not know such an offence. It has been wording similar to the offence of "buggery" of the anglo-saxon law and therefore seems to have been applied to anal intercourse (on the other side it has to be considered that India applied and applies its offence of "carnal knowledge against the order of nature" to all sexual acts which cannot lead to conception). How alien this law seems to have been to the Thais is shown on the penalty prescribed for it: while in the anglo-saxon countries (from where the law originated) stiff penalties have been applied (the death penalty or at least life imprisonment) the Thais established rather low penalties. The law has not been taken over into the Criminal Code 1957 anymore.

[16] The United States Federal Criminal Code establishes a general minimum age of 12 years (§ 2241) and an additional limit of 16, if the partner is 4 or more years older than the adolescent (§ 2243), but these provisions do apply to territories only which come under the special territorial and maritime jurisdiction of the U.S. and to federal correctional institutions.

Mostly under state legislation there is no special age afforded for the older partner. Therefore sexual contacts of youths under the respective age limits always are criminal; even if their partner also is under this limit.

Additionally in most states sexual relations with minors can be prosecuted under the offence of "contributing to the delinquency of a minor" (if the relation contributed to the "moral corruption" of the minor; and if the minor has not already been "delinquent" in this sense before).

The Military Code renders oral and anal intercourse by military personnel a felony (regardless of the age of the partner).

The Federal Crime Bill 1994 introduced a new offence: whoever travels in interstate or international commerce with the intent to engage in sexual contact with someone under 16 is liable to imprisonment of up to 10 years (§§ 2423, 2243 Federal Criminal Code). Liable for prosecution is also who prepares for such a travel. This leads to an obscure legal situation: the minimum age for sexual relations is set at 14 in Hawaii for instance. A couple consisting of a 15 and 21 year old therefore can legally have sex. But when both travel to another U.S.-state or to another country their relation becomes a criminal offence and the older partner can be jailed up to 10 years, even if the relation also is legal in the other U.S.-state (e.g., Florida) or in the other country (e.g., Canada).

Under federal law it is also an offence to "knowingly transport, or knowingly persuade, induce, or coerce any individual to travel in interstate or foreign commerce, or in any territory or possession of the United States, with intent that such individual engage in any sexual activity for which any person can be charged with a criminal offense" (18 U.S.C.A. §§ 2421 [enacted 1948], 2422 [enacted 1948]) (Posner & Silbaugh, *A Guide to America's Sex Laws*, The University of Chicago Press, Chicago & London 1996, 71).

[17] In 1981 the U.S. Supreme Court held that stricter rules for males do not violate the equal protection clause of the Constitution, on the theory that men lack the disincentives associated with pregnancy that women have to engage in sexual activity, and the law may thus provide men with those disincentives, in the form of criminal sanctions *(Michael M. v. Superior Court*, 450 U.S. 464 [1981]).

[18] In 2003 the Supreme Court struck down a total ban of homosexual acts as violating the constitutional right to privacy (*Lawrence et al. vs. Texas*, 2003).

[19] Homosexual penetrations of the vagina, the anus, by parts of the body are by law liable to imprisonment of up to one year and/or a fine of up to 1000 dollars. The *Circuit Court of Pulaski County, Arkansas Sixth Division* however on 23th March 2001 *Picado vs. Jegley* declared the ban to be in violation of the fundamental rights of "privacy" and "non-discrimination".

[20] cf. The People v. T.A.J. (1998)

[21] cf. B.B. v. State (1995)

[22] General age of consent is 16 (Fla. Stat. Ann. § 800.04 [enacted 1993]); Moreover "unlawful carnal intercourse with any unmarried person, of previous chaste character" under 18 is also a felony (Fla. Sat. Ann. § 794.05 [enacted 1892]) (Posner & Silbaugh 1996, 49). The latter provision has been declared unconstitutional by Florida Supreme Court in B.B. v. State (1995).

[23] General age of consent is 16 (Fla. Stat. Ann. § 800.04 [enacted 1993]); Moreover "unlawful carnal intercourse with any unmarried person, of previous chaste character" under 18 is also a felony (Fla. Sat. Ann. § 794.05 [enacted 1892]) (Posner & Silbaugh 1996, 49). The latter provision has been declared unconstitutional by Florida Supreme Court in B.B. v. State (1995).

[24] General age of consent is 16 (Fla. Stat. Ann. § 800.04 [enacted 1993]); Moreover "unlawful carnal intercourse with any unmarried person, of previous chaste character" under 18 is also a felony (Fla. Sat. Ann. § 794.05 [enacted 1892]) (Posner & Silbaugh 1996, 49). The latter provision has been declared unconstitutional by Florida Supreme Court in B.B. v. State (1995).

TABLE VIII (continued)

[25] General age of consent is 16 (Fla. Stat. Ann. § 800.04 [enacted 1993]); Moreover "unlawful carnal intercourse with any unmarried person, of previous chaste character" under 18 is also a felony (Fla. Sat. Ann. § 794.05 [enacted 1892]) (Posner & Silbaugh 1996, 49). The latter provision has been declared unconstitutional by Florida Supreme Court in B.B. v. State (1995).

[26] State v. Anthony Powell, Supreme Court of Georgia (23.11.1998)

[27] State v. Pilcher (1976); formally repealed in 1978

[28] Commonwealth v. Wasson, Supreme Court of Kentucky (1992)

[29] *Williams v. State*, 1998 Extra LEXIS 260, Baltimore City Circuit Court, January 14, 1999; Maryland had two laws criminalizing private adult sex. The "Unnatural and Perverted Sexual Practice" Act made oral sex between people of the same gender a crime, while Maryland's sodomy law prohibited anal sex. The oral sex statute was struck down in October 1998 as a result of an ACLU lawsuit. In order to end the ACLU lawsuit, the state agreed that the sodomy law should be struck down as well. In January 1999 the Baltimore City Circuit Court entered a final judgment prohibiting the state from enforcing either law for private sex acts. Because the state conducts all criminal prosecutions in Maryland, both laws are now invalid and unenforceable.

[30] Commonwealth v. Balthazar (1974)

[31] Age limit of 15 only for "seducers" 18 or over (Minn. Stat. Ann. § 609.352 [enacted 1986]) (Posner & Silbaugh 1996, 54).

[32] Age limit of 18 only for "carnal knowledge" ("illicit connection") with an adolescent of "previous chaste character" and only if perpetrator is "older" than the adolescent (Miss. Code Ann. §§ 97-3-67 [enacted 1917], 97-5-21 [enacted 1857]) (Posner & Silbaugh 1996, 55).

[33] In 1999, a Missouri appeals court, in State v. Cogshell, has construed the sodomy statute not to apply to consensual sexual relations.

[34] Gryczan v State of Montana, Supreme Court of Montana (1997)

[35] The age limit of 16 covers only heterosexual vaginal, anal and oral intercourse, and only if the partner is 18 or over (Nev. Rev. Stat. §§ 200.364 [enacted 1977], 200.368 [enacted 1977]) (Posner & Silbaugh 1996, 56).

[36] The age limit of 16 covers only heterosexual vaginal, anal and oral intercourse, and only if the partner is 18 or over (Nev. Rev. Stat. §§ 200.364 [enacted 1977], 200.368 [enacted 1977]) (Posner & Silbaugh 1996, 56).

[37] N.H. Rev. Stat. Ann. § 645:1 (enacted 1971) (Posner & Silbaugh 1996, 57).

[38] State v. Saunders (1977), State v. Cuiffini (1978); formally repealed in 1979

[39] People v. Onofre (1980), People v. Uplinger (1983)

[40] Okla. Stat. Ann. tit. 21, § 1114 (enacted 1981) (Posner & Silbaugh 1996, 59)

[41] 18 PA. Cons. Stat. Ann. §§ 3121, 3122.1, 3123, 3125, 3126 (enacted 1995) (Posner & Silbaugh 1996, 60)

[42] It is (also) an offense to seduce a female of "good repute", under eighteen, with promise of marriage (18 PA. Cons. Stat. Ann. § 4510 [enacted 1939]) (Posner & Silbaugh 1996, 60).

[43] Commonwealth v. Bonadio (1980); Gesetz formally repealed in 1995.

[44] R.I. Gen. Laws §§ 11-37-8.1 (enacted 1984), 11-37-8.3 (enacted 1984) (Posner & Silbaugh 1996, 60)

[45] S.C. Code Ann. § 16-3-655 (Posner & Silbaugh 1996, 61)

[46] S.D. Codified Laws Ann. §§ 22-22-7, 22-22-7.3 (Posner & Silbaugh 1996, 61)

[47] Campbell v. Sundquist, Supreme Court of Tennessee (1996)

[48] The ban on same-sex acts has been declared unconstitutional in 1992 by two courts of first instance (England v. State of Texas; Morales v. Texas). In *Lawrence & Garner vs. The State of Texas* a panel of the Texas (14th) Appeals Court struck down the law on 8th June 2000. On motion of the state of Texas the full court reheard the case and on 15th March 2001 reversed the decision and upheld the law. The judgement has been appealed to the Texas Court of Criminal Appeals.

[49] Between 15 and (under) 18 it is rebuttably presumed that the minor is incapable of consent (Wis. Stat. Ann. §§ 940.225, 948.09 [enacted 1987]) (Posner & Silbaugh 1996, 63)

[50] Wis. Stat. Ann. § 948.10 (enacted 1987) (Posner & Silbaugh 1996, 64)

[51] Wis. Stat. Ann. § 948.10 (enacted 1987) (Posner & Silbaugh 1996, 64)

[52] cf. Campbell v. State (1985)

[53] In the Northern Territory homosexual contact is an offence if more than two persons are present.

[54] The U.S.Supreme Court in a judgment of 26th June 2003 held that a total ban on homosexual contacts violates ther fundamental right to privacy (*Lawrence et. al. vs. Texas*, 2003).

[55] *Homosexual anal intercourse, homosexual fellatio, homosexual cunnilingus, homosexual anus/vagina-contacts and homosexual penetration of the vagina, anus oder penis* are punishable with a fine of up to 200 dollars regardless of the age of the partners. Respective heterosexual contacts have been decriminalized by law in 1974, after a federal district court declared the law unconstitutional as it comes to consensual acts of married partners (Buchanan v. Batchelor, 308 F. Supp. 729 (N.D. Tex. 1970), cert. denied, 401 U.S. 989 (1971)). The ban on same-sex acts has been declared unconstitutional in 1992 by two courts of first instance (England v. State of Texas; Morales v. Texas). In *Lawrence & Garner vs. The State of Texas* a panel of the Texas (14th) Appeals Court struck down the law on 8th

June 2000. On motion of the state of Texas the full court reheard the case and on 15th March 2001 reversed the decision and upheld the law. The judgement has been appealed to the Texas Court of Criminal Appeals.

[56] In Canada anal intercourse between unmarried partners is an offence if more than two persons are present.

[57] In 2003 the Supreme Court struck down a total ban of homosexual acts as violating the constitutional right to privacy (*Lawrence et. al. vs. Texas*, 2003)

[58] Applies in state prisons only (Cal.Penal Code §§ 286 [enacted 1872], 288a [enacted 1921], 289 [enacted 1978]) (Posner & Silbaugh 1996, 66f)

[59] A State District court judge on 18th May 2001 declared the law to be in violation of the state constitution. This decision however is not a binding precedent in other court districts of the state (St. Paul Pioneer Press, May 21, 2001, http://www.pioneerplanet.com/)

[60] In 2003 the Supreme Court struck down a total ban of homosexual acts as violating the constitutional right to privacy (*Lawrence et al. vs. Texas*, 2003)

[61] Named differently ("Abominable and detestable crime against nature", "Infamous crime against nature", "unnatural and lascivious acts", etc.)

[62] India punishes all sexual penetration which cannot lead to conception ("carnal intercourse against the order of nature").+

[63] In 2003 the Supreme Court struck down a total ban of homosexual acts as violating the constitutional right to pruivacy (*Lawrence et al. vs. Texas*, 2003)

[64] "Unnatrual and lascivious acts" (Fla.Stat.Ann. § 800.02 [enacted 1993]) (Posner & Silbaugh 1996, 67)

[65] In *Michigan Organization for Human Rights v. Kelley*, No. 88-815820 CZ (Mich. Cir. Ct. July 9, 1990) a trial court ruled Michigan's sodomy law unconstitutional under the state constitution. Because the attorney general did not appeal that ruling, Michigan law makes it binding on all state prosecutors, at least absent future litigation that might attempt to resuscitate the sodomy statute.

[66] Consensual heterosexual acts performed in private between unmarried persons (regardless of the age of the partners); for details see Posner & Silbaugh (1996, 98ff).

[67] Heterosexual (unmarried) cohabitation (regardless of the age of the partners); for details see Posner & Silbaugh (1996, 98ff).

[68] cf. however Commonwealth v. Balthazar (1974)

[69] Only seduction of a female of "previous chaste character under promise of marriage".

[70] If "–" is indicated this can either mean that in this jurisdiction a total ban on certain sexual acts never existed or that such a ban still is in force. Where this sign ("–") is given and the country is not listed under II. to V. this means

SUMMARY

All states in Europe and all of the studied non-European jurisdictions do have minimum age limits for sexual relations, do punish sexual relations with persons under a certain age. This age nowhere is set lower than 12 years.

In Europe in nearly 1/2 of the jurisdictions consensual sexual relations with 14-year-old adolescents are legal; in almost 2/3 with 15-year-olds; in a majority also when the older partner has started the initiative (and also when the initiative contains an offer of remuneration). In nearly all jurisdictions such relations are legal from the age of 16 onwards.

Nearly all European jurisdictions set the same age limit in the criminal law for depicting sexual activity as for the sexual activity itself.

Most states apply a higher age limit for contacts in relationships of authority. If authority is not misused this age limit in most jurisdictions is set between 14 and 16; if it is misused between 16 and 18.

Most states make no difference between homo- and heterosexual relations.

CONCLUSIONS

It is not the intention of this presentation to provide final answers to the two questions posed at the beginning. It should rather present a factual comparative law basis for further discussion of these problems.

However, the author does not conceal his belief that[93] in applying the rules established by the European Court on Human Rights in accordance with the recommendations of most of the European governmental expert commissions on the topic and in accordance with experts from the Council of Europe (Horstkotte 1984), sexual acts with prepuberal children should (remain to) be criminalized, that a minimum "age limit of 14 is sufficient and a higher age limit for cases of 'seduction' neither workable nor necessary" (Horstkotte 1984, 198).[94] A higher age limit for contacts in relationships of authority should be set and it should be applied, when authority is used to pressure a young person into consenting to sexual acts. An age of 16 seems to be sufficient in this respect. Depictions of sexual activity within legal sexual relations should not be criminalized. And "the availability of some procedural reliefs should not obscure the fact that in many cases a complete dropping of the procedure and a crisis management by medical and youth welfare services and by private persons and organizations constitute the most efficient support" (Horstkotte 1984, 197). Screening seems indispensable and states should provide for effective remedies for that. Finally, the law should make no differences between heterosexual and homosexual behaviour (Horstkotte 1984, 202).

CITED CASES

Abdulaziz, Cabales and Balkandali v. UK, 94 ECtHR Series A (1985)
A.D.T. vs. UK, ECtHR (35765/97), judg. 31.07.2000
Ashcroft vs. Free Speech Coalition, United States Supreme Court, opinion 16.04.2002, 535 U.S., No. 00-795
B.B. v. State, 659 So.2d 256 (Fla. 1995)
Campbell v. State, 709 P.2d 425 (Wyo. 1985)

Campbell v. Sundquist, Tennessee Supreme Court, 926 S.W. 2d 250, Tenn. (1996)
Christine Goodwin vs. UK, ECtHR (28957/95), judg. 11.07.2002 [GC
Commonwealth v. Balthazar 318 N.E.2d 478 (Mass. 1974)
Commonwealth v. Bonadio, 415 A.2d 47 (Pa. 1980)
Commonwealth v. Wasson, Supreme Court of Kentucky, 842 SW 2d 487, Ky (1992)
Dudgeon v. UK, 45 ECtHR Series A (1981)
Gryczan v. State of Montana, Montana Supreme Court, ND 96-202 (1997)
Halm v. Canada (Minister of Employment and Immigration), 2 F.C. 331, 27 CRR (2d) 23, 28 Imm.L.R. (2d) 252 (1995)
I. vs. UK, ECtHR (25680/94), judg. 11.07.2002 [GC]
Inze v. Austria, 126 ECtHR Series A (1987)
Karner vs. Austria, ECtHR (40016/98), judg. 24.07.2003
Lawrence et. al. vs. Texas, U.S.-Supreme Court, 02-102, dec. 26.06.2003
Limon, Matthew R. v. Kansas, U.S.-Supreme Court, 02.583, 27.06.2003
Lustig-Prean & Beckett vs. UK, ECtHR (31417/96; 32377/96), judg. 27.09. 1999
L. & V. v. Austria, ECtHR (39392/98, 39829/98), judg. 09.01.2003
Marckx v. Belgium, 31 ECtHR Series A (1979)
Matthews vs. UK, ECtHR (24833/94), judg. 18.02.1999;
max.mobil Telekommunikation Service GmbH, Court of First Instance (EU), Case T-54/99 (31.01.2002)
Michael M. v. Superior Court, 450 U.S. 464 (1981)
M.K. vs. Austria, ECmHR, Decision (appl. 28867/95) (1997)
Modinos v. Cyprus, 259 ECtHR Series A (1993)
National Coalition for Gay and Lesbian Equality v. Minister of Justice, Constitutional Court of South Africa (08.05. 1998)
National Coalition for Gay and Lesbian Equality v. Minister of Justice, Johannesburg High Court (09.10.1998)
Norris v. Ireland, 142 ECtHR Series A (1988)
Open Door and Dublin Well Women v. Ireland, ECtHR, press release 468 (29.10.1992)
People v. Onofre, 415 N.E.2d 936 (N.Y. 1980)
People v. Scott, 9 Cal.4th 331, Cal. SC (1994)
People v. Uplinger, 447 N.E.2d 62 (N.Y. 1983)
R v. C.M., Ontario Court of Appeals, O.J. No. 1432 (1995)
R v K & F, EDL 71 (1932)
R v N, (3) ShA 147 (T) (1961)
R v. Roy, 125 Quebec Court of Appeals, Canadian Criminal Cases (3d), 442 (1998)
Rassmussen v. DK, 87 ECtHR Series A (1984)
Salgueiro da Silva Mouta vs. Portuga,l ECtHR (33290/96), judg. 21.12.1999
Segi & Others and Gestoras pro Amnistia & Others vs. 15 member states of the European Union, ECtHR (6422/02, 9916/02), dec. 23.05.2002
S.L. v. Austria, ECtHR (45330/99), judg. 09.01.2003
Smith & Grady vs. UK, ECtHR (33985/96; 33986/96), judg. 27.09.1999
State of Georgia v. Anthony Powell, Georgia Supreme Court (23.11.1998)
State v. Lawrence&Gardner, Texas Supreme Court (according to IGLHRC 1998)
State v. Limon, 41 P.3d 303, 2002 Kan. App. LEXIS 104, (Feb. 1, 2002), review denied (June 13, 2002)

State v. Cuiffini, 395 A2d 904, App. Div. (N.J. 1978)
State v. Pilcher, 242 N.W.2d 348 (Iowa 1976)
Stubbings & Others vs. UK, ECtHR (22083/93 ; 22095/93), judg. 22.10.1996
Sutherland v. UK, ECmHR, Report (appl. 25186/94) (1997)
The People v. T.A.J., Cal. Ct. App., 1st App. Distr., Div.2, A076464, 9th April (1998)
Toonen v. Commonwealth of Australia, Communication No. 488/1992, 50th session, United Nations Human Rights Committee CCPR/C/50/D/488/1992 (1994)
X & Y v. NL, ECtHR, judgement 26.03.1985 (EuGRZ 1985, 297)

NOTES

1. The information given in this paper is based upon a thorough analysis of the respective provisions of the national criminal law and of the jurisdiction of the courts in each state. The author studied the text of the laws, the case-law of the courts, commentaries to the criminal law and other literature and sought information from the Ministries of Justice and from University law schools in the respective countries. The sources are too numerous to represent them here but detailed references to these sources and the full text of the laws are given in the country-by-country survey contained in Graupner (1995, 2, 359-748; 1997b, 2, 359-748). Where information is based on sources not given there or in Graupner (2000), explicit references are given in the text here. The author attempted to be as thorough and encompassing as possible. Due to the nature of such an extensive comparative law study it is however never possible to exclude all possibilities of error, inaccuracy, misunderstanding and deficiencies concerning up-to-date-information. Therefore the author referenced each information in a way to facilitate the reader's way back to the sources.

2. *Dudgeon vs. UK* (1981), *Norris vs. Ireland* (1988), *Modinos vs. Cyprus* (1993), *A.D.T. vs. UK* (2000); *L. & V. vs. Austria* (2003). The Court does not exclude minors from this rule (*S.L. vs. Austria* 2003). According to its case-law also (private) sexual behavior of minors falls under the protection of Art. 8 (1) ECHR (see note 3) and therefore respective state regulation, to be justified, has to meet the requirements set forth in par. 2 of Art. 8 (cf. *Dudgeon v. UK* 1981, par. 41f, 48f, 62). Also the European Commission on Human Rights held that position (cf. *Sutherland v. UK* 1997, par. 35f). U.S.-caselaw however seems to be divided over this issue. While the Florida Supreme Court recognized a (state) constitutional right of privacy for minors to engage in sexual intercourse thereby obliging the state to put forward justification for (criminal law) regulation of juvenile sexuality (*B.B. v. State* 1995: the Court in this case moreover finally did not find the justification put forward well founded and invalidated the contested law criminalizing sexual intercourse of minors "of previous chaste character"), the California Court of Appeals rejected the notion that, under the right to privacy enshrined in California's Constitution, minors "have a constitutionally protected interest in engaging in sexual intercourse" (*The People v. T.A.J.* 1998; cf also *People v. Scott* [Cal. SC 1994]). "While we do not ignore the reality that many California teenagers are sexually active, that fact alone does not establish that minors have a right of privacy to engage in sexual intercourse. We accept the premise that due to age and immaturity, minors often lack the ability to make informed choices that take into account of both immediate and long-range consequences. While they may have the ability to respond to nature's call to exercise the gift of physical love, juveniles may yet be unable to accept

the attendant obligations and responsibilities. For all of these reasons we conclude there is no privacy right among minors to engage in consensual sexual intercourse," the Court stated thereby exempting the state from establishing any (compelling) interest in the law which criminalizes all (penetrative) sex of (even between) minors under 18 (*The People v. T.A.J.* 1998: the case originated in the conviction of a 16-year-old adolescent for engaging in consensual sexual intercourse with a 14-year-old female juvenile). In February 2002 the *Kansas Court of Appeals* confirmed a sentence of 17 years imprisonment for an 18 year old male who had consensual oral sex with a male school mate aged 14 years and 11 months; in addition the maximum sentence would have been 15 months if the couple would have been male-female. The *Kansas High Court* denied review and the case has been brought before the *Supreme Court (State v. Limon,* 2002). The *Supreme Court* on 27.06.2003 vacated the appeals court judgment and remanded the case to the Court of Appeals of Kansas for further consideration in light of *Lawrence v. Texas* (*Limon, Matthew R. v. Kansas*, 2003).

3. Art. 8 European Convention on Human Rights reads:

(1) Everyone has the right to respect for his private and family life, his home and his correspondence.

(2) There shall be no interference by a public authority with the exercise of this right except such as is in accordance with the law and is necessary in a democratic society in the interests of national security, public safety or the economic well-being of the country, for the prevention of disorder or crime, for the protection of health or morals, or for the protection of the rights and freedoms of others.

4. *Dudgeon vs. UK* 1981, *Norris vs. Ireland* 1988, *Modinos vs. Cyprus* 1993, *Open Door and Dublin Well Women vs. Ireland* 1992, *Marckx vs. Belgium* 1979, *Rasmussen vs. Denmark* 1984, *Abdulaziz et. al. vs. UK* 1985, *Inze vs. Austria* 1987, *L. & V. vs. Austria* (2003), *S.L. vs. Austria* (2003); more references in Graupner (1995, Vol. 1, 77, 87f, 101; 1997b, Vol. 1, 77, 87f, 101). Remarkably the Court often does not even require conformity between most of the states but points to discernible international legal trends. Legislation which contradicts such trends affords "very weighty reasons" to stand scrutiny (for a detailed analysis of the respective case-law cf. Graupner 1995, Vol. 1, 75ff; 1997b, Vol. 1, 75ff).

5. Case *X and Y vs. NL* 1985; *Stubbings et. al. vs. UK* 1996

6. Also the Council of the European Union did not proscribe specific detailed offenses to the member states but remained in relatively vague terms and expressly stated that the terms (as "child," "sexual abuse" or "unlawful sexual acts") used by it have to be interpreted according to the national legal systems (Council of the European Union 1997, 2f; for recent acts of the Council in respect to pornography and prostitution see VII. below). Also the Committee of Ministers of the Council of Europe did not define the terms "child" and "young adult" used in its recommendations to the member states on the issue (Committee of Ministers 1993, 22): "for the purposes of implementing the present recommendation in member states, the terms 'child' and 'young adult' are defined in accordance with the age limits laid down in national legislation" (ibid).

7. The German Constitutional Court for instance held that a minor is "from the beginning and increasing with his age (...) a personality protected by Art. 2 I of the German Constitution (the right to free development of one's personality) in connection with Art. 1 I (the right to respect for human dignity)." His competence increases according as his ability to self-determination exceeds his need for protection. In especially a discerning minor should be able to exercise rights on his own, which are central to his personality ("höchstpersönliche Rechte") (see BVerfGE 47, 46 (74) in: NJW

1978, 807; BVerfGE in: NJW 1982, 1375 (1378)). Similarly the case-law of Austrian Supreme Court. In Switzerland even the written law itself does contain this formula. According to Art. 19 II of the Swiss Civil Code "discerning minors" without the consent of their legal representative can exercise the "rights accorded to them on the basis of their personality" (details in Graupner 1995, Vol. 1, 63f; 1997b, Vol. 1, 63f).

8. which introduced an age limit as early as 1285 (at 12 years of age)
9. where in 1572 a fix limit of 12 has been set for vaginal intercourse with girls.
10. Only for vaginal intercourse with girls the age limit was 16 (since 1885).
11. Only for vaginal intercourse with girls the age limit was 16 (since 1885).
12. On the Isle of Man–as a rest of the old total ban (repealed in 1992)–a higher limit of 21 applies to anal intercourse only. The total ban on (heterosexual) anal intercourse is even still in force in Gibraltar, Jersey, Guernsey and in Northern Ireland. In Turkey the higher age limit (of 18) applies to anal and vaginal intercourse only.
13. The only exception being Switzerland (cf. next paragraph).
14. In *England & Wales* 75% of the cases with 13 to 15 year old girls are dropped Also with homosexual contacts most cases are dropped (Walmsley & White 1979, p. 42). In the years 1990-1992 only 9, 10 and 12 men over 21 have been prosecuted for homosexual contact with a young man under 21 (the then age of consent for homosexual conduct lowered to 18 in 1994) (House of Commons 1994, p. 102). Also in the *Netherlands* about 2/3 of the cases are dropped; moreover relations with minors over 12 can be prosecuted only upon complaint (of the adolescent, his legal representatives or the Council for Youth Protection). And as a result of extensive power of discretion granted to the prosecution authorities there have hardly been any prosecutions for sexual relations with 14 and 15 year old adolescents in *Norway* (personal communication Thore Langfeldt, World Congress for Sexology, Valencia 1997). As the Netherlands also *Portugal* (over 12) binds prosecution for (consensual) sexual relations with minors under the minimum age on a complaint (by the minor or his legal representative). But even some countries with an age limit lower than 16 do require a complaint: *Greece, Hungary* (heterosexual acts only), *Italy* (over 10), *Malta, San Marino, Spain* (also the state prosecutor can complain), *Vatican.*
15. Principle of legality means that police authorities are obliged to investigate, prosecutors to prosecute and courts to convict in each and every case. No power of discretion is attributed to them.
16. Proceedings ex officio means that prosecution can take place without complaint or consent of the victim, its legal representative or a certain institution or organisation.
17. Graupner (1997e, 1997f)
18. Case Dudgeon v. UK 1981; Norris v. Ireland 1988; Modinos v. Cyprus 1989
19. A.D.T. vs. UK 2000
20. Case Euan Sutherland v. UK (appl. 25186/94, report 01.07.97)
21. Euan Sutherland v. UK (par. 59, 64)
22. Euan Sutherland v. UK (par. 64f)
23. L. & V. vs. Austria 2003; S.L. vs. Austria 2003
24. S.L. vs. Austria 2003
25. Already the study of Fernand-Laurent (1988) on behalf of the UN-Commission on Human Rights (elaborated by appointment of the Economic and Social Council) called for an end of discrimination of homosexuals and for equal age of limits for homo- and heterosexual contact.
26. CRC/C/15/Add.134, 16.10.2000; CRC/C/15/Add.135, 16.10.2000; *www. unhchr.ch*
27. CRC/C/15/Add. 188, 09.10.2002); *www.unhchr.ch*

28. former Conference for Security and Cooperation in Europe (CSCE)
29. For details cf. Graupner, 1995, Vol. 1, 433ff; 1997b, Vol. 1, 433ff), European Parliament (1997, 1998a, 1998b, 1998c, 2003)
30. Opinion 216 (2000); Rec. 1474 (2000) (par. 7) ; In September 2001 the *Committee of Ministers of the Council of Europe* assured the Assembly "that it will continue to follow the issue of discrimination based on sexual orientation with close attention" (Doc 9217, 21.09.2001).
31. Norway (1981), France (1985, 1986), Denmark (1986), Sweden (1987), Ireland (1989), the Netherlands (1992, 1994), Finland (1995), Austria (1993), Slovenia (1995), Spain (1995), Iceland (1996), Luxemburg (1997), Hungary (1997), Romania (2000), Czech Republic (2001), Germany (2001), Belgium (2003), Lithuania (2003), Malta (2003). South-Africa (1994, 1996), Ecuador (1998) and Fiji (1998) even enshrined the principle of non-discrimination on the basis of "sexual orientation" in their national constitutions. For examples outside of Europe and for sources cf. the extensive survey in Graupner (1998a, 1998c, 1999a, 2003).
32. See *Parliamentary Assembly of the Council of Europe*: Written Declaration No. 227, Febr. 1993; Halonen-Resolution (Order 488 [1993]); Opinion No. 176 (1993); Opinion 221 (2000); *http://assembly.coe.int*
33. CONF/4005/97 ADD 2, *http://europa.eu.int/eur-lex*
34. Art. 13 par. 1 EC: "Without prejudice to the other provisions of this Treaty and within the limits of the powers conferred by it upon the Community, the Council, acting unanimously on a proposal from the Commission and after consulting the European Parliament, may take appropriate action to combat discrimination based on sex, racial or ethnic origin, religion or belief, disability, age or sexual orientation."
35. Directive 2000/78/EC, *http://europa.eu.int/eur-lex*. The directive has to be implemented in all member states until December 2nd, 2003 at the latest (Art. 18).
36. OJ C 364/1-22 (18.12.2000), *http://europa.eu.int/eur-lex*; The Charter is not binding but it is used in interpretation of binding EU-law (see *max.mobil Telekommunikation Service GmbH*, par. 48)
37. *Salgueiro da Silva Mouta vs. Portugal* 1999 (par. 36)
38. *Lustig-Prean & Beckett vs. UK* 1999 (par. 90); *Smith & Grady vs. UK* 1999 (par. 97); *Salgueiro da Silva Mouta vs. Portugal* 1999 (par. 36); *L. & V. v. Austria* 2003 (par. 45, 52); *S.L. v. Austria* 2003 (par. 37, 44)
39. *L. & V. v. Austria* 2003 (par. 45); *S.L. v. Austria*. 2003 (par. 37)
40. *Karner vs. Austria* 2003
41. *Lustig-Prean & Beckett vs. UK* 1999 (par. 90); *Smith & Grady vs. UK* 1999 (par. 97); *L. & V. v. Austria* 2003 (par. 52); *S.L. v. Austria* 2003 (par. 44)
42. *Christine Goodwin vs. UK* (28957/95), judg. 11.07.2002 [GC] (par. 91); *I. vs. UK* (25680/94), judg. 11.07.2002 [GC] (par. 71)
43. All countries which took over the french Code Napoléon or which oriented their criminal law after it, repealed the ban on homosexuality during the 19th century. Homosexuality has not been mentioned in the criminal law anymore, homo- and heterosexual relations were treated equally. Special offenses–as there are higher minimum age limits, bans on homosexual prostitution only or higher penalties in the case of homosexual acts in a public place–did not exist. The (uniform) age limits have been set very low, between 12 and 14 in most states. Some countries in the beginning even had no fixed limit. The countries however which did not come under the influence of the Code Napoléon kept the total ban on homosexuality up to the 20th century. Decriminalization in the 19th century has been confined to the Romanic jurisdictions. But also there discriminatory regu-

lations have been reintroduced, in most cases higher age limits for homosexual relations (for some time). Italy and Turkey have been the only countries in Europe which decriminalized homosexuality in the 19th century and ever since have been treating homosexual relations equally under its criminal legislation. But only Portugal (1912-1945), Spain (1928-1934), Serbia (1929-1994) and Romania (1948-1996) (and the Soviet Union 1934-1993 (year when Russia abolished the law; the Ucraine did 1991, Estonia 1992, Latvia 1992, Lithuania 1993, Belarus in 1994, Moldova 1995) reintroduced the total ban on homosexuality (cf. for details Graupner 1997b, 1998a).

44. In the case of seduction-provisions only two (Färöer, Greece) jurisdiction(s) do establish differences concerning minors (see Table III).

45. Portugal repealed all special laws against homosexual behaviour in 1982 and since 1945 established an equal age limit of 16. The current inequality results from a lowering of the minimum age limit in 1995 for heterosexual contact only (from 16 to 14). The following inequality between hetero- and homosexual contacts has been critized in the literature (Pizarro Beleza 1996, 27).

46. cf. also the similar provisions in Austria, Finland, Italy and Portugal

47. cf. Deutscher Bundesrat (1992), Deutscher Bundestag (1993), Graupner (1995, Vol. 1, 361-408; 1997b, Vol. 1, 361-408)

48. Case-law of the German Supreme Court ("Bundesgerichtshof") on the identical Art. 174 par. 4 CC and the former Art. 175 par. 4 CC. In interpreting Art. 182 par. 4 CC the Federal Court sticks to this case-law (cf. BGH 06.04.1995, 1 StR 82/95).

49. This complaint has to be made within three months after knowledge of deed and perpetrator (Art. 77b CC). The public prosecutor is entitled to prosecution only if due to an outstanding public interest in prosecution he deems prosecution necessary (Art. 182 CC). BGH 06.04.1995, 1 StR 82/95

50. Art. 207b CC; Bertel & Sachwaighofer (2002), Ebensperger & Murschetz (2002), Friedrich (2002), Graupner (2002); *www.paragraph209.at, www.RKLambda.at*

51. See the *Netherlands* where 80-90% of the cases (of seduction of 16 and 17 year old adolescents) are dropped. Many of these countries also bind prosecution upon a complaint (by the adolescent or his legal representative): *Germany* (for the alternative "practicing on lacking ability to sexual self-determination," Art. 182 par. 2 CC), *Monaco* (girls over 15), the Netherlands (over 12; as soon as the minor is 16 even just he himself can complain, legal representatives can do so for minors under 16 only), *Portugal* (over 12), *Spain* (also the state prosecutor can complain). Also the offence of seduction by a false promise of marriage (which has not been considered for this calculation, see table IV/FN 1) in the successor states of the *former Yugoslavia*, in *San Marino* and in *Turkey* can be prosecuted on the basis of a complaint (by the minor or his legal representative) only. The same is true for the offenses of "corruption of minors" in *Malta* and the *Vatican* (see table IV/FN 1).

52. Switzerland and Iceland are the only countries which do allow legally effective consent into "seduction" from the age of 16 only *and* do establish a multistage system *and* do not allow for extensive screening.

53. See table VIII

54. Wyoming set the minimum age limit even as high as 19. Just one of the jurisdictions studied worldwide does establish a higher one: Chile, where the limit is 20. The most restrictive legislation the author found was Canadian legislation between the years 1955 and 1969: homosexual but also heterosexual "gross indecency" (potentially all kinds of sexual contact) has been a criminal offense regardless of the age of the partners. In 1969 the offense has slightly been modified: if not more than two persons were

present *and* the partners were married or both above 21 years of age. In 1988 this law has been abolished (for details cf. Graupner 1997b, 334/46).

55. With the exception of total bans on (certain) homosexual acts in some US-states (see table VIII) homosexual contacts are subject to the same regulations as heterosexual ones. Homosexual conduct (or some kinds of) therefore either is totally illegal or subject to the same regulations. Unequal laws for the protection of youths (as different age limits) for hetero- and homosexual contacts are not known in the US-law.

56. Besides the provisions on "child"-pornography (see VII. below)

57. Art. 64 CC

58. Chapter 1 § 11 CC

59. In 1998 Germany extended this principle of exterritoriality also to its seduction-provision (Art. 182 CC) (cf. IV above and Table III.) (Art. 1 lit. 2b 6th Criminal Law Reform Act 1998).

60. Art. 227-27-1 CP

61. For sexual contacts with persons under 14 only.

62. This is of importance since these countries as a principle do confine the absolute application of their criminal law to offenses on their territory. The question does not arise in countries, which bound their citizens to their criminal law wherever they are and irrespective of the law of the country where the offence occurs (for example the Netherlands, Italy, Poland, the Czech Republic). For Italy see also Art. 604 CP, as amended by law 02.08.1998 (no. 269), in relation to Art. 4ff CP.

63. France applies its law to its citizens and to foreigners permanently residing in France

64. Also Norway applies its respective laws such extensively. But for the prosecution of an offence committed by a non-resident foreigner abroad a decision by the king is afforded.

65. Traditionally the UK restricted the power of its jurisdiction to actions within its own territory. Sexual conduct outside the Kingdom did not fulfill an offence triable by British courts even if the conduct was an offence both at home and abroad. In 1997 the British parliament passed a law however making also (certain) sexual offenses (against persons under 16) abroad triable by its courts. But as a requirement the conduct can only be prosecuted in the UK if it is an offence both in the UK and abroad (s. 7 & 8 Sex Offenders Act 1997).

66. §§ 2252, 2256 Federal Criminal Code. The legislation was introduced in 1978 with an age limit of 16 (Pub.L. 95-225, § 2(a), Feb. 6, 1978, 92 Stat. 7, 8). 1984 the age was raised to 18 (Pub.L.98-292, §§ 4, 5, 7(2), May 21, 1984, 98 Stat. 204, 205, 206).

67. §§ 2251-2256 Federal Criminal Code; Confirmation of Intent of Congress in Enacting Section 2252 and 2256. Section 160003 of Pub.L. 103-322)

68. ch. 46, 40-41-42 Elizabeth II.23.06.1993

69. Council Framework Decision 2004/68/JHA of 22 December 2003 on combating the sexual exploitation of children and child pornography, OJ 13 L/44-48, 20.01.2004, *http://europa.eu.int/eur-lex/en/archive/2004/l_01320040120en.html*. See *http://europa.eu.int/prelex/rech_simple.cfm?CL=en*; COM [2000] 854, OJ C 62 E/327-330, 27.02.2001), *http://europa.eu.int/prelex/detail_dossier_real.cfm?CL=de&DosId=161008#311962*; *www.RKLambda.at* (News)

70. Only *Estonia, France* (Art. 227-23 CC), *Italy* (Art. 600ter CC; exploitation afforded), *Latvia* (Art. 165 CC), *Spain* (Art. 189 CC) *and Sweden* (Ch. 6 § 7 (2) CC; restricted to seduction to making depictions) have an age limit in the criminal law for depicting sexual activity that is higher than the general age-limit for sex. And also none

of the provisions of these countries are nearly as extensive as the offenses prescribed by the EU-Framework-Decision of 2003.

71. The original proposal by the Commission even obliged to criminalize "inducement" of "children" (under 18) into sexual contact. That would even have made it a criminal offence to proposition 17 ½ year-old young men and women. In later versions this offence has been dropped (see www.RKLambda.at [News], http://register.consilium.eu.int/scripts/utfregisterDir/WebDriver.exe?MIval=simle&MIlang=EN).

72. Also the *Cybercrime-Convention* of the Council of Europe (ETS 185, 23.11.2001; *http://conventions.coe.int*) and the 2000 *Optional Protocol* to the UN-Convention on the Rights of the Child "on the sale of children, child prostitution and child pornography" (*www.unhchr.ch*) do not proscribe such extensive offenses. Both do not require possession for private purposes and depictions of (younger looking) adults neither virtual productions to be made crimes. And the Cybercrime-Convention does not oblige member-states to criminalize depictions of persons of 16 years of age and above.

73. See the other chapter of Graupner in this book. In 2002 the *U.S. Supreme Court* held a ban on virtual child pornography, not involving images of real persons under 18, as violating the right to freedom of speech (*Ashcroft vs. Free Speech Coalition*, 2002).

74. The European Court of Human Rights has already held that states can not set aside their obligations under the Convention by transferring competencies to supra-national bodies. So the Court claims its supervising power to also extend to acts of the European Union (or the EC) and to acts of member states determined by Union (or EC) law (see for instance *Matthews vs. UK* 1999; *Segi & Others and Gestoras pro Amnistia & Others vs. 15 member states of the European Union*, 2002).

75. Working Group of Experts on Sexual Offenses (1997-1999); Schweizer Expertenkommission (1977), Swedish Commission on Sexual Offenses (1976), Danish Council on the Criminal Law (1975), Bundesministerium für Justiz (1956-1962)

76. Niederländische Strafrechtsreformkommission (Melai-Kommission) 1980

77. Deutscher Bundesrat (1992), Deutscher Bundestag (1993); Österreichischer Nationalrat (1995)

78. The Norwegian Criminal Law Commission (which recommended to lower the minimum age limit in Norway from 16 to 15; Justis-og politiedepartementet 1997) ; The Finnish Criminal Law Commission 1993 (which recommended to lower the minimum age limit in Finland from 16 to 15; Oikeusministeriön 1993); The Law Reform Commission of Ireland (1990); but also: "Although age limits are necessarily arbitrary, the age in this country of 15 on one view seems particularly difficult to justify . . . No doubt, prosecutorial discretion and flexible sentencing can, and probably does, avoid the grosser injustices which such a law could produce: nonetheless, its retention on the statute book in this form is at least questionable" (The Law Reform Commission of Ireland 1989, 65).

79. Policy Advisory Committee on Sexual Offenses 1981 (and, just adopting its recommendations, the Criminal Law Revision Committee 1984)

80. Niederländische Strafrechtsreformkommission (Melai-Kommission) 1980

81. Working Group of Experts on Sexual Offenses (1997-1999); Schweizer Expertenkommission (1977), Swedish Commission on Sexual Offenses (1976), Danish Council on the Criminal Law (1975), Bundesministerium für Justiz (1956-1962)

82. The Norwegian Criminal Law Commission 1997 (Justis-ogpolitiedepart ementet 1997); The Finnish Criminal Law Commission 1993 (Oikeusministeriön 1993); The Law Reform Commission of Ireland 1990 (only for vaginal and anal (not oral) penetration of (not by) adolescents it recommended an age limit of 17)

83. Policy Advisory Committee on Sexual Offenses 1981 (and just adopting its recommendations the Criminal Law Revision Committee 1984)
84. Swedish Commission on Sexual Offenses (1976)
85. Deutscher Bundesrat (1992), Deutscher Bundestag (1993)
86. Austrian National Council, Committee of Justice, Public Hearing of Experts, 11.12.2003 (minutes to be published at *http://www.rklambda.at/eu_plan.htm*).
87. Policy Advisory Committee on Sexual Offenses 1981 (and just adopting its recommendations the Criminal Law Revision Committee 1984)
88. The Norwegian Criminal Law Commission 1997 (Justis-og politiedepartementet 1997); The Finnish Criminal Law Commission 1993 (Oikeusministeriön 1993); The Law Reform Commission of Ireland (1990), Niederländische Strafrechtsreformkommission (Melai-Kommission) 1980, Schweizer Expertenkommission (1977), Swedish Commission on Sexual Offenses (1976), Danish Council on the Criminal Law (1975), Health Council of the Netherlands (1969)
89. Deutscher Bundesrat (1992), Deutscher Bundestag (1973, 1990, 1993)
90. Österreichischer Nationalrat (1995)
91. June 1998 the House of Commons (by 234:194) rejected a motion to introduce an age-limit of 18 for relationships of authority (Stonewall 1998)
92. cf. Graupner (1995, Vol. 1, 596; 1997b, Vol. 1, 596)
93. For a detailed reasoning see Graupner (1997b, 1999b)
94. The European Court of Human Rights awarded a juvenile considerable compensation payments for–between the ages of 14 and 18–not having been allowed by the law to engage in intimate relations with (adult) partners of his choice (*S.L. v. Austria* 2003). A general minimum age limit of 14 has been upheld by the European Commission of Human Rights (*M.K. vs. Austria* 1997).

REFERENCES

Bertel, Ch. & Schwaighofer, K. (2002), *Österreichisches Strafrecht–Besonderer Teil II*, 5th ed., Springer: Vienna
Bundesministerium für Justiz (1956-1962). *Protokolle der Kommission zur Ausarbeitung eines Strafgesetzenwurfes*, Vienna, Austria.
Criminal Law Revision Committee (1984). *15th Report: Sexual Offenses*, London.
Committee of Ministers (1993). *Sexual exploitation, pornography and prostitution of, and trafficking in, children and young adults–Recommendation No. R(91)11 and Report of the European Committee on Crime Problems*, Council of Europe Press: Strasbourg.
Council of Ministers of the European Union (1997). *Joint Action concerning the combat against trafficking in humans and sexual exploitation of children*, 97/154/JI, OJ L 63/2-6.
Danish Council for the Criminal Law (1975). *Straffelovradets udtalelse om strafferetlige aldersgraenser for seksuelle forhold;* Betaenkning nr. 747, Copenhagen 1975; unpublished translation into German by Mag. Kurt Krickler, Wien 1984; see Council of Europe: Sexual Behaviour and Attitudes and Their Implications for Criminal Law, Reports presented to the 15th Criminological Research Conference 1982, European Committee on Crime Problems, p. 188, Strasbourg 1984.
Demsar, Drago (1981). *Law and Development in Yugoslavia*, in: Contemporary Developments in the Definition and Punishment of Sex Offenses, Nouvelles Études Pénales I, Toulouse.

Deutscher Bundesrat (1992). *Niederschrift über die 9. Sitzung des Ausschusses für Frauen und Jugend am 04. März 1992 in Bonn, Öffentliche Anhörung zum Sexualstrafrecht (§§ 175, 182 StGB),* Bonn

Deutscher Bundestag (1970). *28., 29. und 30. Sitzung des Sonderausschusses für die Strafrechtsreform,* 6. Wahlperiode, Stenographischer Dienst, *Bonn 23., 24. und 25. November 1970,* Bonn.

Deutscher Bundestag (1990). *Aids: Fakten und Konsequenzen, Endbericht der Enquetekommission des 11. Deutschen Bundestages "Gefahren von Aids und wirksame Wege zu ihrer Eindämmung," Zur Sache 90, 13,* Bonn.

Deutscher Bundestag (1993). *Protokoll der 93. Sitzung des Rechtsausschusses am Mittwoch, dem 20. Oktober 1993 in Bonn, Öffentliche Anhörung,* Protokoll Nr. 93, Bonn

Ebensperger, St. & Murschetz, V. (2003), Aufhebung des § 209 StGB durch den Verfassungsgerichtshof, in: *Juristische Ausbildung und Praxisvorbereitung.*

European Parliament (1997). *Resolution on the Respect for Human Rights Within the European Union,* 08 April, A4-0112/97, Strasbourg.

European Parliament (1998a). *Resolution on the Respect for Human Rights Within the European Union,* 17 February, A4-0034/98, Strasbourg.

European Parliament (1998b). *Resolution on Equal Rights of Lesbians and Gay Men in the European Union,* 17 September, B4-0824 & 0852/98, Strasbourg.

European Parliament (1998c). *Resolution on the Respect for Human Rights Within the European Union (1997),* Strasbourg, 17.12.1998.

European Parliament (2000). *Resolution on the Respect for Human Rights Within the European Union (1998/99),* A5-0050/00, Strasbourg, 16.03.2000

European Parliament (2003). *Resolution on Fundamental Rights Right in the European Union (2002),* A5-0281/2003, Strasbourg, 04.09.2003.

Fernand-Laurent, Jean (1988). *The Legal and Social Problems of Sexual Minorities,* UN-Economic and Social Council Document (E/Cn.4/Sub.2/1988/31.06.1988), Commission on Human Rights, Sub-Commission on Prevention of Discrimination and Protection of Minorities, Geneva Friedrich, M. (2002), *Kein Reifezeugnis für die Koalition,* in: *Der Standard,* 11 July 2002.

Graupner, Helmut (1995). *Sexualität, Jugendschutz & Menschenrechte–Über das Recht von Kindern und Jugendlichen auf sexuelle Selbstbestimmung,* 2 Volumes, University of Vienna (Diss. iur.)

Graupner, Helmut (1997a). *Keine Liebe zweiter Klasse–Diskriminierungsschutz und Partnerschaft für gleichgeschlechtlich L(i)ebende,* Rechtskomitee LAMBDA, Vienna.

Graupner, Helmut (1997b). *Sexualität, Jugendschutz & Menschenrechte–Über das Recht von Kindern und Jugendlichen auf sexuelle Selbstbestimmung,* 2 Volumes, Peter Lang, Frankfurt, M/Berlin/Bern/New York/Paris/Vienna.

Graupner, Helmut (1997c). Sexuelle Mündigkeit–Die Strafgesetzgebung in europäischen und außereuropäischen Ländern, *Zeitschrift für Sexualforschung* 10(4), 281-310, Stuttgart.

Graupner, Helmut (1997d). *Austria.* In: West, D.J. & Green, R., *Socio-Legal Control of Homosexuality–A Multi-Nation Comparison,* 269-287, Plenum: New York.

Graupner, H. (1997e), Wider die Gewalt–für die selbstbestimmte Sexualität. Das neue Sexualstrafrecht in Spanien und Italien (Teil I), *Sexus* 1 (II-IV), Aaptos: Vienna

Graupner, H. (1997f). Wider die Gewalt–für die selbstbestimmte Sexualität. Das neue Sexualstrafrecht in Spanien und Italien (Teil II), *Sexus* 2 (II-IV), Aaptos: Vienna
Graupner, Helmut (1998a). *Von "Widernatürlicher Unzucht" zu "Sexueller Orientierung"–Homosexualität & Recht,* in: Roth, R. & Hey, B., Que(e)erdenken. Weibliche/männliche Homosexualität und Wissenschaft, Studienverlag, Innsbruck.
Graupner, Helmut (1998b). *Homosexualität und Strafrecht in Österreich,* 6th ed., Rechtskomitee LAMBDA: Vienna.
Graupner, Helmut (1998c). *Keine Liebe zweiter Klasse–Diskriminierungsschutz und Partnerschaft für gleichgeschlechtlich L(i)ebende,* 2nd ed., Rechtskomitee LAMBDA: Vienna.
Graupner, Helmut (1998d). *Update on Austria.* Euroletter 65 (November).
Graupner, Helmut (1999a). *Keine Liebe zweiter Klasse–Diskriminierungsschutz und Partnerschaft für gleichgeschlechtlich L(i)ebende,* 3rd ed., Rechtskomitee LAMBDA: Vienna.
Graupner, H.(1999b). Love versus Abuse–Crossgenerational Sexual Relations of Minors: A Gay Rights Issue?, *Journal of Homosexuality,* 37 (4) 23-56.
Graupner, H. (2000). Sexual Consent–The Criminal Law in Europe and Overseas, *Archives of Sexual Behaviour,* Vol. 29, No. 5, 415-461
Graupner, H. (2002). Die verhängnisvolle Kinokarte–Vom politischen Mißbrauch einer verfassungsgerichtlichen Entscheidung, in: *Der Standard,* 29 July 2002, 27.
Graupner, H. (2003). *Keine Liebe zweiter Klasse–Diskriminierungsschutz & Partnerschaft für gleichgeschlechtlich L(i)ebende,* 4th ed., Rechtskomitee LAMBDA: Vienna; *www.RKLambda.at* (Publikationen).
Health Council of the Netherlands (1969). *Memorie van Toelichting,* Bijlage 4, Zitting 1969-70–10347; German Translation: Speijer-Report, Pais Press Produkt, Schweiz 1976
Horstkotte, H. (1984). *Ages and Conditions of Consent in Sexual Matters,* in: Council of Europe, European Committee on Crime Problems, Sexual Behaviour and Attitudes and Their Implications for Criminal Law: Reports presented to the 15th Criminological Research Conference 1982, p. 165ff, Strasbourg.
House of Commons (1994). *Minutes of the Debate on the Criminal Justice and Public Order Bill,* 21.02.1994, 48 CD 21/28, London.
Human Rights Committee (1998). *Concluding Observations to the Report of Austria Submitted under Art. 40 International Convenant of Civil and Political Rights,* 46th session, Geneva: 11.11.1998
International Gay and Lesbian Human Rights Commission (IGLHRC) (1998). *IGLHRC Celebrates the 50th Anniversary of the UDHR,* email 11.12.
Justis-og politidepartementet (1997). *Seksuallovbrudd–traffelovkommisjonens delutredning VI,* NOU 1997:23, Oslo.
Ministry of Justice (1997). *Letter to the Author,* 07.07., Kiev.
Ministry of Labour (1998). *Violence Against Women–Government bill 1997/98:55,* Fact Sheet, Swedish Government Offices: Stockholm.
Niederländische Strafrechtsreformkommission (Melai-Kommission) (1980). *Schlußbericht 1980,* see Edward Brongersma, Schutzalter 12 Jahre?–Sex mit Kindern in der niederländischen Gesetzgebung, in: Angelo Leopardi, Der pädosexuelle Komplex, S. 213ff, Berlin/Fft. 1988

Note (1991). Constitutional Barriers to Civil and Criminal Restrictions on Pre- and Extramarital Sex. 104 *Harvard Law Review* 1660

Oikeusministeriön (1993). *Seksuaalirikokset–Rikoslakiprojektin ehdotus.* Oikeusministeriön lainvalmisteluosaston julkaisu 8. Helsinki.

Österreichischer Nationalrat (1995). *Unterausschuß des Justizausschusses, Zusammenfassende Darstellung der Expertenanhörung zu den §§ 209, 220, 221 StGB*, 10.10.1995 (Doc: U-AU-JUS.DOC).

Pizarro Beleza, Teresa (1996). *Sem Sombra de Pecado–O Repensar dos Crimes Sexuais na Revisao do Código Penal*, Lisboa.

Policy Advisory Committee on Sexual Offenses (1981). *Report on the Ages of Consent in Relation to Sexual Offenses*, London.

Posner, Richard A. & Silbaugh, Katharine B. (1996). *A Guide to America's Sex Laws*, The University of Chicago Press: Chicago & London

Rebane, Ilmar (1980). *Commented Soviet Estonian Penal Code*, Eesti Raamat: Tallin.

Schweizer Expertenkommission für die Revision des Strafgesetzbuchs (1977). *Aenderung des Strafgesetzbuches und des Militärstrafgesetzes betreffend die Strafbaren Hanldungen gegen Leib und Leben, gegen die Sittlichkeit und gegen die Familie: Vorentwurf und Erläuternder Bericht zu den Vorentwürfen*, 3.82 600 14786/1, 3.82 1400 14786/2, Bern.

Swedish Commission on Sexual Offenses (1976). Kjellin-Sexualbrottsutredningen, *Sexuella övergrepp*, Stockholm 1976; (1) see Brongersma; E.: The Meaning of "Indecency" with Respect to Moral Offenses Involving Children, British Journal of Criminology, 20, 20-34, 1980; (2) see Council of Europe: Sexual Behaviour and Attitudes and Their Implications for Criminal Law, Reports presented to the 15th Criminological Research Conference 1982, European Committee on Crime Problems, Strasbourg 1984; (3) see Verband von 1974: *Ein Land schafft gleiches Recht–Beitrag zur Diskussion um Paragraph 175 StGB nach amtlichen Drucksachen des Schwedischen Reichstages*, Hamburg 1979

The Law Reform Commission of Ireland (1989). *Consultation Paper on Child Sexual Abuse*, Dublin.

The Law Reform Commission of Ireland (1990). *Report on Child Sexual Abuse*, Dublin.

Walmsley, Roy & White, Karen (1979). *Sexual Offenses–Consent and Sentencing*, Home Office Research Study No. 54, London.

Working Group of Experts on Sexual Offenses (1997-1999), *Protocols of Deliberations*, Ministry of Justice, Vienna (unpublished)

APPENDIX 1. Council Framework Decision 2004/68/JHA of 22 December 2003 on Combating the Sexual Exploitation of Children and Child Pornography

THE COUNCIL OF THE EUROPEAN UNION,

Having regard to the Treaty on European Union, and in particular Article 29, Article 31(1)(e) and Article 34(2)(b) thereof,

Having regard to the proposal from the Commission([1]),

Having regard to the opinion of the European Parliament([2]),

Whereas:

(1) The Action Plan of the Council and the Commission on how best to implement the provisions of the Treaty of Amsterdam on an area of freedom, security and justice([3]), the conclusions of the Tampere European Council and the Resolution of the European Parliament of 11 April 2000 include or call for legislative action against sexual exploitation of children and child pornography, including common definitions, charges and penalties.

(2) Council Joint Action 97/154/ JHA of 24 February 1997 concerning action to combat trafficking in human beings and sexual exploitation of children([4]) and Council Decision 2000/375/ JHA of 29 May 2000 to combat child pornography on the Internet([5]) need to be followed by further legislative action addressing the divergence of legal approaches in the Member States and contributing to the development of efficient judicial and law enforcement cooperation against sexual exploitation of children and child pornography.

(3) The European Parliament, in its Resolution of 30 March 2000 on the Commission Communication on the implementation of measures to combat child sex tourism, reiterates that child sex tourism is a criminal act closely linked to those of sexual exploitation of children and of child pornography, and requests the Commission to submit to the Council a proposal for a framework Decision establishing minimum rules relating to the constituent elements of these criminal acts.

(4) Sexual exploitation of children and child pornography constitute serious violations of human rights and of the fundamental right of a child to a harmonious upbringing and development.

(5) Child pornography, a particularly serious form of sexual exploitation of children, is increasing and spreading through the use of new technologies and the Internet.

(6) The important work performed by international organisations must be complemented by that of the European Union.

(7) It is necessary that serious criminal offences such as the sexual exploitation of children and child pornography be addressed by a comprehensive approach in which the constituent elements of criminal law common to all Member States, including effective, proportionate and dissuasive sanctions, form an integral part together with the widest possible judicial cooperation.

(8) In accordance with the principles of subsidiarity and proportionality, this framework Decision confines itself to the minimum required in order to achieve those objectives at European level and does not go beyond what is necessary for that purpose.

(9) Penalties must be introduced against the perpetrators of such offences which are sufficiently stringent to bring sexual exploitation of children and child pornography within the scope of instruments already adopted for the purpose of combating organised crime, such

as Council Joint Action 98/699/JHA of 3 December 1998 on money laundering, the identification, tracing, freezing, seizing and confiscation of the instrumentalities and the proceeds from crime([6]) and Council Joint Action 98/733/JHA of 21 December 1998 on making it a criminal offence to participate in a criminal organisation in the Member States of the European Union([7]).

(10) The specific characteristics of the combat against the sexual exploitation of children must lead Member States to lay down effective, proportionate and dissuasive sanctions in national law. Such sanctions should also be adjusted in line with the activity carried on by legal persons.

(11) Victims who are children should be questioned according to their age and stage of development for the purpose of investigation and prosecution of offences falling under this framework Decision.

(12) This framework Decision is without prejudice to the powers of the Community.

(13) This framework Decision should contribute to the fight against sexual exploitation of children and child pornography by complementing the instruments adopted by the Council, such as Joint Action 96/700/JHA of 29 November 1996 establishing an incentive and exchange programme for persons responsible for combating trade in human beings and sexual exploitation of children([8]), Joint Action 96/748/JHA of 16 December 1996 extending the mandate given to the Europol Drugs Unit([9]), Joint Action 98/428/JHA of 29 June 1998 on the creation of a European Judicial Network([10]), Joint Action 96/277/JHA of 22 April 1996 concerning a framework for the exchange of liaison magistrates to improve judicial cooperation between the Member States of the European Union([11]), and Joint Action 98/427/JHA of 29 June 1998 on good practice in mutual legal assistance in criminal matters([12]), as well as acts adopted by the European Council and the Council, such as Decision No 276/1999/EC of the European Parliament and of the Council of 25 January 1999 adopting a multiannual Community action plan on promoting safer use of the Internet by combating illegal and harmful content on global networks ([13]), and Decision No 293/2000/EC of the European Parliament and of the Council of 24 January 2000 adopting a programme of Community action (the Daphne programme) 2000 to 2003) on preventive measures to fight violence against children, young persons and women([14]),

HAS ADOPTED THIS FRAMEWORK DECISION:

Article 1

Definitions

For the purposes of this framework Decision:

(a) "child" shall mean any person below the age of 18 years;

(b) "child pornography" shall mean pornographic material that visually depicts or represents:

    (i) a real child involved or engaged in sexually explicit conduct, including lascivious exhibition of the genitals or the pubic area of a child; or

    (ii) a real person appearing to be a child involved or engaged in the conduct mentioned in (i); or

    (iii) realistic images of a nonexistent child involved or engaged in the conduct mentioned in (i);

(c) "computer system" shall mean any device or group of interconnected or related devices, one or more of which, pursuant to a programme, perform automatic processing of data;

(d) "legal person" shall mean any entity having such status under the applicable law, except for States or other public bodies in the exercise of State authority and for public international organisations.

Article 2

Offences concerning sexual exploitation of children

Each Member State shall take the necessary measures to ensure that the following intentional conduct is punishable:

(a) coercing a child into prostitution or into participating in pornographic performances, or profiting from or otherwise exploiting a child for such purposes;

(b) recruiting a child into prostitution or into participating in pornographic performances;

(c) engaging in sexual activities with a child, where

   (i) use is made of coercion, force or threats;

   (ii) money or other forms of remuneration or consideration is given as payment in exchange for the child engaging in sexual activities; or

   (iii) abuse is made of a recognised position of trust, authority or influence over the child.

Article 3

Offences concerning child pornography

1. Each Member State shall take the necessary measures to ensure that the following intentional conduct whether undertaken by means of a computer system or not, when committed without right is punishable:

(a) production of child pornography;

(b) distribution, dissemination or transmission of child pornography;

(c) supplying or making available child pornography;

(d) acquisition or possession of child pornography.

2. A Member State may exclude from criminal liability conduct relating to child pornography:

(a) referred to in Article 1(b)(ii) where a real person appearing to be a child was in fact 18 years of age or older at the time of the depiction;

(b) referred to in Article 1(b)(i) and (ii) where, in the case of production and possession, images of children having reached the age of sexual consent are produced and possessed with their consent and solely for their own private use. Even where the existence of consent has been established, it shall not be considered valid, if for example superior age, maturity, position, status, experience or the victim's dependency on the perpetrator has been abused in achieving the consent;

(c) referred to in Article 1(b)(iii), where it is established that the pornographic material is produced and possessed by the producer solely for his or her own private use, as far as no pornographic material as referred to in Article 1(b)(i) and (ii) has been used for the purpose of its production, and provided that the act involves no risk for the dissemination of the material.

Article 4

Instigation, aiding, abetting and attempt

1. Each Member State shall take the necessary measures to ensure that the instigation of, or aiding or abetting in the commission of an offence referred to in Articles 2 and 3 is punishable.

2. Each Member State shall take the necessary measures to ensure that attempts to commit the conduct referred to in Article 2 and Article 3(1)(a) and (b), are punishable.

Article 5

Penalties and aggravating circumstances

1. Subject to paragraph 4, each Member State shall take the necessary measures to ensure that the offences referred to in Articles 2, 3 and 4 are punishable by criminal penalties of a maximum of at least between one and three years of imprisonment.

2. Subject to paragraph 4, each Member State shall take the necessary measures to ensure that the following offences are punishable with criminal penalties of a maximum of at least between five and ten years of imprisonment:

(a) the offences referred to in Article 2(a), consisting in "coercing a child into prostitution or into participating in pornographic performances", and the offences referred to in Article 2(c)(i);

(b) the offences referred to in Article 2(a), consisting in "profiting from or otherwise exploiting a child for such purposes", and the offences referred to in Article 2(b), in both cases as far as they refer to prostitution, where at least one of the following circumstances may apply:

- the victim is a child below the age of sexual consent under national law,

- the offender has deliberately or by recklessness endangered the life of the child,

- the offences involve serious violence or caused serious harm to the child,

- the offences are committed within the framework of a criminal organisation within the meaning of Joint Action 98/733/JHA, irrespective of the level of the penalty referred to in that Joint Action;

(c) the offences referred to in Article (a), consisting in "profiting from or otherwise exploiting a child for such purposes", and the offences referred to in Article (b), in both cases as far as they refer to pornographic performances, Article 2(c)(ii) and (iii), Article 3(1)(a), (b) and (c), where the victim is a child below the age of sexual consent under national law and at least one of the circumstances referred to under the second, third and fourth indent under point (b) of this paragraph may apply.

3. Each Member State shall take the necessary measures to ensure that a natural person, who has been convicted of one of the offences referred to in Articles 2, 3 or 4, may, if appropriate, be temporarily or permanently prevented from exercising professional activities related to the supervision of children.

4. Each Member State may provide for other sanctions, including non-criminal sanctions or measures, concerning conduct relating to child pornography referred to in Article 1(b)(iii).

Article 6

Liability of legal persons

1. Each Member State shall take the necessary measures to ensure that legal persons can be held liable for an offence referred to in Articles 2, 3 and 4 committed for their benefit by any person, acting either individually or as part of an organ of the legal person, who has a leading position within the legal person, based on:

(a) a power of representation of the legal person;

(b) an authority to take decisions on behalf of the legal person; or

(c) an authority to exercise control within the legal person.

2. Apart from the cases provided for in paragraph 1, each Member State shall take the necessary measures to ensure that legal persons can be held liable where the lack of supervision or control by a person referred to in paragraph 1 have rendered possible the commission of an offence referred to in Articles 2, 3 and 4 for the benefit of that legal person by a person under its authority.

3. Liability of legal persons under paragraphs 1 and 2 shall not exclude criminal proceedings against natural persons who are perpetrators, instigators or accessories in an offence referred to in Articles 2, 3 and 4.

Article 7

Sanctions on legal persons

1. Each Member State shall take the necessary measures to ensure that a legal person held liable pursuant to Article 6(1) is punishable by effective, proportionate and dissuasive sanctions, which shall include criminal or non-criminal fines and may include other sanctions such as:

(a) exclusion from entitlement to public benefits or aid;

(b) temporary or permanent disqualification from the practice of commercial activities;

(c) placing under judicial supervision;

(d) a judicial winding-up order; or

(e) temporary or permanent closure of establishments which have been used for committing the offence.

2. Each Member State shall take the necessary measures to ensure that a legal person held liable pursuant to Article 6(2) is punishable by effective, proportionate and dissuasive sanctions or measures.

Article 8

Jurisdiction and prosecution

1. Each Member State shall take the necessary measures to establish its jurisdiction over the offences referred to in Articles 2, 3 and 4 where:

(a) the offence is committed in whole or in part within its territory;

(b) the offender is one of its nationals; or

(c) the offence is committed for the benefit of a legal person established in the territory of that Member State.

2. A Member State may decide that it will not apply, or that it will apply only in specific cases or circumstances, the jurisdiction rules set out in paragraphs 1(b) and 1(c) where the offence is committed outside its territory.

3. A Member State which, under its laws, does not extradite its own nationals shall take the necessary measures to establish its jurisdiction over and to prosecute, where appropriate, an offence referred to in Articles 2, 3 and 4 when it is committed by one of its own nationals outside its territory.

4. Member States shall inform the General Secretariat of the Council and the Commission accordingly where they decide to apply paragraph 2, where appropriate with an indication of the specific cases or circumstances in which the decision applies.

5. Each Member State shall ensure that its jurisdiction includes situations where an offence under Article 3 and, insofar as it is relevant, under Article 4, is committed by means of a computer system accessed from its territory, whether or not the computer system is on its territory.

6. Each Member State shall take the necessary measures to enable the prosecution, in accordance with national law, of at least the most serious of the offences referred to in Article 2 after the victim has reached the age of majority.

Article 9

Protection of and assistance to victims

1. Member States shall establish that investigations into or prosecution of offences covered by this framework Decision shall not be dependent on the report or accusation made by a person subjected to the offence, at least in cases where Article 8(1)(a) applies.

2. Victims of an offence referred to in Article 2 should be considered as particularly vulnerable victims pursuant to Article 2(2), Article 8(4) and Article 14(1) of Council framework Decision 2001/220/JHA of 15 March 2001 on the standing of victims in criminal proceedings([15]).

3. Each Member State shall take all measures possible to ensure appropriate assistance for the victim's family. In particular, each Member State shall, where appropriate and possible, apply Article 4 of that framework Decision to the family referred therein.

Article 10

Territorial scope

This framework Decision shall apply to Gibraltar.

Article 11

Repeal of Joint Action 97/154/JHA

Joint Action 97/154/JHA is hereby repealed.

Article 12

Implementation

1. Member States shall take the necessary measures to comply with this framework Decision by 20 January 2006 at the latest.

2. By 20 January 2006 the Member States shall transmit to the General Secretariat of the Council and to the Commission the text of the provisions transposing into their national legislation the obligations imposed on them under this framework Decision. By 20 January 2008 on the basis of a report established using this information and a written report from the Commission, the Council shall assess the extent to which the Member States have complied with the provisions of this framework Decision.

Article 13

Entry into force

This framework Decision shall enter into force on the day of its publication in the Official Journal of the European Union.

Done at Brussels, 22 December 2003.

For the Council
The President
A. Matteoli

NOTES

(1) OJ C 62 E, 27.2.2001, p. 327.
(2) OJ C 53 E, 28.2.2002, p. 108.
(3) OJ C 19, 23.1.1999, p. 1.
(4) OJ L 63, 4.3.1997, p. 2.
(5) OJ L 138, 9.6.2000, p.1.
(6) OJ L 333, 9.12.1998, p. 1. Joint Action as amended by framework Decision 2001/500/JHA (OJ L 182, 5.7.2001, p. 1).
(7) OJ L 351, 29.12.1998, p. 1.
(8) OJ L 322, 12.12.1996, p. 7.
(9) OJ L 342, 31.12.1996, p. 4.
(10) OJ L 191, 7.7.1998, p. 4.
(11) OJ L 105, 27.4.1996, p. 1.
(12) OJ L 191, 7.7.1998, p. 1.
(13) OJ L 33, 6.2.1999, p . 1.
(14) OJ L 34, 9.2.2000, p. 1.
(15) OJ L 82, 22.3.2001, p. 1.

Index

Abortion, spontaneous, 27-28
Abraham (biblical character), 26
Abstinence, sexual, 30
  as focus of sex education, 47
ADD Health Survey. *See* National
    Longitudinal Study of
    Adolescent Health
Adolescent males, child sexual abuse
    by, 78-79
Adolescents
  African-American, age of first
      sexual intercourse, 44
  American, sexual behavior of,
      43-53
    non-coital behavior, 45,46
    positive and negative effects of,
        46
    prevalence of, 44-45
    progression behaviors in, 45-46
    same-sex relationships, 49-51
    summer and holiday peaks in, 47
  classification as children,
      9,63-70,142
  classification as young adults,
      56-57
  sexual autonomy of, 12
  sexual relationships of, 47-49
  sexual relationships with adults,
      55-62
    as child sexual abuse,
        56-57,59,60
    heterosexual adolescent
        males/women, 57,58-61
    homosexual adolescent
        males/men, 58-61
Adoption, by same-sex couples, 122
Age discrimination, 69-70

Age of consent
  in ancient Egypt, 26
  in ancient Greece, 28-29
  in ancient Rome, 29-31
  in colonial America, 32-37
  under criminal law, 114-121
    for depiction of legal sexuality,
        140,142
    English law, 32-36,38
    for females, 115,117-118
    French law, 37
    German law, 37
    for homosexual relations,
        121-123,124-128
    Italian law, 37
    Japanese law, 37
    in Latin America, 37
    for lesbians, 115
    for males, 115,117-118
    national commissions'
        recommendations regarding,
        39
    overseas (extraterritorial)
        applications of, 134,136,140,
        145-146,148-151
    within relations of authority,
        130,133-134,137-139,
        141,143-144
    seduction provisions, 114,
        123,128-130,131-133,134,
        135-136
    Spanish law, 37
    Turkish law, 37
  in early United States of America,
      36-37
  in European Union member states,
      9

for females, 26,28,115,117-118
historical overview of, 25-42
implication for child pornography criminal liability, 10,13-14
for lesbians, 115
for males, 26,28-29,115,117-118
for marriage, 28-42
in modern society, 38-39
for oral sex, 38
relationship with marriage age, 29
relationship with puberty onset, 26,27,28,39
under religious law
   Islamic law, 31
   Roman Catholic (Canon) law, 31-32,37,124,135,138,139,141,143
seduction provisions, 114,123, 128-130,131-133,134, 135-136
Albania, minimum age limits for sexual relations in, 117, 125,137,141,143
for homosexual relations, 125
seduction provisions, 135
American Historical Association, 37
Andorra, minimum age limits for sexual relations in, 117, 124,141,143
for homosexual relations, 124
seduction provisions, 123,131
"... And Then I Became Gay" (Savin-Williams), 60
Anemia, of pregnancy, 27-28
Archives of Sexual Behavior, 58-59
Aristotle, 34
Armenia, minimum age limits for sexual relations in, 117, 124,141,143
for homosexual relations, 124
seduction provisions, 135
Ashcroft v. *Free Speech Coalition* 2002, 13
Athens, bethrothal agreements in, 29

Australia, minimum age limits for sexual relations in, 145
Austria
legal definition of child in, 66
minimum age limits for sexual relations in, 66-67,118, 124,137,141
for homosexual relations, 124
seduction provisions, 130,131,135
sex education in, 68
Austrian Society for Sex Research, 12
Authority figures, adolescents' and children's sexual relations with, 130,133-134,1337-139, 141,143-144
Autonomy, sexual, 12
Ayssha, 31
Azerbaijan, minimum age limits for sexual relations in, 117, 124,141,143
for homosexual relations, 124

Belgium, minimum age limits for sexual relations in, 117, 124,137,141,143
for homosexual relations, 124
Belorus, minimum age limits for sexual relations in, 117, 141,143
for homosexual relations, 125
seduction provisions, 135
Bennet, John, 35
Bethrothal agreements, 29
Bisexuals, adolescent, 50-51,52,122
Bosnia-Herzegovina
homosexuality ban in, 125
minimum age limits for sexual relations in, 117,137,141,143
seduction provisions, 135
Brazil, minimum age limits for sexual relations in, 145
Breast feeding, maternal iron loss during, 27

Brerton, Jane, 33
British Criminological Society, 39
"Buddy sex," 49
Bulgaria, minimum age limits for
    sexual relations in, 117,
    125,141,142
  for homosexual relations, 125
  seduction provisions, 131
Bunbury, Elizabeth, 36
Bürgerliches Gesetzubch, 37

Canada, minimum age limits for sexual
    relations in, 145
Canon law, 31-32
Casanova de Seingalt, Giovanni
    Jacopo, 34
Casual sex, 49
Catholic Church
  minimum age limits for sexual
    relations set by, 31-32,37,
    124,138,139,141,143
  seduction provisions, 135
  priest sexual abuse scandal within,
    37,39
Catholic Youth League, 39
Celibacy, clerical, 37
Chandler, Behethland, 36
Chandler, John, 36
Chandler, Stephen, 36
Charles II, King of England
Child, definitions of, 78-81
  age-based, 8-9
  in Austrian law, 66
  under the European Union, 9,10,
    66,69-70,100,140,166
  under German law, 78-81,109
Chile, minimum age limits for sexual
    relations in, 145
China, minimum age limits for sexual
    relations in, 146
Civilization, 98-99
Clergy
  celibacy of, 37
  child sexual abuse by, 37,39

Code Civil, 37
Códgo civile, 37
Codice civile, 37
Coke, Edward, 34
College students
  bisexual, 59
  homosexual, 58,59
  sexual relationship patterns among,
    47-49
College women, attitudes toward
    marriage, 49
Colonial America, age of consent in,
    32-36
Committee on the Rights of the Child,
    121-122
Computers, use in pornography, 11,
    13-15,67,140,142
Condom use, by adolescents, 44
Consensus, marriage by, 31
Contraceptive use, in adolescents,
    44,45
Convention on the rights of the Child,
    9
Cornell University, 58-59
Corpus Juris Civilis, 30
Cosovo
  homosexuality ban in, 125
  minimum age limits for sexual
    relations in, 117,138,141,
    143
  seduction provisions, 135
Council of Europe (COE), 122
  Parliamentary Assembly of, 122
Council of Trent, 31
Courtship, 47-48,49
Crime
  definition of, 90-91
  fear of, 97
  against minors, 80,84
  punishment for, 91
  sexual
    adolescent victims of, 11
    sensationalization of, 97-98
Criminalization, of juvenile
    prostitution, 108-109

Criminal law, regarding juvenile
  sexual behavior, 111-171.
  See also European Union,
  Framework Decision on
  Combating the Sexual
  Exploitation of Children and
  Child Pornography; German
  Penal Code
 definitions in
  child, 78-81,109
  primary or secondary harm,
   77-78
  violence and injury, 76-78
 for depiction of legal sexuality,
  140,142
 English law, 32-36,38
 French law, 37
 German law, 37
 for homosexual relations,
  121-123,124-128
 Italian law, 37
 Japanese law, 37
 in Latin America, 37
 overseas (extraterritorial)
  applications of, 134,136,140,
   145-146,148-151
 for relationships with authority
  figures, 130,133-134,137-139
 seduction provisions,
  114,123,128-130,131-133,
  134,135-136
 Spanish law, 37
 Turkish law, 37
Croatia, minimum age limits for sexual
  relations in, 117,124,143
 for homosexual relations, 124
 seduction provisions, 131,135
Cyprus, minimum age limits for sexual
  relations in, 117,125,141,143
 for homosexual relations, 125
Czech Republic, minimum age limits
  for sexual relations in, 117,
  124,137,141
 for homosexual relations, 124
 seduction provisions, 135

Dating, trends in, 47-49
Davis, Natalie, 37
Denmark
 de facto same-sex marriage in, 122
 minimum age limits for sexual
  relations in, 117,124,137,143
 for homosexual relations, 124
 seduction provisions, 131,135
Discrimination, toward homosexuals,
  121-123
Drug use, associated with juvenile
  prostitution, 106,107
Duke of Southampton, 33
Dutch Bar Association, 39

East Anglia, 34
East Europe, juvenile prostitution in,
  106
Egypt, ancient, marriage in, 26
Elias, N., 98-99
Estonia, minimum age limits for sexual
  relations in, 117,124,141,143
 for homosexual relations, 124
 seduction provisions, 135
European Commission on Human
  Rights, 121
European Convention on Human
  Rights, 65,121
European Court on Human Rights,
  113,121,123
European Region of the International
  Lesbian and Gay Association
  (ILGA-Europe), 12
European Union, 100
 Charter of Fundamental Rights, 122
 condemnation of discrimination
  toward homosexuals by, 122
 Council of Ministers, 12,122
 Framework Decision on Combating
  the Sexual Exploitation of
  Children and Child
  Pornography, 9-24,140
 child pornography provisions of,
  9,10

criticism of, 12-13
deficiencies of, 9-10
definition of child, 10,66,
    69-70,100,140-166
Dutch version, 13
English version, 12-13
European Parliament's approval
    of, 11
European Union's Council of
    Minister's approval of, 15
French version, 13
German version, 13
Italian version of, 12-13,14
Portuguese version, 13
prostitution provisions of, 9-10,
    12-13
sexual inducement provision of,
    9,11
Spanish version, 13
text of, 165-171
proposed criminalization of juvenile
    sexual relations by, 61

Fantasies, sexual
    of homosexual adolescents, 58
    of young women, 48
Färöer, minimum age limits for sexual
        relations in, 117,125,137,143
    for homosexual relations, 125
    seduction provisions, 131,135
Finland
    de facto same-sex marriage in, 122
    minimum age limits for sexual
        relations in, 117,124,137,143
        for homosexual relations,
            124,141
        seduction provisions,
            121,123,131,135
France, minimum age limits for sexual
        relations in, 117,124,138,143
    for homosexual relations, 124
    seduction provisions, 135
Friends, sexual relations with, 49,59,60
    among lesbians, 50-51

Geer, Nancy, 35
Geographia (Strabo), 28
Georgia, minimum age limits for
        sexual relations in, 117,
        124,141
    for homosexual relations, 124
German Lesbian and Gay Association,
    12
German Penal Code, regarding
        juvenile sexual behavior,
        90-96
    application to sexual aggression and
        child abuse, 95-103
    aptitude or expediency principle
        (Geeignetheit) of, 92
    categories of suboffenses under,
        74-75
    certainty principle *(Bestimmtheit)*
        of, 92
    Chapter 13,71-87
        structure of, 73-75
    constitutional background of, 91-92
    constitutionality of, 91
    definitions in
        child, 78-81,109
        primary *versus* secondary harm,
            77-78
        violence and injury, 78-81
    historical background to, 72-74
    human rights protection under, 91
    inconsistency of sanctions under,
        95-96
    interdisciplinary approach in,
        102-103
    interpretation of, 96-97
    law enforcement's power of
        intervention under, 95
    legal protection concept in, 76
    moral paradigm of, 90
    necessity principle
        (Erforderlichkeit) of, 91
    objective of, 76
    protection of legal goods principle
        (Rechtsgüterschutz) of, 90-94
    rationale for, 76

relationship with public opinion and values, 83-84
scientific justification for, 76
sexual self-determination protection principle of, 73-75,82-83
structure of, 73-75
theories of punishment (*Strafzwecke*) of, 92
unlawfulness and guilt principle (*Unrechts-Schuldprinzip*) of, 92
victim doctrine (*Victimodogmatik*) of, 93-94
Zweckrationalität of, 96
German Sexological Association, 39
German Society for Sex Research, 12
Germany
  child prostitution in, 105-110
    among homosexual adolescents, 106,107
    criminalization of, 108-109
    drug use associated with, 106,107
    juvenile welfare system's response to, 108,109-110
    motivation for, 106,107
  child sexual abuse in
    age of perpetrators, 78-79
    prevalence of, 78-79,81
  de facto same-sex marriage in, 122
  minimum age limits for sexual relations in, 117,124,138, 141,143
    for homosexual relations, 124
  minimum age limits for sexual relations in, 117,124,138,143
  seduction provisions, 121, 123,132
  sexual crime prevalence in, 101
Ghana, minimum age limits for sexual relations in, 145
Gibraltar, minimum age limits for sexual relations in, 117,125
  for homosexual relations, 125,141

governmental expert commissions' examination of, 142-144
Gratian, 31-32,33
Greece
  ancient, age of consent in, 28-29
  minimum age limits for sexual relations in, 117,124,138,143
    for homosexual relations, 124
  seduction provisions, 121,123, 132,135
Greenland
  de facto same-sex marriage in, 122
  minimum age limits for sexual relations in, 117,124,141,143
    for homosexual relations, 124
  seduction provisions, 132,135
Guernsey, minimum age limits for sexual relations in, 117,125, 141,143
  for homosexual relations, 125

Halfhide, Sarah, 35
Hamburg, Germany, institutionalization of adolescents in, 109-110
Hathaway, Mary, 32
Hathaway, Thomas, 32
Hemmings, Sally, 36-37
Heritage Foundation Reports, 46
Herrmann, Horst, 68
Hippies, 49
Homosexual adolescents, 50-52
  prostitution among, 106,107
  sexual fantasies of, 58
Homosexuality
  in ancient Greece, 28-29
  declassification as mental illness, 122
  illegality of, 38,123,125,134
Homosexual relations, minimum age limits for, 121-123,124-128
Homosexuals, discrimination toward, 121-123
"Hooking up," 48,49

Howard League of the United Kingdom, 39
Hulse, George, 33
Human rights, 91
Hungary, minimum age limits for sexual relations in, 117, 138,143
  for homosexual relations, 124
  seduction provisions, 135

Iceland
  de facto same-sex marriage in, 122
  minimum age limits for sexual relations in, 118,124,139,143
    for homosexual relations, 124
    seduction provisions, 123, 128,132
Incarceration
  of adolescent sexual perpetrators, 11
  of sexual delinquents, 95-96
Incest, 130,133
  feminist campaign against, 56
Indentured servants, 34
India, minimum age limits for sexual relations in, 145
Infantilization, of adolescents, 68-69
Inquisitions Post Morten, 32-33
Institutionalization, of adolescents, 109-110
International Classification of Diseases (ICD), 122
International Covenant on Civil and Political Rights (ICOR), 121
International Lesbian and Gay Association, European Region of, (ILGA-Europe), 12
Ireland, minimum age limits for sexual relations in, 117,125,141,143
  for homosexual relations, 123,125
  seduction provisions, 132,135
Iron-deficiency anemia, 27-28
Isaac (biblical character), 26

Islam, 31
Isle of Man, minimum age limits for sexual relations in, 118, 124,125
  for homosexual relations, 141,143
  seduction provisions in, 135
Italy, minimum age limits for sexual relations in, 118,124,125,139
  for homosexual relations, 124
  seduction provisions, 132

Jäger, Herbert, 73,76
Japan, minimum age limits for sexual relations in, 145
Jefferson, Thomas, 36-37
Jersey, minimum age limits for sexual relations in, 118,141,143
  for homosexual relations, 125, 141,143

Kaiser Foundation, 45-46
Khadijah, 31

Labeling, 98,100-101
Lactation, maternal iron loss during, 27
Latin America, juvenile prostitution in, 106
Latvia, minimum age limits for sexual relations in, 118,124,141,143
  for homosexual relations, 124, 141,143
  seduction provisions, 135
Lesbians
  adolescent, 50-51
  sexual relations with adolescents, 80
Liechenstein, minimum age limits for sexual relations in, 118,124, 139,141,143
  for homosexual relations, 124
  seduction provisions, 132,135

Lithuania, minimum age for sexual
    relations in, 118,124,141
  seduction provisions, 135
Lolita (Nabokov), 34
Luxembourg, minimum age limits for
    sexual relations in, 118,124
  for homosexual relations, 141,143

Macedonia, minimum age limits for
    sexual relations in, 118,
    124,138,141,143
  for homosexual relations, 124
  seduction provisions, 135
Malta, minimum age limits for sexual
    relations in, 118,124,141
  for homosexual relations, 124
  seduction provisions, 135
Man-boy relationships, in ancient
    Greece, 28-29
Manichaeism, 30
Marriage
  age of consent for, 28-42
  of children, 31-32
  college women's attitudes toward, 49
  by consensus, 31
  de facto, of same-sex couples, 122
  false promises of, 128-129
Marriage age
  in ancient Greece, 28-29
  in ancient Rome, 29-31
Masterpiece (Aristotle), 34
Masturbation
  incitement to, 120
  mutual, 45,46
Media
  influence on adolescent sexual
    behavior, 44
  sensationalization of sexual crime
    by, 97-98
"Melai" Commission, 39,142
Middle Ages
  iron-deficiency anemia during,
    27-28
  marriage age during, 30-32

Miller, Alice, 68
Moldova, minimum age limits for
    sexual relations in, 117,
    124,141,143
  for homosexual relations, 124
Monaco, minimum age limits for
    sexual relations in, 118,
    124,138,141,143
  for homosexual relations, 124
  seduction provisions, 132,135
Montenegro, minimum age limits for
    sexual relations in, 117,
    138,141,143
  for homosexual relations, 124
  seduction provisions, 135
Muhammed, 31

National Council of Civil Liberties
    (U. K.), 39
National Longitudinal Study of
    Adolescent Health (ADD
    Health Survey), 47,50
National Longitudinal Survey of
    Adolescent Health, 44-45
National Longitudinal Survey of
    Youth, 44-45
National Survey of Family Growth,
    44-45
Natural law, 91
Netherlands
  adolescent male/adult female
    relationships in, 58
  Bar Association, 39
  "Melai" Commission, 39,142
  minimum age limits for sexual
    relations in, 118,124,138,143
  for homosexual relations, 124
  seduction provisions, 132,135
New York Times, 44-45
New Zealand, minimum age limits for
    sexual relations in, 145
Norway
  de facto same-sex marriage in, 122

minimum age limits for sexual
relations in, 118,124,138,143
for homosexual relations, 124

On the Education of Children
(Plutarch), 29
Oral sex
in adolescents, 45,46
adolescents' attitudes toward, 48
age of consent for, 38
Organization for Security and
Cooperation in Europe
(OSCE), 122

Pall Mall Gazette, 38
Papua New Guinea, minimum age
limits for sexual relations in,
145
Pennsylvania State University, 59
Perrot, Richard, 35
Philippines, minimum age limits for
sexual relations in, 145
Plato, 29
Plutarch, 29
Poland, minimum age limits for sexual
relations in, 118,124,138,141
for homosexual relations, 124
Pornography, child, 100
criminal liability for, 13-14
definition of, 10
legal sanctions against
criminalization of adolescents
under, 68-69
of European Commission, 9
of European Union, 140,166,167
"virtual," 14-15
Austrian Criminal code
sanctions against, 67
Portugal, minimum age limits for
sexual relations in, 118,
125,143
for homosexual relations, 123,125

seduction provisions, 132,135
Pregnancy
anemia associated with, 27-28
first, maternal age at, 27-28
Pregnancy rate, adolescent, 46
Priests, sexual abuse by, 37,39
Projectable identification, 98
Prostitutes, juvenile, social work
interventions with, 12
Prostitution, child, 38
definition of, 12-13
European Commission's provision
against, 9,13-15
European Union Framework
provisions regarding, 140
in Germany, 105-110
among homosexual adolescents,
106,107
criminalization of, 108-109
drug use associated with,
106,107
juvenile welfare system's
response to, 108,109-110
motivation for, 106,107
in Thailand, 134
Psychotherapy, for sexual perpetrators,
97
Puberty
onset age of, 26
in females, 27
in German girls, 81
in males, 27
relationship with age of consent,
26,27,28,39
relationship with age of first
sexual intercourse, 44
physical signs of, 27
Public opinion, "hysterization" of, 97
Punishment, for crime, 91

Rape
definition of, in 16th-century
England, 38
feminist campaign against, 56

by husbands, 32
    incestuous, 56
"Registered partnerships," 122
Repatriarchilization, of adolescents, 68
Republic (Plato), 29
Return of Martin Guerre, The, 37
Romania, minimum age limits for
        sexual relations in, 118,
        124,138,141,143
    for homosexual relations, 124
    seduction provisions, 132,135
Roman law, regarding marriage age,
        30-31
Rome, ancient
    age of consent in, 29-31
    marriage age in, 29-31
Romeo and Juliet (Shakespeare), 32
Russian Federation, minimum age
        limits for sexual relations in,
        117,124,141
    for homosexual relations, 124
    seduction provisions, 135

St. Augustine, 30
Same-sex couples
    adoption by, 122
    de facto marriage of, 122
Same-sex relationships
    of American adolescents, 49-51
    in ancient Greece, 28-29
San Marino, minimum age limits for
        sexual relations in, 118,124,
        141,143
    for homosexual relations, 124
    seduction provisions, 135
Serbia, minimum age limits for sexual
        relations in,
        117,125,138,141,143
    for homosexual relations, 125
    seduction provisions, 135
Servants, indentured, 34
Sex education, 46-47
    abstinence-based, 47
    in Austria, 68

Sex in the City (television program), 49
Sex manuals, 34
Sexological associations, German, 12
Sex ratio, on college campuses, 48
Sex tourism, 134,136
Sexual abstinence, 30
Sexual abuse, of children
    by adolescent males, 78-79
    in Germany
        age of perpetrators, 78-79
        prevalence of, 78-79,81
    by priests, 37,39
Sexual crimes
    adolescent victims of, 11
    sensationalization of, 97-98
Sexual delinquency, societal basis for,
        96
Sexual delinquents, imprisonment of,
        95-96
Sexual intercourse, in adolescents,
        onset age of, 44,47-48
Sexuality, public, 96
Sexual offenders
    adolescent, incarceration of, 11
    criminal records of, 75
    deviant labeling of, 98,100-101
    diagnosis and treatment of, 97
Sexual partners, age of, 44
Sexual relations, intergenerational, 39
Sexual self-determination, offenses
        against
    German Penal Code provisions
            regarding, 71-87
    international agreements regarding, 84
Slovakia, minimum age limits for
        sexual relations in, 118,
        124,138,141,143
    for homosexual relations, 124
Slovenia, minimum age limits for
        sexual relations in, 118,
        135,141,143
Socrates, 29
Somerford, John, 33
South Africa, minimum age limits for
        sexual relations in, 145

South Korea, minimum age limits for sexual relations in, 145
Spain, minimum age limits for sexual relations in, 118,124,138,141
  for homosexual relations, 124
  seduction provisions, 132,135
Stead, W. T., 38
Strabo, 28
Strangers, sexual relations with, 59-60
Stubbes, Philip, 34
Summer of '41 (movie), 58
Sweden
  de facto same-sex marriage in, 122
  minimum age limits for sexual relations in, 118,124,138, 143
    for homosexual relations, 124
    seduction provisions, 132,135
"Swept away," 48
Swinburne, Henry, 33
Switzerland, minimum age limits for sexual relations in, 118, 124,139,141,143
  for homosexual relations, 124

Taiwan, minimum age limits for sexual relations in, 145
Thailand, minimum age limits for sexual relations in, 145
Toledo, Ohio, adolescents' sexual behavior in, 44
Toonen v. Commonwealth of Australia, 121
Treaty of Amsterdam, 122
Treaty on the Foundation of the European Community, 122
Turkey, minimum age limits for sexual relations in, 118,124,141, 143
  for homosexual relations, 124
  seduction provisions, 132,135
Tuvalu, minimum age limits for sexual relations in, 145

U. S. v. Knox, 10
Ukraine, minimum age limits for sexual relations in, 117, 124,141,143
  for homosexual relations, 124
United Kingdom
  adolescent male/adult female relationships in, 58
  minimum age limits for sexual relations in, 118,124, 138,141,143
    for homosexual relations, 124, 125,141
United Nations, Rights Committee, 121
United Nations Convention on the Rights of the Child, 65-66
United States, minimum age limits for sexual relations in, 134-136, 145-146
United States Federal Criminal Code, 134,136
  child pornography definition of, 10,12

Vatican. *See* Catholic Church
Vermont, adolescent same-sex sexual behavior in, 50
"Victim doctrine," of criminal law, 93-94
Victims, of sexual crimes, 100,101
  adolescents as, 11
Vietnam, minimum age limits for sexual relations in, 146
Violence, 98-99,101
  sexual, German Penal Code provisions regarding, 74,75,76-77,78
  toward children, European Commission's proposed regulation of, 9

"Webcam-sex," 11,13-14,140,142
Weber, Max, 96
Williams, William, 32
Women's movement, 56
Wood, Mary, 33
World Association for Sexology, 12
World Health Organization, 122

Xenophon, 29

BOOK ORDER FORM!

Order a copy of this book with this form or online at:
http://www.haworthpress.com/store/product.asp?sku=5494

Adolescence, Sexuality, and the Criminal Law
Multidisciplinary Perspectives

____ in softbound at 29.95$ ISBN: 0-7890-2781-X.
____ in hardbound at $49.95 ISBN: 0-7890-2780-1.

COST OF BOOKS _____	❏ **BILL ME LATER:** Bill-me option is good on US/Canada/Mexico orders only; not good to jobbers, wholesalers, or subscription agencies.
POSTAGE & HANDLING _____ US: $4.00 for first book & $1.50 for each additional book Outside US: $5.00 for first book & $2.00 for each additional book.	❏ Signature _____ ❏ Payment Enclosed: $ _____
SUBTOTAL _____ In Canada: add 7% GST. _____	❏ **PLEASE CHARGE TO MY CREDIT CARD:** ❏ Visa ❏ MasterCard ❏ AmEx ❏ Discover ❏ Diner's Club ❏ Eurocard ❏ JCB
STATE TAX _____ CA, IL, IN, MN, NJ, NY, OH, PA & SD residents please add appropriate local sales tax.	Account # _____
FINAL TOTAL _____ If paying in Canadian funds, convert using the current exchange rate, UNESCO coupons welcome.	Exp Date _____ Signature _____ (Prices in US dollars and subject to change without notice.)

PLEASE PRINT ALL INFORMATION OR ATTACH YOUR BUSINESS CARD

Name _____
Address _____
City _____ State/Province _____ Zip/Postal Code _____
Country _____
Tel _____ Fax _____
E-Mail _____

May we use your e-mail address for confirmations and other types of information? ❏ Yes ❏ No We appreciate receiving your e-mail address. Haworth would like to e-mail special discount offers to you, as a preferred customer. **We will never share, rent, or exchange your e-mail address. We regard such actions as an invasion of your privacy.**

Order from your **local bookstore** or directly from
The Haworth Press, Inc. 10 Alice Street, Binghamton, New York 13904-1580 • USA
Call our toll-free number (1-800-429-6784) / Outside US/Canada: (607) 722-5857
Fax: 1-800-895-0582 / Outside US/Canada: (607) 771-0012
E-mail your order to us: orders@haworthpress.com

For orders outside US and Canada, you may wish to order through your local sales representative, distributor, or bookseller.
For information, see http://haworthpress.com/distributors

(Discounts are available for individual orders in US and Canada only, not booksellers/distributors.)
Please photocopy this form for your personal use.
www.HaworthPress.com

BOF05

PREVIOUS SPECIAL THEMATIC ISSUES OF JOURNAL OF PSYCHOLOGY & HUMAN SEXUALITY™ ARE AVAILABLE BOUND SEPARATELY

SAVE! 25% on each book!

Gain important insight and a broader perspective on where, why, and how sex workers conduct their business
CONTEMPORARY RESEARCH ON SEX WORK
Edited by Jeffrey T. Parsons, PhD
$24.95 soft. ISBN-13: 978-0-7890-2964-5 / ISBN-10: 0-7890-2964-2.
$49.95 hard. ISBN-13: 978-0-7890-2963-8 / ISBN-10: 0-7890-2963-4.
Available Summer 2005. Approx. 222 pp. with Index.
published simultaneously as JPHS 17(1/2)

Contains evidence-based information on improving the quality of care provided to lesbian and bisexual women
LESBIAN AND BISEXUAL WOMEN'S MENTAL HEALTH
Edited by Robin M. Mathy, MSW, LGSW, MSc, MSt, MA, and Shelly K. Kerr, PhD
$19.95 soft. ISBN-13: 978-0-7890-2682-8 / ISBN-10: 0-7890-2682-1.
$34.95 hard. ISBN-13: 978-0-7890-2681-1 / ISBN-10: 0-7890-2681-3.
2004. 235 pp. with Index.
published simultaneously as JPHS 15(2/3)(4)

Explore multidisciplinary perspectives on the sexual rights of adolescents and the legal issues that threaten their sexual autonomy
ADOLESCENCE, SEXUALITY, AND THE CRIMINAL LAW
Multidisciplinary Perspectives
Edited by Helmut Graupner, JD, and Vern L. Bullough, PhD
$29.95 soft. ISBN-13: 978-0-7890-2781-8 / ISBN-10: 0-7890-2781-X.
$49.95 hard. ISBN-13: 978-0-7890-2780-1 / ISBN-10: 0-7890-2780-1.
Available Spring 2005. Approx. 222 pp. with Index.
published simultaneously as JPHS 16(2/3)

Provide humane, dignified, effective treatment to sexual offenders
SEX OFFENDER TREATMENT
Accomplishments, Challenges, and Future Directions
Edited by Michael H. Miner, PhD, and Eli Coleman, PhD
$22.95 soft. ISBN-13: 978-0-7890-1983-7 / ISBN-10: 0-7890-1983-3.
$39.95 hard. ISBN-13: 978-0-7890-1982-0 / ISBN-10: 0-7890-1982-5.
2003. 125 pp. with Index. published simultaneously as JPHS 13(3/4)

Look beyond the taboos and cultural misconceptions to see how masturbation can promote sexual health
MASTURBATION AS A MEANS OF ACHIEVING SEXUAL HEALTH
Edited by Walter O. Bockting, PhD, and Eli Coleman, PhD
$17.95 soft. ISBN-13: 978-0-7890-2046-8 / ISBN-10: 0-7890-2046-7.
$29.95 hard. ISBN-13: 978-0-7890-2047-5 / ISBN-10: 0-7890-2047-5.
2003. 147 pp. with Index. published simultaneously as JPHS 14(2/3)

What normal sexual thoughts and desires do we experience as children?
CHILDHOOD SEXUALITY
Normal Sexual Behavior and Development
Edited by Theo G. M. Sandfort, PhD, and Jany Rademakers, PhD
$29.95 soft. ISBN-13: 978-0-7890-1199-2 / ISBN-10: 0-7890-1199-9.
$49.95 hard. ISBN-13: 978-0-7890-1198-5 / ISBN-10: 0-7890-1198-0.
2001. 136 pp. with Index. published simultaneously as JPHS 12(1/2)
Translated into Hebrew! 2001. 136 pp. with Index.

Explore new research into treatment and rehabilitation options for sex offenders
SEXUAL OFFENDER TREATMENT
Biopsychosocial Perspectives
Edited by Eli Coleman, PhD, and Michael Miner, PhD
$14.95 soft. ISBN-13: 978-0-7890-1018-6 / ISBN-10: 0-7890-1018-6.
$39.95 hard. ISBN-13: 978-0-7890-1017-9 / ISBN-10: 0-7890-1017-8.
2000. 118 pp. with Index. published simultaneously as JPHS 11(3)

What is the future of HIV prevention for gay and bisexual men?
NEW INTERNATIONAL DIRECTIONS IN HIV PREVENTION FOR GAY AND BISEXUAL MEN
Edited by Michael T. Wright, LICSW, MS, B. R. Simon Rosser, PhD, MPH, and Onno de Zwart, MA
$24.95 soft. ISBN-13: 978-1-56023-116-5 / ISBN-10: 1-56023-116-5.
$59.95 hard. ISBN-13: 978-0-7890-0538-0 / ISBN-10: 0-7890-0538-7.
1998. 167 pp. with Index. published simultaneously as JPHS 10(3/4)

Stay current on the concerns, challenges, and concepts of postsecondary sexuality education
SEXUALITY EDUCATION IN POSTSECONDARY AND PROFESSIONAL TRAINING SETTINGS
Edited by James W. Maddock, PhD
$34.95 hard. ISBN-13: 978-0-7890-0027-9 / ISBN-10: 0-7890-0027-X.
1997. 193 pp. with Index. published simultaneously as JPHS 9(3/4)

Re-think your assumptions on sexual coercion with this new research
SEXUAL COERCION IN DATING RELATIONSHIPS
Edited by E. Sandra Byers, PhD, and Lucia F. O'Sullivan, PhD
$19.95 soft. ISBN-13: 978-1-56024-844-6 / ISBN-10: 1-56024-844-0.
$59.95 hard. ISBN-13: 978-1-56024-815-6 / ISBN-10: 1-56024-815-7.
1996. 179 pp. with Index. published simultaneously as JPHS 8(1/2)

HOW TO:
PLACE AN ORDER!
Please see order form on the reverse side.
Use promo code HEC25 to get the 25% off discount online

FIND MORE INFORMATION ABOUT THESE BOOKS
http://www.HaworthPress.com
and use our QuickSearch Catalog

The Haworth Press, Inc.
10 Alice Street, Binghamton, New York 13904-1580 USA

Improve your caregiving with these important insights on the impact of HIV and AIDS on sexuality
HIV/AIDS AND SEXUALITY
Edited by Michael W. Ross, PhD, MPH
$22.95 soft. ISBN-13: 978-1-56023-068-7 / ISBN-10: 1-56023-068-1.
$59.95 hard. ISBN-13: 978-1-56023-730-2 / ISBN-10: 1-56024-730-4.
1995. 206 pp. with Index. published simultaneously as JPHS 7(1/2)

Discover information on the clinical management of gender dysphoria in this insightful book
GENDER DYSPHORIA
Interdisciplinary Approaches in Clinical Management
Edited by Walter O. Bockting, PhD, and Eli Coleman, PhD
$22.95 soft. ISBN-13: 978-1-56024-473-8 / ISBN-10: 1-56024-473-9.
$59.95 hard. ISBN-13: 978-1-56024-459-2 / ISBN-10: 1-56024-459-3.
1993. 155 pp. published simultaneously as JPHS 5(4)

This vital book discusses the impact of HIV on people's lives and how infected individuals cope
SEXUAL TRANSMISSION OF HIV INFECTION
Risk Reduction, Trauma, and Adaptation
Edited by Lena Nilsson Schönnesson, PhD
$19.95 soft. ISBN-13: 978-1-56023-024-3 / ISBN-10: 1-56023-024-X.
$59.95 hard. ISBN-13: 978-1-56024-332-8 / ISBN-10: 1-56024-332-5.
1992. 176 pp. published simultaneously as JPHS 5(1/2)

Join Dr. Money's fellow sexologists in honoring his distinguished career through their own original articles that further contemporary scientific knowledge of sexuality
JOHN MONEY: A TRIBUTE
Edited by Eli Coleman, PhD
$64.95 hard. ISBN-13: 978-1-56024-190-4 / ISBN-10: 1-56024-190-X.
1991. 198 pp. published simultaneously as JPHS 4(2)

Textbooks are available for classroom adoption consideration on a 60-day examination basis. You will receive an invoice payable within 60 days along with the book. **If you decide to adopt the book, your invoice will be cancelled.** Please write to us on your institutional letterhead, indicating the textbook you would like to examine as well as the following information: course title, current text, enrollment, and decision date.

CALL OUR TOLL-FREE NUMBER: 1-800-429-6784
US & Canada only / 8am–5pm ET; Monday–Thur; Fri–8am–2pm.
Outside US/Canada: + 607-722-5857

FAX YOUR ORDER TO US: 1-800-895-0582
Outside US/Canada: + 607-771-0012

E-MAIL YOUR ORDER TO US:
orders@haworthpress.com

VISIT OUR WEB SITE AT:
http://www.HaworthPress.com

SPECIAL OFFER! 25% on each book!

Order Today and Save!

TITLE	ISBN	REGULAR PRICE	25%-OFF PRICE

- Discount available only in US, Canada, and Mexico and not available in conjunction with any other offer.
- Individual orders outside US, Canada, and Mexico must be prepaid by check, credit card, or money order.
- In Canada: Add 7% for GST after postage & handling. Residents of Newfoundland, Nova Scotia, and New Brunswick, also add an additional 8% for province tax.
- CA, IL IN, MN, NJ, NY, OH & SD residents: Add appropriate local sales tax.

Please complete information below or tape your business card in this area.

NAME _____
ADDRESS _____
PLEASE ATTACH YOUR BUSINESS CARD
CITY _____
STATE _____ ZIP _____
COUNTRY _____
COUNTY (NY residents only) _____
TEL _____ FAX _____
[please type or print clearly]
E-MAIL _____
May we use your e-mail address for confirmations and other types of information?
( ) Yes ( ) No. We appreciate receiving your e-mail address. Haworth would like to have e-mail discount offers to you, as a preferred customer. We will never **share, rent, or exchange** your e-mail address. We regard such actions as an invasion of your privacy.

POSTAGE AND HANDLING:
If your book total is: Add
up to $29.95 — $5.00
$30.00 – $49.99 — $6.00
$50.00 – $69.99 — $7.00
$70.00 – $89.99 — $8.00
$90.00 – $109.99 — $9.00
$110.00 – $129.99 — $10.00
$130.00 – $149.99 — $11.00
$150.00 and up — $12.00

☐ **BILL ME LATER**
(Bill-me option is not available on orders outside US/Canada/Mexico. Service charge is waived for booksellers/wholesalers/jobbers.)

Signature _____

☐ **PAYMENT ENCLOSED** _____
(Payment must be in US or Canadian dollars by check or money order drawn on a US or Canadian bank.)

☐ **PLEASE CHARGE TO MY CREDIT CARD:**
☐ AmEx ☐ Diners Club ☐ Discover ☐ Eurocard ☐ JCB ☐ MasterCard ☐ Visa

Account # _____ Exp Date _____

Signature _____

May we open a confidential credit card account for you for possible future purchases? ( ) Yes ( ) No

US orders will be shipped via UPS; Outside US orders will be shipped via Book Printed Matter. For shipments via other delivery services, contact Haworth for details. Based on US dollars. Booksellers: Call for freight charges. • If paying in Canadian funds, please use the current exchange rate to convert total to Canadian dollars. • Payment in UNESCO coupons welcome. • Please allow 3–4 weeks for delivery after publication. • Prices and discounts subject to change without notice. • Discount not applicable on books priced under $15.00.

The Haworth Press, Inc.
10 Alice Street, Binghamton, New York 13904-1580 USA

(16)(20) 07/05 BBC05